HENRY SHAW

HENRY SHAW
His Life and Legacies

William Barnaby Faherty, S.J.

University of Missouri Press
Columbia, 1987

Copyright © 1987 by
The Missouri Botanical Garden
University of Missouri Press, Columbia, Missouri 65211
Printed and bound in the United States of America

Library of Congress Cataloging-in-Publication Data
Faherty, William Barnaby, 1914-
      Henry Shaw, his life and legacies.

      Bibliography: p.
      Includes index.
      1. Shaw, Henry, 1800–1889. 2. Saint Louis (Mo.)—
Biography. 3. Missouri Botanical Garden—History.
4. Tower Grove Park (Saint Louis, Mo.)—History.
I. Title.
F474.S253S523   1987   977.8'65   87–5935
ISBN 0–8262–0644–1 (alk. paper)

∞™ This paper meets the minimum requirements of
the American National Standard for Permanence of Paper
for Printed Library Materials, Z39.48, 1984.

Frontispiece: Henry Shaw in about 1860, photographer
unknown.
Illustration on p. vi: Henry Shaw at age 35, oil painting
owned by the Missouri Botanical Garden, artist
unknown.

To the Trustees
of the
Missouri Botanical Garden

HENRY SHAW.
1835

Acknowledgments

◆◆

The author wishes to thank, above all, Dr. Peter H. Raven for inviting him to undertake this life of Henry Shaw and for his continued interest in the project. He wishes to thank also these members and former members of the Garden staff: Richard H. Daley, Patricia E. Rich, and Lee Fox; Martha J. Riley and Barbara Mykrantz, archivists at the Missouri Botanical Garden Library; and Librarian Connie Wolf and her assistants.

These other librarians and archivists were also most helpful: Lenore Thompson at the Archives of the Royal Botanic Gardens, Kew; Ven. Charles F. Rehkopf of the Archives of the Episcopal Diocese of Missouri; Jeanne Mino at the Rochester Public Library; Leland Hillegoss, Martha Hillegoss, Noel Holobeck, Eric Stocker, Gail Mitchell, and Niki Ehrenberger of the St. Louis Public Library Research Departments; Dorothy Claybourne, Miriam Joseph, Brian Forney, Kathryn Thorpe, Jo Ann van Schaik, John Waide, and Catherine Weidle of the Pius XII Library at St. Louis University; Anita Karg of the Hunt Institute for Botanical Documentation; Virginia Renner and Mary Wright at Huntington Library; Beryl Manne, Archivist at Washington University; and a number of thoroughly cooperative individuals at the Sheffield (England) Public Library.

The following individuals appraised a trial copy of this work in whole or in part and offered valuable suggestions from their vantages as historians, botanists, scientists, writers, or literary critics: Rev. Lucius F. Cervantes, S.J., Dr. Marshall R. Crosby, Dr. John D. Dwyer, Bernice Gurney, Dr. Thomas Hall, NiNi Harris, Eldridge H. Lovelace, Dr. Mildred Mathias, Mrs. Nancy Merz, Dr. James Neal Primm, Dr. David Roediger, Rev. John Martin Scott, S.J., and Mrs. Frances Stadler.

The author was able to interview the following: Harriet Bakewell, Louis G. Brenner, Jr., Mrs. Oscar Buder, Dr. Thomas B. Croat, Dr. Marshall R. Crosby, Dr. William G. D'Arcy, Robert Denison, Bertha Dodge, Bernice Gurney, Dr. Thomas Hall, Henry Hitchcock, Gerhardt Kramer, Anne Lehmann, Catherine Lieneman, Dr. Mildred Mathias, Dr. Robert Mohlenbrock, Dr. Roy Moore of Mill Hill, Dr.

James Neal Primm, Charles Pring, Tamra Raven, James Reed, Deni and Dr. Russell Seibert, and Dr. Julian A. Steyermark.

Edna Suermann helped with the maps. Lisa DeLorenzo, Tom Dewey, and Don Martin took some of the photographs. Sister Dionysia, S.S.N.D., Curator of the Swekosky Photo Collection, graciously granted permission for use of photographs, and Norbury Wayman made available his sketches of early St. Louis. Barbara Mangona, Suzie Poole, and Mollylu Vonland typed various sections of this work.

W. B. F., S.J.
St. Louis
April 1987

Contents

❖❖

Chronology

◆◆

1800, 24 July	Born in Sheffield, England.
1811–1816	Attends Mill Hill School.
1818	Leaves for Canada with his father.
1819, 4 May	Arrives in St. Louis to sell cutlery.
1820	Sends money to his mother and sisters in England.
1822	His mother and sisters come to upstate New York.
1823	Opens a store on North Main.
1825	Visits his family in Pittsford, N.Y.
1828, Summer	Purchases a slave woman.
1836	Builds a house for his family in Rochester.
1839	Closes the books on cutlery sales and engages in money lending with property as security.
1840, July—1842, June	Tours Europe.
1842, 8 August	Buys property in Prairie des Noyers, an area southwest of St. Louis.
1843, 4 July	Becomes naturalized citizen.
1843, July—1846, August	Visits Europe a second time.
1849	Commissions George I. Barnett to build his town house and country home.
1850, 16 October	Buys slaves at public auction at Court House.
1851	Begins extensive tree-planting at country home.
1851, 12 May	Makes first will.
1851, June-December	Visits Europe a third time; goes to Chatsworth; determines to start a garden at his country home.
1856, 11 February	Seeks guidance of Sir William Jackson Hooker.
1856, 9 April	Dr. Engelmann writes Dr. Gray about Shaw's plans.
1856, May	Consults Engelmann.
1859, 14 March	Act of legislature authorizing garden.

◆◆

1859, 27 May	Sued for breach of promise by Effie Carstang.
1859, 3 June	Loses suit; his lawyers appeal.
1859, 15 June	Garden opens.
1860, March	Goes to court a second time.
1860, 31 March	Wins appeal.
1864, 5 February	Appointed commissioner of projected city park.
1867, 9 March	Act authorizing Tower Grove Park.
1869, 1 May	Celebrates fiftieth anniversary of arrival in St. Louis.
1872, June	Visits Colorado.
1874, 20 July	Charles Kingsley, English author, visits Garden.
1877, 16 July	Joseph Hooker, Director of the Royal Botanic Gardens, Kew, visits Park and Garden.
1883	Mark Twain praises Park and Garden.
1884	Publishes *The Vine and Civilization*.
1884, 4 February	Dr. George Engelmann dies.
1885, 1 January	Makes last will.
1885, 28 May	Elected to Board of Trustees of Washington University.
1885, 8 June	Gives endowment for School of Botany at Washington University.
1885, 6 November	Dr. William Trelease gives inaugural address at School of Botany.
1886, 12 October	Statue of Columbus unveiled in Tower Grove Park.
1888, 7 October	Gilmore's Matchless Band plays at Garden.
1889, 25 August	Dies at 3:15 a.m.
1889, 2 September	Will submitted to Probate Court.
1889, 7 September	Trustees of Garden organize with Rufus Lackland as president.

Introduction

❖❖

Henry Shaw, a successful merchant from the distant American state of Missouri, meditated as he walked through the beautiful gardens of Chatsworth in central England in 1851. He had left his native town of Sheffield, twenty-five miles away, thirty-three years before to test the uncertain business conditions of the American frontier at the small town of St. Louis. He had succeeded beyond hope. In 1840, already wealthy, he had left the day-to-day conduct of his business affairs to an agent and visited various parts of Europe. He then returned to St. Louis, the center of his commercial ventures, and in 1849 built a town house and an Italianate villa in the country. The Great Exhibition of 1851 had brought him back to his native land and at that moment to Chatsworth.

Shaw was impressed by the duke of Devonshire's magnificent residence, palatial inside and out. But he marveled even more at the gardens to the south along the River Derwent and on the hills to the southeast. Earlier dukes had designed the gardens, but the sixth duke, ten years older than Henry Shaw, and his friend, Joseph Paxton, a famous gardener, had created the estate as Henry Shaw saw it.

On the hillside to the east stretched the "Cascade," a two-hundred-yard-long staircase of water. At its foot stood four statues of Carrara marble, typical of the works of art the duke had spread through the garden. To the south Shaw viewed the ring pond and beech hedge, and a bit farther along the hillside, the iron and glass conservatory that housed flowers and plants from diverse areas of the world. Joseph Paxton had built this plant house between 1836 and 1840 and then used it as the model for his Crystal Palace in the Great Exhibition in London the year of Shaw's visit. This last creation, incidentally, was bringing him the honor of knighthood.

At the foot of the hill below Paxton's conservatory, a canal pond about thirty feet wide and three hundred feet long led the eye back to the Emperor Fountain, which could throw a stream of water two hundred and ninety feet into the air. This highest jet in Europe was named in honor of Czar Nicholas I of Russia, even though the monarch, who had planned to visit Chatsworth, failed to arrive. Beyond the fountain to the north, seeming to rise out of the water of the canal pond, stood Chatsworth House.

As Shaw walked, he thought of his many acres four miles from the downtown area of St. Louis. The city had been a frontier village of at most thirty-three hundred people without a paved street when he had arrived in 1819. The Indian frontier had been only two hundred and fifty miles farther west. Now the city numbered over seventy-seven thousand inhabitants and was growing with floods of immigrants from Germany and Ireland. The state of Missouri was becoming one of the most populous in the nation. Houses were going up so fast and so close together that people had little chance to see the beautiful world of nature.

"Why may I not have a garden, too?" Shaw asked himself. "I have enough land and money for the same sort in a smaller way."[1] Could he, even in his most expansive dreams, have imagined that someday his garden would outshine the one at Chatsworth and even rival the Royal Botanic Gardens at Kew along the Thames above London?

He sailed back to the states and set to work. He sought guidance from Sir William Jackson Hooker, the director of Kew, who in turn urged him to seek advice and help from physician and botanist Dr. George Engelmann, one of the founders of the Academy of Science of St. Louis. Shaw also wrote to the greatest American botanist of the day, Dr. Asa Gray of Harvard University.

Shaw would devote most of his attention to his botanical garden until his death in 1889. All the while he would remain a most private person. The following pages will tell the story of Henry Shaw—his life, his times, and his garden.

I. A Son of Sheffield and Mill Hill

❖❖

The hilly region of Sheffield, where Henry Shaw was born, greatly resembles the areas near its American steel-producing counterparts, Pittsburgh, Pennsylvania, and Birmingham, Alabama. A small river, the Don, comes down into the city from the northwest. In the west section of Sheffield, a small stream, the Rivelin, flows into the Don from the south. A mile and a half farther on, a second waterway, the Sheaf—whence the name Sheffield—joins the Don in the center of town, and the river turns northeast. Where Lady's Bridge crosses the Don, the altitude is only 160 feet, while High Neb, a hill southwest of the city in Shaw's day but now within city limits, soars 1,502 feet above sea level. The people of the area have mined coal in the surrounding hills since the days of Richard the Lionhearted.

By 1800, four main roads, not well paved, led into the town from the northwest, northeast, southeast, and southwest.[1] The more than a hundred streets in Sheffield were narrow and well paved.[2] The streets ran up and down the hills. Two-story houses, mostly of stone, piled close together on the slopes, their porchless fronts edging the sidewalks. These 7,720 residences housed 31,314 persons.

At the start of the new century, Sheffield monopolized the English cutlery industry. Smiths and cutlers in the town made the Sheffield "Thwitel" (the common knife) that Chaucer mentioned in the *Canterbury Tales* and the blade that, as the "Bowie Knife," would become famous on the American frontier. More than one hundred relatively small concerns, operating with little capital and often in restricted premises, brought the Sheffield steel industry into prominence.[3] The Company of Cutlers, set up by an act of Parliament in 1624, ran everything. The master cutler, in fact, presided at the main civic functions.

The typical Sheffield craftsman had traditionally owned his tools, controlled his hours of work, purchased raw materials, and employed apprentices. The men who made the knives, sickles, scythes, saws, razors, shovels, axes, and other tools did not face the factory conditions or live in the smoke-saturated atmosphere that would oppress succeeding generations; but they had their complaints, and agitated often.

3

1. The Green Lane Works, Sheffield, England, where Robert Jobson and Joseph Shaw produced grates and other fireplace equipment.

In the late eighteenth century, a man named Joseph Shaw had come to Sheffield from Leicester, twenty miles to the south on the road to London, which lay two hundred miles beyond. Shaw began to manufacture grates, pokers, tongs, and related ironware with a partner, Robert Jobson. They opened their plant on Green Lane, a street that wound along the Don River for a few blocks at the north end of town.

"With his partner, Mr. Jobson," Sheffield historian R. E. Leader recalled years later, "[Shaw] laid the foundation of that trade which has obtained for Sheffield [leadership in] the manufacture of stoves and fenders [metal guards for fireplaces] previously claimed by Edinburgh and London."[4] Joseph Shaw, Leader pointed out, "was a Baptist, and he not only held service in his works on Sunday, but established a Sunday School as well."[5] The Society of Baptists, incidentally, built Townhead Chapel on an elevated piece of ground in Townhead Street during those years.[6] The church stood only three blocks up the hill south of the Shaw-Jobson plant. Jobson, in contrast, adhered to the Church of England.

Shaw had married Sarah Hoole, one of six children of a prominent family of Sheffield, just before the turn of the century. Sarah's older brother, William, who manufactured cutlery, also belonged to an emerging group of merchant-capitalists who had begun to control the distribution of Sheffield products. A younger brother, James, set out for London to engage in merchandising. An eloquent nephew, Henry E. Hoole, was to chair a local committee of the Liberal party in 1852; the citizens of Sheffield would elect another of Sarah's nephews, Francis Hoole, mayor in 1853. The Hooles were destined to remain prominent in the area.[7]

Sarah and Joseph had four children: Henry (born 24 July 1800), Sarah, Caroline, and a boy who died in infancy. The Shaws lived in Netherthorpe, a hilly area in Sheffield a few blocks south of the factory on Green Lane, not far from the Baptist chapel. The residence was later to house a school.

As a boy Henry went to school at Thorne, a village on the river Don not far north of Sheffield. The only recollection of this period of Henry's life came from a classmate, Richardson, who distinctly remembered a severe flogging he and Henry had to endure for running away to look at the river Don in time of flood.[8] A man by the name of Wilson ran the school, and no doubt did the flogging.

After his primary education, Henry entered Mill Hill School near London at the age of eleven. The school occupied Ridgeway House, the former home of botanist Peter Collinson (1693–1768), a Quaker and a friend of the American statesman Benjamin Franklin and of the Swedish naturalist and physician Carl Linnaeus. Collinson had planted larches, cypresses, and plane trees at Mill Hill. Linnaeus reputedly visited Collinson's Garden in 1737 and put in two cedar trees.[9]

At this lovely place, London Baptists, Presbyterians, and Congregationalists had founded Mill Hill School to give a classical education to their sons, who could not enter the great public schools of Eton and Harrow, restricted as they were to members of the Church of England. The Mill Hill School stood nine miles north of London on a high ridge four hundred feet above sea level. The site offered a magnificent view over four counties. From the terrace the students could make out Epsom Downs and Windsor Castle in the distance and the spires of Harrow ten miles to the west. The school gave a fine classical education.[10] The principal during the school's first forty years, Rev. John Pye-Smith, attempted "to combine on an extensive scale the advantages of a religious education with solid and correct erudition, and general knowledge."[11] The fact that the principal was the son of a Sheffield bookseller may explain Henry's attending Mill Hill School.

The school sent its graduates principally into law, the ministry, medicine, education, and "the higher forms of commerce." The undergraduates followed the strict routines common to nineteenth-century religious-based schools, with instruction in catechism.[12] The classical languages formed the core of the curriculum, but Mill Hill also stressed the study of the French language, English composition, and handwriting.

Shaw did well in all three secular subjects and developed a life-long interest in the classics. He learned to write impressively in English and French, with a style of handwriting easy to read, although he had a strange habit of using dashes for periods. His fluency in French would later prove especially valuable.

The term at Mill Hill lasted ten months, with one month's Christmas vacation and one month's holiday in summer. The school gave limited time to recreation, expended none of its resources on playground equipment, and did not record scores of the cricket contests,[13] but sports did not seem to be Henry's concern. In Shaw's time Mill Hill boasted a boy's garden.[14] A twentieth-century historian of Mill Hill, Norman G. Brett-James, stated, "While at school he (Shaw) took a great interest in gardening, and in after years was wont to tell of the delight with which he used to gaze on the cedars and other famous trees, and to cultivate his own tiny plot."[15] In another chapter the author insisted that Shaw gained at Mill Hill "a taste for botany."[16] After Shaw's death seventy years later, a friend recalled that Henry had spoken to him of the plots the students tilled at Mill Hill.[17] No contemporary evidence, however, supports this assertion that Henry Shaw showed an interest in flowers and trees so early in life.

The Register of Mill Hill School (1807–1926) includes a twenty-four-line sketch of Shaw's career, which tells that Shaw remained six years at the school.[18] He returned to Sheffield in 1816, presumably to help his father in business. Joseph Shaw needed more help than a son could provide, however. While visiting Liverpool, he had met a fellow Baptist from the American state of Tennessee who convinced him to try the American market and ship consignments of goods to New Orleans and Canada. During the course of this business venture, Joseph Shaw borrowed large amounts of money from the banking house of Remington and Young and asked the husband of his sister, Sarah Cornthwaite, to stand surety.[19] Sheffield's economic historians would agree that Joseph Shaw was correct in looking to the United States as the best market for Sheffield-made goods at the time.[20] He was presumably not as wise, however, in the choice of his business partner in the venture. The man from Tennessee, whose name Shaw never mentioned, neglected the shipments to New Orleans. To add to Joseph Shaw's discomfort, his partner Jobson also broke with him at this time. Shaw Senior was ready to leave for the New World.

Without knowing that his father was fleeing creditors, eighteen-year-old Henry willingly looked to the opportunities across the seas. The two Shaws embarked for Canada in June 1818 on an old Danish prize vessel and reached Quebec after seventy-four days at sea. While Joseph Shaw would not recoup his losses in the New World, his son, an unimpressive-looking young man with no exceptional gifts of personality or physique but with an evident ability to work at his desk and keep exact accounts, would soon be on the road to prosperity.

2.   Henry Shaw Comes to St. Louis

◆◆

Early in 1819, while his father prepared to move to English-speaking Canada, Henry left Quebec and went by sled across the snowy trails of upper New York State. Reaching Manhattan, he took a boat along the coast to New Orleans, where he was able to find the consignment of tools his father had sent in agreement with his Tennessee associate. As Henry had expected, most of the shipment was unsold: saws, files, planes, chisels, and wood screws—an assortment that amounted to over £400 in value.[1] The glutted market in New Orleans made Henry look into the interior of the western country.

Henry planned to go upriver to St. Louis and, perhaps, to visit Louisville later. If business kept him occupied into the summer, he would not go back to Canada that year, but return to New Orleans for the winter.[2] On 25 March, he boarded the steamboat *Maid of Orleans.* Even though eighteen-year-old Shaw had crossed the ocean, gone up

2. The *Pike,* the first steamboat to reach St. Louis, arrived in 1817, two years before Henry Shaw came upriver from *New Orleans* on the more ponderous *Maid of Orleans.* Sketch by Norbury Wayman.

the St. Lawrence River, and traveled down the Hudson Valley, his first trip on the Mississippi left a distinct imprint on his memory. He remembered the ponderous structure and limited power of the steamboat, the rugged bluffs of Vicksburg, a Cherokee Indian swimming across the wide river, and the names of several of his fellow passengers.

On reaching St. Louis on 4 May, he noticed the pleasant appearance of the houses, some of them with wide verandas like those he had seen in the South, and fruit trees in blossom alongside the houses, forming a striking contrast with the moss-covered oaks of Louisiana. Several steamboats, a half-dozen barges, and several mackinaw boats were moored at the landing.[3]

James Haley White, another newcomer who arrived only seven days later, had a less cheerful first impression. He remembered the long, dirty quicksound beach, the many empty keelboats tied to stakes driven into the sand, and the rugged limestone bluff that allowed only two narrow passageways from beach to the Rue Principale (First or Main Street).[4]

When the War of 1812 had ended just four years before Shaw arrived, the village of St. Louis still occupied the same area that Pierre Laclede, the founder, had platted fifty years before. Three blocks deep east and west, it stretched a mile along the river. Between several impressive stone mansions stood homes of upright logs, some pointed and driven into the ground in the French manner. Beyond the second terrace on Third Street, a charming countryside rose in waves to the west, neither hilly nor level, but rising gradually for several miles. Close to the town a mill dam formed a beautiful lake called Chouteau's Pond that provided opportunities for boating, swimming, fishing, and picnicking in summer and for skating in winter.[5] The village occupied one of the best sites along the Mississippi, on a limestone terrace safe from flood waters, about fifteen miles below the confluence of the Missouri and Mississippi rivers and forty miles below the junction of the Illinois with the Father of Waters.[6]

In 1816, the town had burst out of its fifty-two-year-old limits and sprawled onto this second terrace from Fourth to Seventh streets and from Spruce on the south to the road to St. Charles on the north. Bilingual St. Louis had contained about 1,400 inhabitants in 1810, with 720 of French background, 280 Anglo-Americans, and 400 "people of color." Its population would reach 4,900 by 1820. Most of the new arrivals between 1804 and 1816 had come from American states, with almost a third of them from Virginia, which had given twice as many as Pennsylvania and four times as many as Maryland. A few families had arrived from Connecticut and Massachusetts, five families from France,[7] and at least a dozen from Ireland.

The fur trade had been the cause of St. Louis's origin and the main business in its early years. Later the town became the outfitter and depot for lead-mining operations, first in the area near the Missouri town of Potosi, about sixty miles south of St. Louis, and later in northwest Illinois along the Fever River. While conflicts between British and American traders on the upper Mississippi and Missouri rivers during the War of 1812 had hurt the fur trade, these troubles had indirectly helped commerce. The national government thought it necessary to keep a large force of men on the frontier to protect the settlers against the northern Indians allegedly provoked by the British. The government stationed these troops at Fort Bellefontaine on the Missouri, about fifteen miles north of the city. This added an additional sixty thousand dollars annually to the St. Louis economy. The value of goods coming into the village approached a quarter of a million dollars every twelve months.[8]

On 2 August 1817, the *Pike,* the first steamboat to try the Mississippi above the Ohio, had reached St. Louis and brightened the prospects of the rapidly developing territory. By 1818, the year before Shaw arrived, St. Louis had forty retail stores selling luxury items as well as essentials. It numbered several manufacturing concerns, a post office, a federal land office, two banks (both were to last only a short time), a courthouse, a theater, and three churches. Virginia-born John Darby, who came to St. Louis about the time Henry Shaw arrived and was to be elected mayor in the 1830s, described the people many years later in romantic recollection: ". . . the inhabitants were, beyond doubt, the most happy and contented people that ever lived. They believed in enjoying life. There was a fiddle in every house, and a dance somewhere every night. They were honest, hospitable, confiding, and generous. No man locked his door at night."[9] In the forty years that the colonial town had stood in the heart of Indian country, it had numbered only one major crime.

About the time of Shaw's arrival, Missourians began to agitate for statehood. At the time, debates in Congress concentrated on the slavery issue. The organization of Missouri as a slave territory shortly after the

Louisiana Purchase had given the cause of slavery a tremendous boost. A proslavery group led by French colonial leaders and such newcomers as Thomas Hart Benton, who was later elected as a United States senator and ultimately broke with the proslavery forces, had prevailed over their free-soil opponents and the wishes of President Thomas Jefferson.

In the succeeding years, the majority of newcomers to outstate Missouri, some of them slaveholders, came from the upper tier of slave states: Virginia, Kentucky, Maryland, North Carolina, and Tennessee. They moved into counties west and northwest of St. Louis, along the upper Mississippi, and on the north bank of the Missouri River west to Jefferson City and on both banks beyond. The territorial population, an estimated twenty-five thousand in 1814, would reach sixty-five thousand by 1820. By Shaw's arrival, much of outstate Missouri was strong slave territory, though only 10 percent of Missouri families owned slaves.

St. Louis's prosperity appeared boundless. "Thomas Hart Benton, who settled there in 1815 with $400," economic historian Richard Wade was later to point out in his book *Urban Frontier,* "was 'comfortably established' four years later. His only lament was that if he had brought $20,000 he might be worth a quarter of a million."[10] New settlers on the farmlands as well as in the towns brought capital, needs, skills, and energy. Benton was probably not exaggerating by too much when in 1819 he described the rise of real estate prices since 1815: "Ground around St. Louis then selling for $30 an acre sells at this day for $2,000."[11]

The fur trade had not recovered from the war, but the lead industry continued to prosper. Commerce with the Indians, long centered in Mackinac on the Straits between Lake Michigan and Lake Huron, gravitated quickly to St. Louis once the peace settlement lessened English influence in the north. The Indian trade would reach an annual value of $600,000 by 1821.[12] Four groups of settlers needed the supplies available from St. Louis merchants: soldiers at frontier posts, farmers in the hinterland, emigrants moving west, and residents of St. Louis. Another three groups outfitted themselves in the town: the Indian traders, army officers, and surveyors for the land office. Within a short time two million dollars in goods would come into the city annually.

Henry Shaw was moving into a new frontier at the right time. He would become one of the merchants with the foresight Benton spoke about.

3.   Budding Businessman

◆◆◆

Within a month of his arrival in Missouri, eighteen-year-old Henry Shaw made his first sale of merchandise to St. Louis merchants Edward Tracy and Charles Wahrendorff. Further, Shaw succeeded in securing space in the Tracy-Wahrendorff establishment at Four North Main, on the west side of the street between Market and Chestnut, as his warehouse and office. He resided, cooked his meals, and sold his goods in one rented room on the second floor of the building. The goods that he could not move in New Orleans, he sold at a good profit in St. Louis. But he had difficulty in getting money acceptable in the Louisiana metropolis.

At the riverfront he saw boats going upriver and on to Mackinac loaded with furs. On inquiry he found that a certain Monsieur La Croix had left in the middle of June with a batteau for Montreal. When La Croix reached Michilimackinac, he would transfer his cargo to birchbark canoes. The entire trip took forty to fifty days. Shaw contrasted that with the direct water route from London to St. Louis via steamboat from New Orleans. Shaw also considered buying beaver from the Missouri Fur Company.[1]

By July he had sold half of his goods in St. Louis, but the consignment still in New Orleans had found few customers. He ordered more hardware items and considered the possibility of shipping furs.[2] On the last day of September he sent his uncle James Hoole a bill of exchange to remit to his mother.[3] He planned a retail auction and gave thought to buying furs. In early October he looked over prospects in St. Charles, on the Missouri River northwest of St. Louis, soon to be the state capital for a short period. He also planned to sell to country dealers from Illinois at 10 to 15 percent under the usual prices.[4] Not waiting for the dealers to come to St. Louis, he sent an agent to the growing town of Edwardsville, Illinois, twenty miles northeast of St. Louis, one of the two towns connected by a stage and ferry route to St. Louis. The shipment included, among other items, two corkscrews worth $1.05 each; six cast-steel handsaws at $2.00 apiece; and two dozen pocketknives that totaled $15.60.[5]

While his agent sold his cutlery in the Illinois town, Shaw left for the South. He found a yellow fever epidemic in New Orleans but decided to

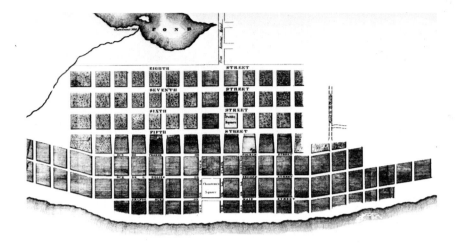

9. St. Louis as it appeared shortly after Shaw's arrival. Map by Lewis Caleb Beck, originally published in *Beck's Gazetteer* (1823).

stay for the winter. He received three letters from his father that gave "mixed signals"; Henry had no clear idea what his father wanted him to do.[6] He began to make his own judgments and not wait for his father to give consistent directions. New Orleans soon gave him more worries than the fear of yellow fever, for he found it one of the worst places in the world to remain idle. "Gambling is incredible," he wrote.[7] Whether he spoke from sad experience is uncertain, but his carefully kept financial records show no unaccountable losses at the time. He did write to his mother a short time later, assuring her that her image and memory were deterring him from misconduct and the evils that befall so many young men.[8]

Taking advantage of good weather early in 1820, Henry went to St. Louis again. In mid-February he proposed to buy buffalo robes for the Canadian market, using sugar and coffee as barter. Such robes could be shipped at a cost of $6.00 per bale to Mackinac, $9.00 to Montreal, and $2.00 to New York.

He still had $400 in merchandise unsold in St. Louis. He felt that he had done as well as could be expected with his goods there, considering the involved political situation of the territory still trying to get into the Union. Henry had momentarily become disenchanted with St. Louis.[9]

The question of Missouri's admission to the Union held the forefront of public discussion. Even though Missouri had taken a big step in an effort to settle the basic question of whether it would be a slave or a free area back at the organization of the territory immediately after Jefferson's purchase of Louisiana, the U.S. House of Representatives had wider issues to face. While the Congress debated under what circumstances the state would be admitted, the territorial legislature considered a proposal to exclude all free blacks from the area in preparation for its imminent statehood. It also proposed a debt moratorium, known in contemporary parlance as a "stop law." Henry called it "a law to encourage villainy."[10] He wrote, "This is truly a country of knavery, oppression and slavery."[11] He questioned whether slavery would be a benefit.[12]

The debate in Washington and throughout the country previewed the arguments that would later convulse the nation. Finally both houses of Congress passed the Thomas Amendment, which allowed Missouri to be a slave state but prohibited further introduction of slavery into the area of the Louisiana Purchase above the line $36°$ $30'$, the southern boundary of Missouri. That would mean the territory of Arkansas could welcome slaves while all the other territories would be free-soil. To match Missouri's admission, Maine came into the Union as a free state.

But big matters of politics and economics did not dominate Henry's life. He had time to write his mother to assure her of his affection and of his recognition of his responsibilities, and he was anxious to tell his sisters about the country he now worked in. He made it a rule never to pass through a country without learning all he could about the people and the customs. The Creoles of Louisiana, for instance, contrasted interestingly with other Americans, reminding him of people in some parts of the West Indies. The Louisiana bayou country, he believed, was "the most valuable and wealthy part of the United States."[13]

About this time (1820) Henry sent eleven hundred dollars to his family in Sheffield[14] and urged his mother and sisters to move to Canada.[15] His father, in turn, was asking him to go to England to settle family business problems. Joseph presumably gave Henry some inkling of the extent of his indebtedness, for the young man lectured his father on the risk of extending credit.[16] What presumption on the part of a twenty-year-old!

While Henry could not leave St. Louis in the summer of 1820, by October he was ready to consider a trip to Canada via New Orleans and then a voyage to England.[17] Still in St. Louis in November, Henry fretted that his remittance of eleven hundred dollars had not yet reached Sheffield.[18] Three weeks later he was in New Orleans and still had no assurance that the money had reached England.

Even though trade was slow, a good many young men had come from the East to buy and sell. As a result, Henry considered a trip to Campeche, Mexico, and then to Havana with a young German named Moller, the son of a merchant of Bremen.[19] Henry carried out neither intention at the time, nor did he visit England. Before the end of 1820, Henry sent his uncle James Hoole another bill of exchange for his mother. "If my mother needs a little cash," he went on, "give it to her and I will remit it on my return to the amount of 20 pounds or so . . . ."[20]

Less than six months later, on 30 April 1821, he registered with the justice of the peace "all the goods, wares and merchandise received at the store of Henry Shaw in the city of St. Louis for the last six months."[21] This, incidentally, was the first explicit mention by Shaw himself of having a "store" in St. Louis. Since John Paxton's *Directory,* published that year, did not carry the name or business address of Henry Shaw,[22] the term may have meant his depot or warehouse at Tracy and Wahrendorff's on Main Street.

In spite of the obvious advantages of frontier St. Louis for an enterprising merchandiser, young Shaw, who already spoke a "tolerable Creole French," had not yet made up his mind to stay there.[23] In the summer of 1821 he was chronically ill in St. Louis and thought of trying Nashville for a year, or perhaps Louisville, where he had gotten 30 percent more for his cutlery than in St. Louis. Looking on Canada with contemporary prejudice and little evaluation of resources, he considered it perhaps the least valuable part of the British Empire. He advised his father against opening a store in Kingston, Upper Canada, and urged him instead to forward what money he could to further Henry's enterprises in the States. Henry intended to remain in the Mississippi Valley as long as his father stayed in Canada, but if Joseph returned to England, the son would follow. Even though a repressive regime ruled Britain in those years after the downfall of Napoleon, Henry retained his regard for his native land. "I prefer," he wrote, "to live under the British government even in the most distant and worst regulated colony England possesses than in these Free States."[24]

Young Shaw could not send a remittance to his mother from New Orleans in the fall of 1821 for two reasons: a quantity of his goods remained unsold in Louisville, and a bank failure in Missouri caused him to lack cash.[25] Since he had been ill during the summer in St. Louis, he decided to try the climate in the winter of 1821–1822. It proved a mistake for him physically. He wrote to his father in January: "Even the winter in St. Louis does not agree with me, and if I do not enjoy better health this next year, I would rather stay altogether in New Orleans."[26]

At that time, Henry's mother and sisters were determined to travel to America with an uncle, Benjamin Shaw, who was visiting Sheffield for a reason unknown to his nieces. Uncle Benjamin planned to sail for America in April 1822.[27] While one uncle was ready to leave for the New World, another uncle, James Hoole, was shipping a large quantity of Sheffield ware to his nephew in America in care of William Alderson in New Orleans. Chisels, gouges, files, razors, adzes, squares, wood screws, and various types of saws and knives made up the shipment.[28]

In good health again by midsummer, Henry could report that he had sold more than half the hardware in New Orleans. He sent £200 to his uncle: £150 to his account and £50 for his mother. He asked Uncle James Hoole to get Queensware from Liverpool, as he believed it would sell, and balls of sewing cotton from Manchester. He begged his uncle's indulgence for asking him to order so far afield; hitherto the consignments had consisted mainly of hardware from Sheffield. Henry also planned to ship flannels to St. Louis.[29]

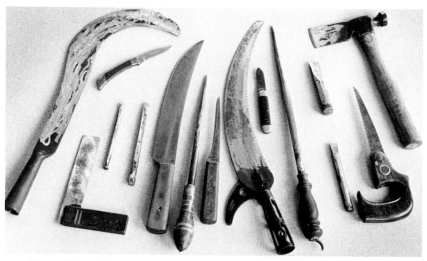

4. Young Henry Shaw shipped knives, hatchets, chisels, and saws from Sheffield to St. Louis.

A friend of Shaw's in later years, James D. Butler, pointed out that Henry "was the first hardware importer by the water route," England to New Orleans to St. Louis.[30] Harvard business historian N. S. B. Gras wrote of Shaw, "Importation . . . was the nucleus of his business."[31] Besides importing from England, Shaw hoped to ship American commodities such as cotton and lead to Europe. He sold domestic products locally. In 1822, for instance, he sold fifty bales of south Alabama cotton, averaging three hundred pounds per bale and retailing at ten cents a pound.[32] Shaw also joined with Tracy and Wahrendorff in selling sixty barrels of flour at $5.50 a barrel, a transaction that netted $50. The partners suggested a venture in sugar. "We are willing to embark with you in this or any other little speculation."[33] They also promised to forward any of Henry's letters, but none as yet had reached the office.[34]

The town Henry knew at this time stretched seven blocks west and twenty-four blocks north and south. An extant map, allegedly drawn in 1822 but probably made several years later, shows that the east-west streets bore the names of trees, following the Philadelphia practice, except Market Street and the last one on the south, Vandeventer. The names Pine, Olive, Chestnut, Walnut, and Poplar were to endure. Prune, Willow, and Pear would disappear over the years. West of Fourth Street on the north end, several streets bore the names of national heroes: Washington, Green, Morgan, and Franklin. On the south end of town, six streets west of Fourth bore the names of prominent early French families: Soulard, Labbadie, Chouteau, Papin, Gratiot, and Cerré. The north-south streets were numbered west from the river.

St. Louis felt the slump following the Panic of 1819 only tardily and pulled out of this delayed reaction quickly. By 1822 the *Missouri Republican* noted that the once-deafening cry of hard times had gone with the return of the green leaves in April. "Trade and navigation from this port are becoming immense," the editor claimed in September of that year. "Steamboats are daily arriving and departing. . . . A bright prospect is before us."[35] Shaw recognized these advantages and slowly came to settle on St. Louis as his central place of business.

His mother's chronic illness and her resultant unhappiness took the edge off his business success. In the summer of 1822 he sent her and his sisters £50, no doubt to help them come to America in the near future. His father had sold the store and the farm in Prescott, Ontario, and was probably not writing lest his whereabouts become known to his creditors in England. As to his own business ventures, Henry paid his Uncle James and ordered more goods, expecting to make a profit of about £400.[36] Shortly after receiving Henry's remittance, his mother and two sisters left for America. They reached New York, intending to join Joseph Shaw in Canada.[37]

The recurrence of yellow fever in New Orleans made Henry wary of spending considerable time there. He had repeatedly commented on the prevalence of the illness, once during the previous summer, for instance, when the epidemic had sent many residents out of the city,[38] and again in December. For that reason, the St. Louis area appealed to him more than the Louisiana bayous, "nothing withstanding its [St. Louis's] numerous disadvantages."[39] He did not list those disadvantages as he saw them.

During 1822 also, the newly elected legislature of the recently admitted state of Missouri had authorized a vote of St. Louis residents on the incorporation of the town. Many members of the colonial French families seemed happy to leave matters as they were. The newly arrived Anglo-Americans preferred to incorporate, and they prevailed in a close vote in 1823.

The townspeople chose an unusually versatile mayor in Dr. William Carr Lane, a Federalist, who defeated Auguste Chouteau. Lane had come west from Pennsylvania as an army surgeon during the War of 1812. Like many other soldiers, he remained in the area after his term of enlistment had ended. Through much of the 1820s, the often-reelected Mayor Lane would open each year with a "State of the Town" address that outlined the needs and offered legislative programs. In accord with his Federalist views, Lane saw a place for government action and planned ahead for the future. He urged the building of levees on the waterfront, the reservation of space for parks, and the planting of shade trees along the streets, all the while insisting on a balanced budget.[40] Mayor Lane looked ahead with enthusiasm, and so did Henry Shaw.

By mid-March 1823 Henry had not heard from his father in a year and a half. He presumed that he had offended the old gentleman by not agreeing with his whims. Henry suggested that his mother should return to England if anything happened to the elder Shaw.[41] Even though Henry still spent the winters in New Orleans and traveled regularly between there and St. Louis, he opened a store at 58 North Main, on the west side of the street between Olive and Pine, in the summer of

1823.[42] John Mullanphy, a wealthy Irish-born businessman, had built this small brick structure, as well as the one adjoining it, later occupied by N. B. Atwood Drugs.[43]

Henry preferred to take care of his own merchandise, not because he presumed others were dishonest, but rather because non-owners gave less attention to business. In July he recorded a shipment of tools from Sheffield and one of goods from Birmingham, including gunflints, large fish hooks, long-handled frying pans, and anvils,[44] and other miscellaneous items such as earthenware, tin plate, gun parts, and steel to make beaver traps for Indian trappers. Two ships, the *Constitution* and the *Three Jesters,* brought this merchandise across the sea.[45]

The inclusion of the names of the ships that carried his imports to America displays an amazing quality of young Shaw. In the otherwise bustling and transitory life on the American frontier, Henry showed a meticulous concern for detail. "It is interesting to note," N. S. B. Gras wrote, "that Shaw himself wrote out the long lists as well as the accompanying letters and commonly both were sent in duplicate or triplicate. In addition, a fair copy of the same had to be made and kept on hand."[46] Gras also commented how fortunate for Shaw to have as purchasing agent in London "his own uncle who was benevolent, prompt, solicitous and discriminating."[47]

When Shaw noticed troops in St. Louis on the way to the upper posts because of Indian disturbances, he decided to look into the Indian trade later. He had an acute observation on frontier troubles. Indians had killed several traders in the northern part of the country. Rumor blamed the British, Henry wrote, "at least in the imagination of these jealous Yankees who are continually infringing on the rights of the natives. If they [the natives] revenge themselves, it is attributed to British influence."[48]

Writing to his mother in early September 1823, Henry had misgivings about his father's ever accomplishing anything. Chances of visiting his parents were slight at the time, for retail sales were slow and he had no one to take care of business while he was away. If his mother intended to write him after 25 October, he told her, she should address her letters in care of William Alderson in New Orleans.[49]

4. Sinking Roots in Missouri Soil

◆◆

When Henry was away from Missouri in the early 1820s, the St. Louis firm of Tracy and Wahrendorff kept him informed of market trends and events in St. Louis.[1] But he gradually was sinking roots in the city. He advertised in the *St. Louis Enquirer* on 17 November 1823 that he had on hand ". . . tin plate, the best blue printed liverpoolware, assorted knives, files, dry goods," and the like.[2] A month and a day later, he reported to his uncle that the most recent shipment of tin plate had found a ready market in St. Louis.[3]

By early 1824, Henry's family had taken a house in Pittsford, near Rochester in upstate New York. His sister Caroline notified Henry that an installment was due the previous owner, a certain Mr. Stone, who was getting impatient. She also told him that the Cornthwaites, Joseph Shaw's sister and brother-in-law, had again asked for help and complained of the Shaw family's indifference.[4] Henry felt that his father had little chance of extricating himself from his financial difficulties. "His mismanaged speculations," he wrote, "have injured himself and others."[5] Henry stepped in to compensate, at least in part, for his father's mistakes. "I am deeply grieved at the injury Mr. Cornthwaite has sustained from my father," Henry wrote to his Uncle James. "You can advance him any amount of money you think proper."[6]

In other letters to James Hoole, Shaw deplored the lack of a bank in St. Louis; nonetheless, business moved briskly. By way of contrast, the South faced hard times. Even though three hundred square-rigged vessels anchored opposite New Orleans, many planters in Louisiana feared the economy would decline.[7] The Tariff of 1824, which raised the duty from less than 25 percent of the value of goods to a new high of 37 percent, played a part in this distress. "This is decidedly against the interests of the southern states," Henry rightfully noted.[8]

At this time, Henry gave power of attorney to S. Eadon and Company to receive goods and bring them through the customhouse in New Orleans. William Alderson served as his agent there; when Alderson died a decade later, Alexander Grant took his place.[9] A sales account for August 1824 showed the extent of the goods Shaw offered for sale besides cutlery from Sheffield: bleach and shirting, gingham robes, boxes of essence, combs, tea canisters, looking glass, flannels, lindsey, trunk locks, and Indiana glass.[10] Shaw sent a consignment of lead to England, his first evident venture in the lead business.[11] In this way he did not have to send money to England to pay for the manufactured products. Over the years he paid for his imported goods by shipping American cotton, lead, beeswax, and furs to Europe.[12]

By this time Henry had developed rapport with the shopkeepers in the country around St. Louis. He noticed that the tariff that had hurt the cotton-producing states had increased the lead business in Missouri by 25 percent. The population of the state had risen to 80,000, including 14,000 slaves, by 1824. The city population had been 4,598 in 1820 and would reach only 5,852, one-fourth of whom were nonwhite, by 1830—a surprisingly slow growth at a time of national expansion. Further, the city needed a strong bank.

Shaw waited with concern for his goods that left New Orleans on the *Plough Boy* in August 1824. Eventually word came that the *Plough Boy* had not moved beyond the junction of the Ohio and Mississippi rivers—a cholera epidemic had carried off the captain and the entire crew.[13] Finally Henry recovered his consignment, and business picked up, especially the sale of winter goods, flannels, and woolens.[14]

In the fall of 1824 Shaw obtained a contract for all the hardware needed at Fort Dearborn on Lake Michigan, located at the spot where the village of Chicago would get its start ten years later.[15] He bought sugar at a low price in New Orleans and sold it with a substantial markup to Gen. Henry Atkinson for use at Fort Snelling on the upper Mississippi River.[16] Shaw also sold dry goods, coats,[17] and blankets to the military.

In letters to his maternal uncle James Hoole in December 1824, Henry showed a growing awareness of his father's injustice and offered to sell millsaws for "Uncle Cornthwaite." He also urged Uncle James to help the Cornthwaites more;[18] he promised a position in his store in St. Louis for his cousin Henry E. Hoole[19] and offered to send three hundred dollars to defray travel expenses.[20] Cousin Henry appreciated the offer, but remained in England.

By this time Shaw, only twenty-five years of age, had an enviable business position. Residing on a frontier that needed goods, he brought in by water the manufactured goods of his native land at lower costs than others could bring American-made products from the Atlantic sea-board. The strong hand of his Uncle James Hoole back in England supported his ventures.[21] He himself possessed a relentless energy and showed amazing business skill. Further, he had a quality not always found among the energetic men of the frontier: the capacity for endless work at the desk, for painstaking care in recording all transactions even to the names of the ships that brought his merchandise from England. He recorded everything, even the cost of the coffin of one of his traders.

By the beginning of 1825, after six years in the country, Shaw had decided to make St. Louis his permanent business headquarters. All thoughts of returning to England seemed to have gone now that his father, mother, and sisters were settled in upstate New York, and he no longer talked with enthusiasm about Louisville. And while he still went to New Orleans regularly, he had planted no roots there. He seemed to have committed himself definitely to St. Louis as the focus of his commercial activities.

Shaw's store was located on the west side of Main between Olive and Pine Streets; it was the only store in that block.[22] The city market was situated on the bank of the river at the foot of Market Street three blocks from Shaw's store. Across from the market between Main and Second streets stood the stately residence of Auguste Chouteau, then a venerable gentleman nearly seventy years old. His brother Pierre had built a similar house several blocks to the north between Washington and Vine, Main and Second. Shaw's hardware store was situated between these two. Many other Creole families lived on Main Street, including the Prattes, Cabannés, Gratiots, Roubidoux, and Sarpys. Eight or nine brick houses graced Main Street. Gen. William Clark, superintendent of Indian affairs, lived in one of them, with a council house adjoining it. Many early French settlers still referred to St. Louis as *La Village*. New Orleans was *La Ville,* the city.[23]

During these years St. Louis established its predominance in the area. In colonial times, the older Missouri town of Ste. Genevieve, situated on the river near the French stronghold of Fort de Chartres, just east of the lead-mining region, seemed destined for regional leadership on the west bank. Long before the 1820s, however, St. Louis had clearly surpassed Ste. Genevieve. It also easily rebuffed the momentary challenge of Edwardsville, Illinois, not far to the northeast, and outgrew a scarcely threatening rival, St. Charles, Missouri, on the Missouri River twenty miles to the northwest. An economic historian of frontier cities, looking back from the mid-twentieth century, stated plainly, "St. Louis enjoyed unprecedented prosperity."[24]

The population of St. Louis would leap dramatically between 1835 and 1875. But in the early years of the century, the increase was less spectacular, going from little more than a thousand in 1800 to slightly less than six thousand in 1830. Most of the early newcomers were Anglo-Americans from other states or immigrants from Ireland or Scotland who readily established themselves in business or politics. Beginning in the late 1820s and continuing until 1875, German immigrants would come in great numbers, some to St. Louis, more, at the outset at least, to the rural areas immediately beyond the town limits. Here they developed farms and sold their products at markets in St. Louis. Even more German immigrants settled in Illinois towns not far east of St. Louis and in the counties along the Missouri River to the west, especially after 1829 when steamboats began to go up the Missouri. A second and poorer group of Irish people would come after the famine of 1846 to 1848, brought on by a blight on the potato crop and abetted by British embargo laws.

A few prominent families of French ancestry came from the West Indies, and some came from Canada, but no great numbers came from France itself. In the *St. Louis Directory* of 1823, the publisher Paxton stated that he could find only 155 families of the "original and other French."[25] But the influence of these pioneers remained strong. They had established themselves early, intermarried with other prominent Creoles and with upwardly mobile Anglo-American newcomers, and set the enduring mood of the city. The chief components of that distinct Gallic spirit were the relaxed quality of life, the lack of acquisitiveness, the tolerance of various opinions, their Catholic religious heritage, and a joy that contrasted sharply with the righteous and somber puritanism of New England.[26]

The two central elements in the St. Louis economy, fur and lead, expanded quickly in the late twenties. The agents of the fur companies did business over the whole expanse of wilderness stretching to the Pacific Ocean. The fur industry was the city's largest employer as well as its biggest exporter; its prosperity involved the entire community. In mining, too, St. Louis was the outfitting center, the "grubstaker" of the workers in the pits. It provided the workers, the capital, and the merchandise and afforded transportation and storage for the ore on its way to the market. The Fever River fields near Galena, in northwestern Illinois, were especially rich, and operations there were expanding.

Further, though St. Louis possessed an essentially commercial character, its leaders constantly tried to lure money into manufacturing. Working men and newspapers continually urged St. Louisans to manufacture goods. Since mercantile channels were so lucrative, money went only slowly into local industries. But St. Louisans gradually began making things themselves, moving into steamboat building, for instance, in the ensuing decades.

Since goods were now coming from New Orleans in any season, Shaw expected Louisville and St. Louis eventually to be ports of entry for foreign goods. He reported to his uncle that he had received invoices for the usual commodities he sold: hardware from Birmingham, earthenware from Staffordshire, and tools and knives from Sheffield.[27] Shaw also began to bring in goods from the eastern seaboard, especially ironware, tea kettles, waffle irons, axes, spades, nails, smith supplies, and glass tumblers.[28]

The four-candidate presidential campaign of 1824, decided by a vote in the House of Representatives, brought from Shaw one of his few recorded political comments. "The presidential election in these states," he wrote to his uncle James Hoole in spring 1825, "has terminated in the choice of Mr. Adams by a small majority over General Jackson, whose popularity is a cause of regret in the sober-minded part of the community."[29] Whether he agreed with the "sober-minded" who saw no questionable political maneuvering in the Adams-Clay agreement that gave the former the presidency and the latter the office of secretary of state, Shaw did not say. But he gave his views on the political atmosphere in the United States: "Politics claim a very small part of my attention.... People in this country meddle too much in this way. Idleness is somewhat a trait in the American character, scheming speculation in place of labour and industry."[30]

Moving back into his more accustomed territory in this same letter, he notified his uncle that he was leaving an agent by the name of Herbert Guion in charge of his store during the six weeks he would visit his family in Pittsford, New York.[31] Henry bought his family a cozy frame house there for seven hundred dollars. He thought it better than the country places in England.[32] He accompanied his sisters to church and later offered the opinion that their friend Elizabeth Guernsey was "the handsomest lady in Pittsford."[33] Beyond that, neither Henry nor his sisters left any further comment on the visit. Nine years later, however, Sarah could still refer to the family reunion as "unforgettable."[34]

Early the following year (1826), Joseph Shaw wrote to son Henry that he was offered a job as manager of an iron foundry for six hundred dollars and board. It might, however, require a purchase of shares. Taking this job might be a good solution to his problems, but Joseph, who was now fifty-nine, feared that the shock of Robert Jobson's "deviousness" had left him incapable of being effective in a mercantile business again.[35] Henry did not offer money to buy shares in the iron foundry, and his father presumably did not take the position of manager at that plant.

In an early spring (1826) Shaw's shipment of goods from England showed a constantly expanding variety of merchandise: hinges, locks, shovels, tongs, spring bolts, nails, pincers, and padlocks.[36] A summer shipment included two categories of commodities: tableware from London and a wide variety of cutting tools from Sheffield.[37] Earlier, Shaw had often complained about shipments, but now he found less reason to complain of inferior quality of goods or of merchandise he had not ordered or that was not in demand on the frontier. In short, all went well with him.

His sisters, however, had problems with their father. While others imposed upon him, they could get no support from him.[38] He had decided to open a store and used the front room of their little home for that purpose. He rejected advice from his daughters and resented their mother's suggestions.[39] To add to the Shaw family troubles, a Mr. Newbould from Sheffield, representing the firm of Remington and Young, visited Joseph Shaw later that year about the money he owed.[40] Shaw obviously had no way of paying his debts. At the same time, in spite of his questionable treatment of the Cornthwaites, self-righteous Joseph Shaw could disapprove of Caroline's attending dancing school.[41]

When Henry proposed to send goods for his family to sell, perhaps in the front room store, his sisters hoped that he understood fully how irresponsible their father was. They repeated their earlier monitions that Joseph, so easily imposed upon, squandered all the family's money.[42] He next opened an accountancy office in Rochester in early 1828, where he seemed to get much business but little return.[43] He had had more than a year to settle his accounts from previous enterprises, but had failed to do so. He would not even discuss his ventures in Kingston, Ontario.[44] He had failed to pay the rent on his old shop there, and two notes had already come due.[45] (Henry obviously had not inherited his business acumen from his father.) Instead of putting his affairs in order, Joseph Shaw accused his daughters of alienating his son, blaming their "false representations of his conduct"[46] for his son's failure to write him.

Henry suggested later in the year (1828) that his father might come out to St. Louis and help him with his account books. This brought a long letter from Caroline that gently and tactfully tried to squelch any such plan.[47] Joseph Shaw had talked for many months of going to Lockport, New York, fifty miles away, to look after some goods he had left there two years before. He finally made the trip and finished this business in three weeks. But then he remained there and wrote a religious treatise on Saturday as the only true sabbath. Joseph had already sent out order blanks for the as-yet-unpublished book *Zion's Trumpet* and was planning two more books to follow. Hoping to convince Henry of the fatuity of inviting their father to help in St. Louis, Caroline wrote during the next year of her father's "want of judgment"[48] and "an imbecility of mind brought on by old age and misfortunes."[49]

In the meantime, Henry had purchased a slave, Peach, from Henry Dodge in the summer of 1828.[50] This marked a dramatic turn in Shaw's social attitudes. Eight years before, he had condemned slavery and deplored American politics; now he became a slaveowner, but still retained his English citizenship even though he would not have been eligible to vote—so restricted was the English ballot—had he returned to his native land. This business transaction of purchasing a slave put him in touch with another of the great names of the frontier. Henry Dodge would become colonel of the First U.S. Dragoons, governor of Wisconsin Territory, and United States senator, and would give his name to frontier cities in three states. In 1829, Shaw had business dealings with other men prominent in the opening of the West: John Jacob Astor, president of the American Fur Company; Pierre Chouteau, that company's St. Louis agent; Gen. William Clark, territorial governor, Indian agent, and explorer; and Bernard Pratte, Louis A. Benoist, Joseph Roubidoux, and Antoine Soulard, Creole merchant traders.[51]

These men profited, as did Shaw, from the presence of the six military posts in the West, all supplied from St. Louis: Jefferson Barracks, a

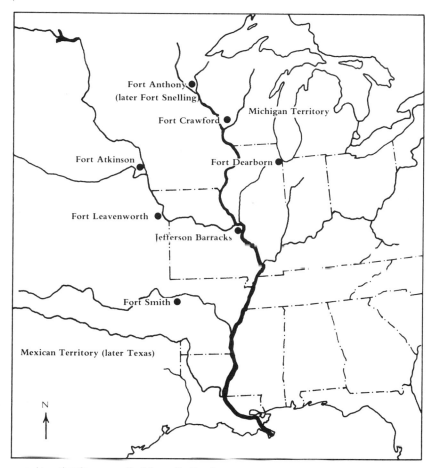

5. Frontier forts supplied from St. Louis

short distance south of the town; Fort Crawford, at what is now Prairie du Chien, Wisconsin; Fort Dearborn, manned spasmodically, at the southern tip of Lake Michigan; Fort Anthony (later Snelling), in what is now Minnesota; Camp Missouri (later Fort Atkinson), on the Missouri River northwest of Council Bluffs, Iowa; and Fort Leavenworth, on the Missouri River in the Kansas Territory. Later a seventh was added, Fort Smith, on the Arkansas River at the western border of the Arkansas Territory.

The officers of the Army congregated in St. Louis in greater numbers than they did in any other point. "It was no uncommon occurrence," contemporary writer Caleb Atwater noted, "for forty officers to sit down at the table to dinner, at Town's, where I lodged; and I saw them in other parts of the city daily and in considerable numbers."[52]

The heavy trade with New Orleans saw several steamboats of the largest class arriving and departing each day. Some continued up the Mississippi, and in a few years specially built steamers would hazard the Missouri River. "The trade in lead, manufactured either in Missouri or in the mineral regions of the Upper Mississippi, has been a great business," that careful observer, Caleb Atwater, pointed out. "The manufacture of lead into the form of shot has been carried on to a

6. John O'Fallon, prosperous St. Louis merchant and sutler for the military on the frontier, purchased supplies from Shaw. When O'Fallon died in 1865, Shaw served as an honorary pallbearer. Engraving by A. H. Ritchie.

considerable extent at Herculaneum, below this town."[53] He estimated the commerce and trade of St. Louis at that time at ten million dollars annually.[54] During these years, Shaw continued to prosper, supplying merchandise much needed on the frontier.[55]

Business historian Gras was to list five advantages Shaw had in his pursuit of business success: he located in a new and growing region; he personally managed well; he worked with able and honest agents in New Orleans and London; he purchased directly from London rather than through Philadelphia, the leading port on the East Coast at the time; and lastly, he received three distinct profits on goods sold at retail—the importer's, the wholesaler's, and the retailer's.[56] Newspaperman Thomas Dimmock, who later knew Shaw well, described his approach:

> He put off nothing to tomorrow that could as well be done today. Whatever he did himself was well done, and what he could not do himself he placed in competent hands, and whenever possible gave it careful personal supervision. . . . He managed business matters on strictly business principles, and in so doing knew no difference between a friend and a stranger. He would take no advantage, however legal, of either; but he expected both the friend and the stranger to be as faithful in the discharge of financial obligations and contracts as he himself was.[57]

In early June 1829, Shaw wrote his sister Sarah that he was looking for a wife with countless good qualities and a dowry of ten thousand dollars. His sister Sarah knew just such a girl, her friend Elizabeth Guernsey, whom Henry had met on his visit to Pittsford in 1825. Henry had even commented on her beauty at the time. Twenty-one-year-old Elizabeth would be a prize even if she lacked the dowry, but her father was rich. Elizabeth was highly accomplished, of a beautiful figure, five feet three inches in height, with lovely dark hair and hazel eyes, bright, industrious, but not extravagant in dress. Sarah concluded that Elizabeth had "too many good qualities to enumerate."[58] Further, the undaunted Sarah went on, if Henry did not want to court Elizabeth, he could consider her younger sisters, who were equally beautiful and, of course, equally rich.[59]

Perhaps Henry feared that marrying one of the Guernsey girls would make him subservient to the business interests of their father; for whatever reason, he did not court Elizabeth or any of her sisters. A friend in

7. Chouteau Pond, recreation area of early St. Louis.

St. Louis, Frederick Billon, thought Henry intended to return to England and find a wife there. Billon, who played chess regularly with Shaw at this time, pointed out that Henry went to parties only occasionally.[60] No newspaper accounts of social gatherings or memoirs of prominent socialites of the time mention Shaw's name. Except for an occasional horseback ride, he apparently refrained from the ordinary recreations of young men of his time, which included, according to a contemporary, James C. Essex, hunting, swimming, and fishing in summer, or skating in winter on Chouteau Pond.[61]

No others besides Frederick Billon claimed Shaw as a friend during those years—and Billon made the claim while reminiscing many years later. Perhaps the extra-attentive young businessman had little time to make many friends. In his *Personal Recollections,* Mayor John Darby gave lengthy tributes to most of his contemporary prominent St. Louisans in the period before the Civil War. He mentioned Shaw's name once in a list of citizens with neither warmth nor ill feeling.[62] In *Persimmon Hill,* William Clark Kennerly recalled the family tradition that Shaw, on his arrival in St. Louis, often stopped by his grandmother's garden to admire the flowers and to talk.[63] And he himself recalled accepting Shaw's invitations years later, after Kennerly had returned from the

Mexican War, to come to Shaw's home on Seventh Street for a glass of wine on occasion.[64] Elihu Shepard had business dealings with Shaw, but he omitted Henry's name in the account of those times.[65] Shaw obviously cut no great swath in contemporary social life.

No evidence indicates that he ever indulged in costly recreations so common among the wealthy Creole merchants and the southern planters of the time, namely betting on horse races or taking part in high-stake poker games, such as the one described by Kennerly in *Persimmon Hill*[66] that involved the transfer of a row of houses, or the one of Archibald Stuart, father of Civil War general J. E. B. Stuart. Having gambled and lost his entire estate in Virginia, Stuart threw himself and his family on the hospitality of his father, retired judge Alexander Stuart, who lived at the time in Florissant, Missouri.[67] Henry Shaw's cautious ways extended beyond his business dealings.

5. The Thrifty Thirties

◆◆

When Henry mentioned his "outdoor exercise" in a letter, Caroline took it for granted that he referred to horseback riding. "It must be very pleasant," she wrote, "to ride in the prairies. I am told they are covered with beautiful flowers."[1] Occasionally in later life, Henry was to speak of riding out into the open country during his early years in St. Louis. At least once his sister Sarah was to comment on his "favorite horse."[2] But not until 1844 did he regularly note "horse-related expenses" in his account books.[3] Henry raced no horses himself and placed no bets on the races, even though there was a track on property he would soon own. He did not join any of the expeditions going west to hunt buffalo on the Great Plains with the Cheyenne or Pawnee, as many St. Louisans were to do in the years ahead.

"Is it true," Caroline asked him, in another vein, "that the 'business gentlemen' mingle very little with society until they have accumulated a fortune? If so, there must be danger of some of them becoming crusty old bachelors before they attain their object."[4] She said that she did not despair, though, of Henry's capacity to find a willing girl in her teens who would make a good wife.[5] But a few months later, a wedding in Pittsford of a lieutenant from Jefferson Barracks who had met Shaw provoked Caroline to comment on the fact that she, Henry, and Sarah would probably remain "three old maids."[6] Singleness seemed to be a characteristic of Shaws and Hooles of that generation; only one out of eight cousins of the trio was thinking of marriage.

While Henry admitted that he did not enjoy himself too much socially,[7] he continued to prosper in business. He brought in hardware, blankets, cutlery, and gun parts in 1830,[8] and copper, beads, tin plates, iron kettles, field tools, anvils, smith tools, and harness parts in 1831.[9]

In August 1831 Joseph Shaw offered to come west and keep books for Henry. He would bring with him some of Henry's Latin and Greek books that the family had brought from England. Since the seventh day (Saturday) was the only real Sabbath, Joseph Shaw would not work on that day. He hoped that would not inconvenience his son.[10] Henry

heeded his sister's earlier warnings of their father's growing irrespon-
sibility and did not urge him to come. The elder Shaw's erstwhile partner, Robert Jobson, died early in the next year. His obituary in the
Sheffield paper gave a quite different view of his qualities than Joseph
Shaw had done.[11]

In March 1832, Aunt Sarah Cornthwaite thanked Henry for his two
gifts of £10 each that had helped to carry them over an unusually difficult
winter. Aunt Sarah could not refrain from mentioning that it would
have been so much better had her brother, Joseph Shaw, sent the
money.[12] But Joseph never wrote his sister or brother-in-law in spite of
their kindness to him.

Henry sent money to his chronically ailing sister Sarah for a trip to
the curative waters of Saratoga Springs during the summer of 1833[13] and
in the fall offered to build a brick house for his family in Pittsford. Sarah
answered that the old one would do until he quit business and came to
live with them.[14] (This was the first suggestion either that Shaw might
quit business or that he might leave St. Louis.) While her mother and
sister attended lengthy Christmas services at St. Luke's Episcopal
Church in Rochester, Sarah wrote Henry that she had never met a more
strict Episcopalian than Caroline, who had only recently joined that
congregation and had taken to reading *Pilgrim's Progress* over and over
again. Sarah herself preferred Gibbons's *Decline and Fall of the Roman
Empire,* but had no inclination to read it over and over again.[15] On
Christmas Day she wrote to thank Henry for his Christmas gifts and his
constant concern for them.[16]

When in May 1834 Henry made it known that he planned to travel on
the continent of Europe when he gave up his business, Sarah hoped that
he would do so soon and invite her to accompany him as far as England.[17] She did not mention that she was at the time having violent ner-
vous headaches.[18] Caroline told Henry of the family's dire financial
situation, and he responded with a gift of $200 for living expenses and
$50 as a down payment on a house either in Rochester or Pittsford that
best suited them.[19] He promised to send them $3,000 in the fall of 1834 to
purchase a new home. They found a house for $3,500 and wondered if
Henry would approve their going over the figure he offered.[20] Apparently, they decided not to purchase this house.

When Sarah mentioned that she had been drinking wine for her
health, even though the rest of the family in Pittsford belonged to the

Temperance Society, Henry sent six cases of wine and brandy. He himself took brandy with water whenever he felt symptoms of cholera.[21]

At that time Sarah wrote that their cousin Frank Hoole—later to be mayor of Sheffield—had announced his plans to marry a young lady named Alathea Tattershall. Henry gave the opinion that Frank's marriage was not likely to add "to his domestic comfort."[22] Sarah wondered whether her brother had heard negative remarks about Alathea, or was it, she asked, "that you think matrimony never adds to anybody's domestic comfort?"[23]

Sarah's health continued to deteriorate throughout the year. Her lungs weakened; she needed a warmer climate. Henry had suggested a move to Philadelphia, but Caroline did not think the weather sufficiently warmer there.[24] Early the following year (1835) Sarah was to complain of more intensive pain during the previous four months than at any time in her life.[25]

Caroline found a temporary home in Rochester.[26] The place would be adequate, Sarah believed, until such a time as Henry retired, when he could superintend the building of such a house as he wanted there or in any place he liked better. "Any place where we could have the pleasure of your society," Sarah wrote, "would be delightful to us. Mother says: 'tell her dear boy how happy we would all be if we lived together.'"[27] The Shaw family rented the house in Rochester for twenty dollars a month and moved there from Pittsford in early fall.[28]

All the while Henry's business ventures prospered. He entered the fur trade directly in the mid-1830s by hiring French-American woodsmen who combed the Missouri and upper Mississippi valleys on horseback, exchanging hardware and dry goods for furs and skins harvested by pioneer farmers and Indians.[29] On 14 June 1834, for instance, Shaw paid trapper Jean Baptiste Roy for an assortment of furs.[30] In that same year, Roy wrote from Black Snake Hills (later St. Joseph, Missouri), complaining that he had not received from Shaw the whole amount of Indian goods that had been promised.[31]

Between 1836 and 1838, Shaw's records listed thirty-five different traders of French background, who dealt with him in amounts ranging from $6 to $370. Only one was well known: Joseph Robidoux, founder of St. Joseph, Missouri.[32] At that time, incidentally, one of the traders, Pierre Bertrand, died at St. Joseph during the time he was under contract to Shaw. Henry paid for his coffin.[33]

8. Charles Marion Russell, Shaw's neighbor, drew this sketch of a French-Indian trader, typical of the woodsmen who worked for Shaw in the late 1830s.

Early in 1836, the Shaws purchased a lot in Rochester for $800 and found a dependable contractor named Loomis. He estimated the cost of the house at $3,000 and the well at $300. While all expressed confidence in Loomis, Joseph Shaw continued to baffle his daughters. He had hesitated to tell them that creditors had a claim to the lot the Shaws purchased for their new house. As a result they almost lost the lot and ended by paying an extra $300 to get clear title.[34] Joseph, furthermore, wanted two rooms in the new residence for himself and continually interfered with progress. Sarah protested, "If we waited for him, we would not get the house built in three years . . . his business facilities are worn out."[35]

Autumn had set in by the time the Shaws moved into the finished residence in late October. They found it to their liking.[36] The final cost of the house was $3,400—not too much for Henry, who was doing so well in business. Since bad weather threatened and Caroline wanted to go to church two or three times a day, she bought India rubber boots—a novelty at the time. Their mother went along, while Sarah, so often ill, stayed home and read or wrote letters to her brother.[37]

Midway through 1836, Henry had purchased another slave, Juliette by name, this one from Antoine Chenier, a grandson of pioneer merchant-traders Joseph Papin and Louis A. Chenier.[38] Two years later, Shaw would buy from Christian Eaker of Cape Girardeau County a third slave girl, Bridgette, who had been raised in the Chenier household.[39] By this time one could readily conclude that Shaw had come to accept the slave system that he had abhorred twenty years before. The social and economic situation of the times made household slavery seem an acceptable institution. No free household help was available; St. Louis was an immigrant city, and few unmarried women immigrated, except under special sponsorship. Within ten years the St. Louis census would show 11,000 more men than women in a population of 77,860.[40] Further, deaths in childbirth were so high that most substantial frontiersmen married several times. There must have been very few unmarried white women available for household chores outside their own home.

The name of the seller of these last two slaves also has historical implications. The French slave code had been quite superior to other colonial codes, requiring that the master see to the training of his bondspeople in the Christian religion, that he not separate families, and that he refrain from molesting female slaves. Many French masters freed their slaves in their wills.[41] The French, in general, had the reputation of never selling their slaves. H. A. Trexler, historian of slavery in Missouri, recalled this tradition and mentioned the Chenier family as one that belied the belief.[42] Bridgette would remain with Shaw. He would remember her and her previously unmentioned son, Cass, generously in his first will fifteen years later.[43]

9. Antoine Chenier, St. Louis fur merchant and son of Marie Thérèse Papin, daughter of Joseph Papin and Marie Louise Chouteau, sold slaves to Shaw.

During those years when he purchased the few slaves and helped his family with their home in Rochester, he continued to sell at a substantial profit. An ever-widening variety of merchandise had come over on the ships *Glenarm, Oileana,* and *Saladen* during 1835[44] and the *Mohawk* and *Thomas* in 1836[45] and would come on the *Ambassador* and *McClellan* in 1837.[46] During these years Shaw purchased a number of lots in the city, including one at Seventh and St. Charles, not far from where he would build his town house in future years. He also purchased several pieces of property in the Rochester area.[47]

In the spring of 1837 the company of Remington and Young wanted Henry to pay his father's large debt. James Hoole wrote Henry to that effect on 25 April 1837.[48] A cousin of Henry, also named Henry Shaw, wrote from Sheffield to James Hoole in October, discussing Joseph Shaw's debt. "Remington and Young," he wrote, "surmised that Henry [in St. Louis] had possessed himself of his father's effects and thus benefitted himself at their expense; and so was bound in honour to liquidate the debt which by that time amounted to nearly £12,000."[49]

Shaw had planned to visit his family in early spring 1837, but at year's end he still had not done so. He did go to New Orleans on business and sent to his father several packs of buffalo robes to sell. By the time they arrived in Rochester, they were in such bad shape they could hardly be sold.[50] Since President Jackson had failed to recharter the national bank, much currency was questionable, and Shaw was careful of bank notes originating in Illinois and Indiana.[51]

Ever alert to new business opportunities, in 1838 Shaw discussed with Capt. Ethan Allen Hitchcock of the Indian Department the possibility of furnishing goods for the Omaha tribe and three bands of the Sioux. In the summer of that year, Shaw pursued his proposal by investing $10,521.82 in outfitting his field men in an attempt to trade with Indian tribes of the Plains—the Omaha, the Kansa, and four branches of the Sioux—and with tribes that had come from east of the Mississippi, uprooted by Jackson's Indian-removal policy. The Indian agent, Lawrence Taliaferro, originally appointed by President Monroe himself and destined to be for twenty years the most important civic official on the upper Mississippi, acknowledged the receipt of presents for various bands of the Sioux.[52] These efforts at direct trade with the tribes presumably did not prove as gainful as other of Shaw's ventures, probably because early traders were too well entrenched.

Almost every year Shaw added something new to his order from England. In 1838, the fresh items were trout hooks, horseshoe nails, and miners' shovels.[53] During the following year, the ships *Chester, Jane Ross,* and *Monticello* would bring over the usual hardware, along with anvils, gunpowder, and brightly colored cloth.[54]

Henry's father had not written in three years. In August 1838 the elder Shaw explained his silence: he had been researching the Scriptures.

Thereupon, jumping from the spiritual to the material, he urged Henry to invest in land in upstate New York and outstate Massachusetts.[55] Henry ignored his father's advice, both spiritual and economic.

Another man whose advice on investments Henry refused to heed was a certain Franco Brichta of Natchitoches, Louisiana. Aware that Shaw intended to travel to Europe, Brichta wrote a letter to a Dr. Poppen in Trieste introducing "his friend Henry Shaw." In the envelope with this letter of introduction, Brichta wrote a glowing account of lands along the Sabine in the newly independent Republic of Texas. He urged Henry to invest in these properties and followed with several other flamboyant real estate proposals in succeeding months,[56] but shrewd Shaw ignored his advice.

When Henry itemized his assets on 1 January 1839, he had a total of $47,678.39 in inventoried merchandise on hand; $15,766.08 in gold and silver; $92,575.68 in bonds and mortgages for money lent; and $33,923.11 in various other properties. The total was $189,943.26.[57]

With his business going well in the spring of 1839, Henry freed his slave Juliette, but gave no reason for the manumission.[58] He sent money to Caroline for a trip to Niagara[59] and gave Sarah power of attorney to sell the family residence in Pittsford to a Mr. Parmely.[60]

Sarah, in turn, thanked Henry for a portrait he had sent, but she did not think it a good likeness. All were happy that Henry was coming to visit. She had deduced that Henry intended to close his business.[61] Sarah and Caroline planned to take out citizenship papers and expressed surprise that Henry had not yet done so. They appreciated Henry's gift of $100 and the certificate of deposit for $350. News of the troubles with the newly formed bank in St. Louis had reached as far as Rochester.[62] The country still felt the effects of the Panic of 1837.

As the time of Henry's proposed visit approached, his mother urged Sarah to recount stories of antislavery demonstrations in Rochester to dissuade him from bringing along one of his slaves. A guest from the South had brought a slave girl along on a visit; the five blacks in Rochester had surrounded the house, stirred up a mob, and broken a few windows before the owner got the girl out of the way. This was only one of several such incidents, Sarah wrote.[63] Henry did not go to Rochester at that time, but when he did visit later, he brought no slaves.

By the end of 1839, Henry had amassed a fortune that totaled nearly $250,000. His profit in various ventures during that one year had come to

$22,876.34.[64] Tradition has it that Henry decided that was enough for anyone to make in a single year, and retired.

As dramatic and interesting as this often-repeated myth is, it does not give the full economic picture. Shaw did stop selling cutlery from Sheffield and goods from neighboring places in England, but he probably did so because economic realities made this a wise move. Canals and railroads were making it easier for firms on the Atlantic seaboard to move their products into the American interior, and the northeastern states were pushing for higher tariffs on imports. As a result, domestic manufacturers could now compete so effectively with imported ware that Henry's unique advantage disappeared. Sheffield historian Mary Walton wrote that "the Sheffield exports to America virtually ceased at the end of the 1830s."[65] Astute businessman that he was, Henry foresaw the end of an era.

In another facet of the economic picture, a severe depression in business was spreading from the East. Land prices plummeted and banks in Illinois, Kentucky, and the South staggered. Many mercantile houses in St. Louis failed, among them M'Gunnegle and Way, Walker and Kennett, and Meyer and Hustall. Shaw had long exported furs, lead, cotton, beeswax, and tobacco. He could now buy them at depression prices and hold them in St. Louis, New Orleans, or London until the prices favored sale. When he announced his "retirement," he was buying lead in Galena, Illinois, and tobacco and beeswax (for candles, crayons, and polishes) in western Missouri.

At the same time, in line with many other merchants, Shaw moved into the real estate business indirectly. He loaned money to many people, a practice banks avoided. Some of these debtors, unable to pay, offered mortgages for security, as historian James Neal Primm pointed out.[66] Many defaulted on their mortgages. While the early French settlers had a reputation of nonacquisitiveness, and the merchants among them, so often related by marriage ties, dealt informally with one another, Shaw tended to separate social relationships from business dealings.

Shaw placed his business affairs in the hands of Peter Lindell, an astute merchant and fellow bachelor who happened to be a close friend, and the law firm of Spalding and Tiffany. They would write regularly to keep him abreast of the local economic picture. Uncle James Hoole would offer a similar service from his vantage in London. In July 1840

Shaw listed some of the assets he left in Lindell's care: "Bonds and notes left with Peter Lindell my agent for collection and safekeeping, July 1840. Total $167,026.32. Left $2,230.53 cash with him."[67] The firm of Pierre Chouteau, Jr., and Company had the largest debt: $21,172.77. Thomas Jefferson Payne, owner of much land in the Prairie des Noyers section southwest of the city, was the largest individual debtor, with a total debt of $18,543.55. Joseph Charless's mortgages totaled $18,480, those of Meriwether Lewis Clark $8,500, that of Marion College, a Presbyterian school near Hannibal in northeast Missouri, $7,000, and those of Henry and Julia Soulard totaled $6,804.

Many other prominent Anglo and Creole neighbors owed lesser amounts. Two clergymen owed Shaw money: the black minister and educator John Berry Meachum owed Shaw $2,750, and Bishop Rosati had borrowed $683.70. In this latter instance, Shaw asked no security of the bishop, who was to make his ten-year report to Pope Gregory and then to travel as the pope's emissary to Haiti in the Caribbean.[68] Shaw also listed obligations and accounts that he left for collection with Spalding and Tiffany in July 1840 that amounted to $13,993.33.[69]

These are typical of the transactions during the next few years: C. W. Taylor, a merchant, secured a $3,000 loan with business property at Main and Pine streets that brought $1,800 annually in rents; John and William Finney secured a $6,000 loan with two riverfront lots; James Thomas, later to be mayor of St. Louis, offered two hundred acres in the Soulard subdivision as security for his loan; and James S. Lane borrowed $4,000 at 10 percent with a building at Third and Pine as security.[70] Shaw was to have revenue-producing property as well as bonds and mortgages worth $166,943.82 by the mid-1840s.

With the home base thus secure, Shaw could relax and travel at ease.

6. Years of Travel

◆◆◆

Shaw set out on his journey on 11 July 1840, going on the steamboat *Fayette* up the Illinois River as far as the town of Peru, Illinois, the highest navigable point on the stream. At that place, the eighteen people in the party divided into two stagecoaches, with nine passengers each, for the trip across the prairies to Chicago. The state of Illinois had completed only half of the work on the canal connecting Lake Michigan and the Illinois River at the time.

Shaw kept a journal, recording his day-to-day impressions as the trip progressed.[1] He thought Chicago a dull place but enjoyed the cool breezes from the lake, both in the town and on the lake steamer *Great Western*. At Mackinac Island, Shaw and the party thought they saw the northern lights.

When the boat arrived at Detroit on Sunday morning, 19 July, Henry visited the Presbyterian, Catholic, and Episcopalian churches for a few minutes each. A day later, he described Cleveland as a bustling place with mock magnificence in its newly erected buildings. He reserved his greatest praise for Buffalo. "The flourishing port of Buffaloe (*sic*)," he wrote in his journal, gave "evidence of a more extensive commerce than have yet observed at any place since leaving Saint Louis . . . ."[2]

On his arrival in Rochester, on 21 July, he had the pleasure of joining his parents and sisters.[3] Henry found all members of his family in good health. He liked their neat, comfortable little dwelling and dubbed it "Economy Hall."[4] He spent two days at the Shaw home and then took his mother and sister Sarah to Buffalo, where they met Julia Guernsey, a younger sister of Elizabeth, the young lady Sarah had wanted her brother to marry eleven years before. Even though Henry and Julia— along with Sarah and his mother—shared a visit to romantic Niagara Falls, Henry left no special mention of the young lady in his diary. Once again, Sarah failed as a matchmaker.

The three ladies did not join Henry on the trip under the cataract. He treasured the certificate signed by Capt. Isaiah Starkey that testified to his having "passed behind the great falling sheet of water."[5] The four visited the rapids of the river and the whirlpool below the falls. They

10. The St. Louis waterfront would have looked much like this when Shaw left in mid-July 1840 on the steamboat *Fayette*. Sketch by Norbury Wayman.

stopped at Lewiston on the lower level on the night of 29 July. Henry rose early the following morning and hiked alone to higher ground to gain a last view of the area before his mother, sister, and Julia awoke.

After returning to Rochester, Henry took Caroline to the Finger Lakes region. He found the town of Ithaca most pleasant for its lovely setting, fine buildings, and "a number of the fair sex—the gallant manners and dress of some of the younger and more handsome very refreshing to my bachelor eyes."[6] Occasionally his sisters would suggest they visit a lady friend, but none of these young women elicited more than a passing mention in Henry's journal.

Henry went back to Rochester for ten days (8–18 August), and then he and his sisters said goodbye to their aged parents and started by stage and rail for New York City. On the day of farewell he handed Sarah $2,500 and Caroline slightly less.[7] After visiting the metropolis, Sarah returned home, while Caroline would go with Henry to Ireland and England. When Sarah arrived in Rochester, she received a letter from Peter Lindell asking her to keep him informed of her brother's whereabouts.[8]

Shortly after Henry left, Joseph Shaw complained in a letter to his son of losses caused by Robert Jobson, his former business partner in Sheffield, and admitted walking out on their in-laws, the Cornthwaites, who had helped him secure a loan of £12,000.[9] Joseph wrote again to Henry in New York a little over a week later, telling his son—presumably for the first time—of his disastrous venture with the Tennessee trickster. Joseph again admitted defaulting on loans to his brother-in-law and blamed Jobson for his business failures.[10]

Henry usually kept a journal of his travels. Even when he did not record his daily activities, however, he still made it easy to trace his whereabouts by keeping receipts of all the hotels he stayed at from Killarney to the eastern Mediterranean. He retained all other bills, too, principally from tailors, shirtmakers, cobblers, and watchmakers. He landed first in Ireland, touring the Killarney Lake country and then going to Dublin before crossing the Irish Channel. He visited his relatives in Sheffield and saw the sights in Oxford and London. While Caroline stayed with relatives in England, Henry took a boat from Dover for the Continent. He spent New Year's in Paris and attended the Grand Opera. Later he went to Lyons and to Marseilles. He visited Italy next, stopping at Leghorn, Florence, Rome, and Naples. He saw the sights and attended Mass at various churches.

While Henry enjoyed traveling in Europe, only bad news came from Rochester. The family physician had forbidden Sarah to walk because of her spinal condition. Her back became ulcerated. To add to the domestic difficulties, the servant girl could not brook Mrs. Shaw and left to take a position with another family. The substitute proved totally unsatisfactory.[11]

Henry did not note in his journal what effect all this gloom had on him. He went to Smyrna in Asia Minor in June and there purchased two Persian rugs. When he shipped the rugs on the American ship *Illinois,* he saw an account in a New York paper of the murder of Jesse Baker, Lindell's nephew. Shaw wrote in his journal that the laws were too lenient on murderers.[12] Santa Sophia in Constantinople did not impress him as much as he expected because of the flatness of its dome;

he had trouble picking it out from the other mosques. But he did purchase a piece of mosaic as a souvenir.

In a series of letters to Henry during 1841, Sarah thanked her brother for the rugs and for other gifts to family and friends. She assured him that his agent, Mr. Allison, had sent money to his family in his absence. If, by chance, he had any information he did not want their father to know, she suggested that he write in French. Lastly, she expected Caroline back from London in July.[13] Caroline did return, and in September 1841 notified her brother, then in Venice, of that fact. She appreciated his promise of a watch and told him what kind she wanted.[14]

When Shaw traveled through the Ionian Islands in September, he singled out a scene that brought back memories. "I could not but admire it," he wrote, "bringing to my recollection the journey with my sister to Bantry, among the rocks and bays of Ireland about a year before."[15] Normally, however, he recalled memories of classical antiquity: Xerxes and his bridge over the Hellespont, Jason and the Argonauts, and the siege of Troy.[16]

He saw the Lippizan horses at Trieste, attended Mass at San Antonio Necchio, where he found the worshipers as fashionable but not as devout as those in Naples and Rome, and wrote his Uncle James to remit money in his name to the American consul in Venice, Mr. Holme. He attended the opera in Venice as he had in Trieste, but found the prima donna "a good singer, but in a family way and very ugly."[17]

In 9 October, Shaw noted in his journal, "I am told Vienna is a gay place and the girls are very pretty."[18] This promise proved correct. He was to stay five weeks and take daily lessons in German from a tutor. He attended Mass on two successive Sundays in the Royal Chapel in the Schönbrunn Palace and found it as beautiful as the Sistine Chapel in Rome. Shaw described the empress as a good-looking lady of thirty, brunette, with a lovely mouth and an intelligent look who followed the ceremony with devotion.

He heard Johann Strauss—"a small, strait-limbed, neatly made man in black"[19]—conducting music of his own creation in the imperial Volksgarten. Shaw spent three hours in the art gallery of Prince Lichtenstein and attended the ballet in the presence of Ferdinand I and the empress.[20] He praised the grounds at the imperial Schönbrunn Palace and wrote about the botanical garden there.[21] This was the first written

11. The Conservatory at the Schönbrunn Palace in Vienna, visited by Shaw in 1841.

statement of Shaw relative to botanical gardens found in his multi-faceted papers.

He visited the Plain of Wagram where, thirty-two years before, Bonaparte had defeated the Austrian archduke whose forces outnumbered the French two to one. Shaw's guide claimed to have taken part in that disaster.[22] A week later, on All Souls' Day, Shaw attended a military memorial Mass at the Augustinian Church for the men who fell in the battles against Napoleon.[23]

Turning abruptly to more pleasant thoughts, Shaw described a young woman by the name of Caroline as having a "beautiful mouth, white, regular teeth . . . an oval face, rather pale, eyes modest, but of a celestial lustre." Her "hair was fine, silky and dark brown . . . her neck and bosom whiter than drifted snow." In person she was "small, delicate and beautifully proportioned."[24] Even though he wrote so appreciatively of the petite Caroline, he did not court her with equal ardor, and did not mention her further.

Shaw had hoped to see Prince Metternich, the elder statesman of Europe, before he left Vienna, but was not able to do so. He met a famous *danseuse,* Cerrito, and invited her to tour America, as another entertainer, Fanny Elssler, had done a short time before. Miss Cerrito said that sea voyages were not to her liking, but she would see him in London on her spring tour.[25]

With cold weather setting in, Shaw bought a fur coat and prepared to cross the Alps to Venice. He concluded his visit with a general tribute to the charming ladies of Vienna. Several times during his last days in Vienna and the first few in Venice he mentioned his traveling companion, Demosthenes (Demo) Simos. On 7 December, he wrote in his journal, "Simos says I let pass very good opportunities—but I don't see he makes much better progress with his Greek fair ones."[26]

Henry received a letter from his seriously ill sister Sarah shortly after Christmas 1841. He confided in his journal that he did not think she would be around much longer.[27] On the last day of the year he visited the Monastery of San Lazzaro, where the poet Byron had spent some time. Shaw happily noted that he found among the names of American visitors in the guest book that of Bishop Joseph Rosati of St. Louis.[28] At this time, Demo Simos wrote from Florence, recalling pleasant memories of the various young ladies they had met.[29]

When cousin Henry Hoole wrote from Sheffield, on Green Lane Works stationery, he tried his hand at matchmaking. "Should you feel strongly disposed toward Matrimony," Hoole wrote, "your cousin Mary still remains in her state of pure virginity and no doubt living in hope as other maidens do."[30] Cousin marriage, incidentally, was common among Hooles. Two months later, Hoole thanked cousin Henry for a painting he had sent.[31] Sarah also received a painting as a gift from her brother at this time, Annibale Carracci's *Madonna*. She stated flatly that she had never seen anything more beautiful.[32]

While on his journey, Shaw corresponded with Pierre Chouteau, Jr. Chouteau responded in French, urging Shaw to keep him informed of politics, improvements, amusements, and even ladies. Chouteau's son planned to go to Europe the following year. If he could go in Shaw's company, the elder Chouteau would be most happy.[33] While Henry toured Europe, Peter Lindell kept him informed on the status of business. Among items that Lindell looked into, he paid the fees for Dr. Vitalis's visits to the slave Bridgette and for the delivery of her baby in 1842, and the wages for "Bridgette Shaw" and a previously unmentioned "Peter Shaw" from midsummer 1840 to 1842.[34] Presumably, Shaw's servants had followed a social custom of the time and taken the family name of their owner with his consent.

Lindell wrote that the economy had picked up two years before with the election as president of William Henry Harrison in 1840. But Harrison had died the following year, and his successor, John Tyler, vetoed a congressional effort to recharter a national bank. By 1842, Lindell complained of business troubles and blamed President Andrew Jackson's war on the bank. Moving from the major national troubles to the problems of one individual, Lindell wrote that Rev. John Berry Meachum, whose payments Shaw had extended in May 1840,[35] had filed for bankruptcy.[36]

Among the many others who borrowed money from Henry Shaw, Thomas Jefferson Payne, a nephew of former territorial governor Gen. Benjamin Howard, owed the most by this time, $18,543.55. Payne had come to St. Louis in the late 1820s and in a few years had gained possession of a large tract of fertile land beyond the fourth terrace that marked the gradual rise of the land west of the Mississippi. Some years later, Grand Avenue would run along this ridge. Payne enclosed a portion on the west end, erected a small house with stables for the keeping of blooded horses, and laid out a trotting track. A grove of trees stood in the center of this oval.

In colonial times, a fence running along the ridge at the east end of these lands separated the Commons from grants of land by the Spanish lieutenant-governors to the Dodier, Labbadie, Marly, Roubidoux, LeBeaume, and other families. The French customarily divided lands into strips rather than into sections as the Anglo-Americans did. The strips usually measured an arpent (about 180 feet) wide by four arpents deep and stretched from east to west. Some colonists cultivated corn and wheat; others left them in natural grass, to cut for hay.

In the French-Spanish days a man by the name of Louis des Noyers kept the gate or *barrière* of the fence that bounded the Commons of St. Louis. As a result the early French called the area Prairie des Noyers or Barrière des Noyers. No trees grew there except two or three ancient cottonwoods along a water course running north to Rock Springs and thence to Chouteau's Mill Pond. Tall prairie grass covered the area, with an occasional patch of wild strawberries.[37] On his eighty-first birthday Shaw was to recall his first look at this area on his arrival in St. Louis in 1819.[38] In no extant record from his early days in St. Louis, however, does Shaw allude to such a visit to the locality.

An 1840 map of the area shows the Prairie des Noyers stretching all the way from Chouteau Avenue to Gravois Road; beyond that to the south lay the Common Fields of Carondelet; to the north the Cul de Sac Fields; and beyond, to the northwest of the city, lay the Grand Prairie

Common Fields. Arsenal Street ran all the way from the Mississippi through the Prairie des Noyers to the River Des Peres—the only city street ever to run that entire distance. Magnolia and Tower Grove avenues, both unnamed, appear on the map as secondary roads. Kingshighway and Old Manchester Road ran through the Prairie des Noyers, and Grand Avenue, not yet an unbroken artery, bounded it on the east.

While Shaw was in Europe, on 8 August 1842, his agents picked up land belonging to Payne and fifteen others at a sheriff's sale. The records bear this cryptic comment: "to satisfy judgments against them."[39] In another sheriff's sale nineteen days later, Shaw's representatives acquired four strips of land between Grand and Tower Grove Avenue north of Arsenal.[40] Shaw and Lindell together gained acres on the south side of Arsenal east of Kingshighway at the same time. At another sheriff's sale, Shaw gained possession of a sizable property on the west side of Kingshighway a few blocks south of Arsenal.[41]

During the last third of 1842 and all of 1843, Shaw's agents took indentures on 119 acres and ten farm houses and deeds to three pieces of land in Prairie des Noyers belonging to the heirs of early French settlers, the Dodiers, De Lisles, Lalandes, and others.[42] Shaw also picked up property in downtown St. Louis, including two stone warehouses on Front Street between Pine and Olive. In June 1842 Dennis Byrnes[43] signed a contract to lay a sidewalk in front of these structures.

In the meantime, Henry Shaw, still overseas, had invited his sister Caroline to move to St. Louis to handle some of his business affairs.[44] Shaw left Venice, visited Verona, Milan, and Turin, and pushed through Chambery and Lausanne to Geneva. From Le Havre he went to Southhampton, and after some time in England, he took a boat for the United States. He registered at the Astor Hotel in New York City on 13 June 1842.[45] He visited his family in Rochester, and a short time later returned to St. Louis and occupied a suite at the new Planters' House. Built while he was overseas to replace an earlier structure, it was the city's most elegant inn.

During the previous year, Uncle James Hoole had discussed business in various letters to Henry. He approved of Caroline's taking charge of Henry's affairs in St. Louis. By late January, Caroline was in St. Louis and, according to her sister, enjoying herself. Sarah, now in better health, was relaxing, going to parties and the theater in Rochester. "I

12. The South Side of St. Louis, 1853.

suppose our good sister will not like that," she wrote to her brother.[46] Sarah had drunk up all the claret Henry had sent and had found some port wine. She and her mother were no longer suffering from cold in the house. They kept good fires burning, now that Caroline was not there "to preach about extravagant burning of too much wood."[47]

Henry's main endeavor during his few months in St. Louis before going back to Europe was attempting to finalize property relationships in the Prairie des Noyers. Thirteen different colonial French families had owned strips of land in that area where Shaw began to garner ownership. Shaw had picked up lands originally belonging to Savarre by purchasing claims and bought outright the property first owned by Gabriel Dodier. From the trustees of Thomas Jefferson Payne, he had received some strips that had belonged initially to Guitard, Lalande, Dacine, and Reynald. He purchased the arpents of Motard. The last

13. The new Planters' House, where Shaw resided when he returned from Europe in the summer of 1842. His sister Caroline lived there later. Sketch by Norbury Wayman.

two plots of that area he would not get until 1850: the one belonging earlier to François Fostin from the Payne trustees; and that of François Belleste from Louis Bompart in 1850.[48]

Shaw signed an agreement with Thomas Payne on 28 April 1843, with Judge Bryan Mullanphy acting as arbiter. The first provision called for Payne to quit the house and lands on Henry Shaw's property within ten days. Second, a man by the name of Dye would have a lease of the trotting track at $2.50 per acre. Third, the fence on the trotting track farm would be moved wherever Shaw desired. Fourth, Shaw would move the fence on a line between his and Chambers's property (the Berda, Dorlac, and Beaugenon strips). Fifth, all instruments of the title surveys and other documents relating to the ownership of the land would be delivered to him. Sixth, Shaw would give up all claims he held against T. J. Payne connected with the deed of trust on said land. Payne, on his part, would assist in defending the titles to the property. Judge Bryan Mullanphy would take the notes and claim and keep them until the time of compliance.

In an addendum to the agreement, Shaw agreed to pay for the extension of the fence eastward, but he did not give up any title to property north of the fence. A proper tribunal should settle that. Payne's only objection was the price of the lease to Dye; he insisted that it should be only $1.25 per acre until March of the following year.[49] Shaw had come into possession of a remarkably rich area near St. Louis, and presumably only a few matters of boundary dispute remained. These would arise in the next few years.

In early spring, Pierre Chouteau, Jr., repeated his request to have his son Charles join Shaw in his travels. This time he wrote in English: "If it would be agreeable with you to have Charles as a companion, be pleased to let us know; but, on the contrary, should it in any manner be likely to interfere with your views, I trust you will . . . say so."[50] Charles wrote a short time later asking to be Shaw's traveling companion, assuring Shaw that he had no trouble with Spanish or French and understood Italian fairly well.[51] Young Charles ultimately did accompany Shaw.

Now that Shaw had visited his native land, he was ready to commit himself permanently to the United States. On 3 July 1843, he agreed to "abjure forever all allegiance and fidelity to Victoria, Queen of Great Britain," and was admitted as "a Citizen of the United States." He had lived the required time in the country and the state of Missouri and had shown himself "a man of good moral character, as required by law."[52] Also in early July, the St. Louis Court of Common Pleas recognized Caroline's position as holding the power of attorney.[53] Caroline resided at the Planters' House and rented a pew at Christ Church.[54]

About the time Shaw was leaving for Europe, Bernard O'Halloran, the caretaker at his country place, discovered that the Shaw-Payne agreements had not ended the dispute with Prairie des Noyers neighbors. He received a threatening letter from Mary Jones, one of the settlers on the old Payne properties. "Remove the rails," she wrote, "or in ten days I will consider them my property. I have just learned that Shaw is to enclose my land by force. Don't drop any more rails or commit any depredation on my land."[55] She warned him to continue only "at your risk or peril."[56]

"You don't own the land," O'Halloran answered three days later. "Shaw bought it at a sheriff's sale . . . . I shall put up the fence and you will resist at *your* peril."[57]

7.   Caroline Shaw: Businesswoman

◆◆

While Henry Shaw traveled in Europe and Caroline took care of his business interests in St. Louis, Sarah found life much more pleasant in Rochester. Parsimonious Caroline was not hounding her mother, father, and sister about minor household expenditures. Sarah thanked Henry for his gift of money; she was using it to travel and planned to go to New York or Boston the following summer.[1]

Out on the Prairie des Noyers, Thomas Jefferson Payne proved troublesome for Bernard O'Halloran. The caretaker notified Shaw in England of Payne's "mid-night depredations, burning and pulling down of fences, threats and open and avowed hostilities."[2] Had O'Halloran known he would be faced with such conduct, he would never have taken the post. But once taken up, he would fight it through. "We must get rid of him—Payne," he wrote. "I have never met such a man. I am disgusted with his low cunning. He even says that the Motard arpent on which I live is his."[3] O'Halloran advised against renting any property, for Payne would only deceive the renter into thinking he still owned the property.[4]

Shaw wrote O'Halloran on 17 October 1843, telling of his pleasant trip through the Scottish Highlands and enclosing newspaper clippings of interest. O'Halloran answered with a three-page letter on 19 December. In his clear and distinctive script, O'Halloran thanked Shaw for his letter and the enclosures. He contrasted the "romantic scenery" Shaw had found in Scotland with the "dull monotony of the Mississippi Valley."[5]

At this juncture, Henry Hoole brought "Cousin Mary" to Shaw's attention again,[6] combining his earlier role as matchmaker with that of banterer concerning Shaw's amorous adventures on the Continent. Wearing the first hat, he wrote: "Our cousin Mary was quite a lion during her stay in Sheffield. She had a great many parties given in honor of her visit."[7] Then donning the other hat, Hoole joked about a "little warbling and interesting amiability" that cousin Shaw had met in France, perhaps a young woman by the name of Aimée Dupont. He offered to be godfather in case that friendship should grow intimate. He thought Shaw would temporarily miss the young lady when he crossed the Pyrenees, but assured him that "the dark eyed girls of Spain will make ample amends."[8] He wondered lastly how his cousin's young companion Chouteau occupied himself while Shaw attended mademoiselle.[9]

No indication of Shaw's reaction to his cousin's banter has come down to posterity. This was the only evidence of humor at Shaw's expense throughout his life; he obviously carried his serious business approach into social life. His sisters never wrote to him with a light touch, and none of the existing accounts of Shaw written by his contemporaries contain an element of humor. If he ever related a funny anecdote, the occasion escaped the record books. His many writings contain only one indulgence in whimsicality: the story of how the French explorer Du Tisne outwitted hostile Indians.[10]

A short time later, Shaw received from Rochester far more serious news than the items Cousin Henry wrote about from England. Sarah wrote him on 27 April 1844 that their father was dying.[11] She followed with a letter three days later telling of Joseph Shaw's death.[12] There was no way Henry could get back from Europe for the funeral.

In the meantime out in St. Louis, Caroline had already showed her business rigidity. Marshall Brotherton had borrowed money from her brother with a clearly defined program of repayment. Now he wanted to "take up his interest notes by repaying the principal."[13] Caroline obviously "could make no such arrangements."[14] Early the following year, she engaged extensively in the purchase and sale of tobacco. The steamer *Iatan* brought consignments from the Chariton River area in the "Little Dixie" country of west-central Missouri. She paid $3,000 for tobacco in July 1844 and $4,050 in August.[15]

Even more important, Caroline picked up downtown property during that year, including warehouses and four-story buildings. Ultimately Shaw would have 103 indentures covering 46 downtown lots, along with 760 acres in St. Louis County, almost all of it in the area of Prairie des Noyers.[16]

Caroline made a loan of $1,200 at 10 percent interest to Mr. Bompart on the security of his sixty arpents (roughly fifty acres) in Barrière des Noyers. "We do not think he can repay," Caroline wrote, "and you have always wanted his land and could buy it under a deed of trust."[17] Many individuals, including some of the old Creole families and fur mer-

14. Caroline Shaw, Henry's younger sister.

chants, borrowed Shaw money, using property as security. Joseph Robidoux already had debts and Judge Wilson Primm sought a loan.[18] In May 1844, René Paul asked Caroline, "How much interest do Peter Chouteau and I owe your brother?"[19] Anglo-Americans came to the

Shaw financial well also. Prof. Elihu Shepard, who was to write a history of the city, borrowed $5,000 from Caroline in that year.[20] While Henry had extended payments and interest on a note of Rev. John Berry Meachum,[21] Caroline sent the constable to levy on the prominent black minister's goods because he had been "so indifferent about paying his rent punctually."[22]

Caroline was not all business, however. As her brother's business prospered, she throve. She gained twelve pounds and, no doubt presuming that the added poundage enhanced her looks, had her picture taken. The family thought the daguerreotype a good likeness. She kept Henry informed on local events, such as the sinking of the steamboat *Shepherdess* with the loss of fifty lives two miles below the city in the winter of 1843–1844,[23] and commented on local personalities, such as the new minister, Rev. Cicero S. Hawkes, an excellent preacher.[24] She wondered about the long betrothal of Henry's traveling companion, Charles Chouteau, and Chouteau's cousin, Julia Anne Gratiot.[25]

At the time of the greatest flood in the history of the central Mississippi Valley during June 1844, Caroline gave each tenant a month's free rent to help them over the period of flood damage.[26] Some of the tenants, such as George Witsel, sharecropped in lieu of rent.[27] During that same election year, rumors spread that the government might move from Washington to a place more central to the nation. St. Louis, the leading city of the West, was the favorite alternative, with some talk having the new capitol on the bluff north of Jefferson Barracks. Sarah noted how valuable Shaw's property in Prairie des Noyers would be in that eventuality.[28] During the following year she wrote that river trips to St. Louis were becoming fashionable.[29]

In early 1845 Caroline fretted about difficulties she was having with O'Halloran.[30] On 3 March of that year, O'Halloran quit,[31] and Cornelius Phelan took his place. He was to remain only three years.[32] Also in 1845, Caroline took part in a questionable practice of a few slaveowners at this time: she "hired out" Bridgette to a river captain. At the end of the season the young woman came back from south Missouri without adequate winter clothing. Caroline provided warm clothes and promised that Bridgette would go back on the boat in the spring.[33]

When Kemper College, an Episcopal school on the southwest corner of Kingshighway and Arsenal, declared bankruptcy in late 1845, the county court purchased the property for a poorhouse. Caroline warned her brother, "I fancy the location will not enhance the value of your property in that direction."34

Unperturbed by these events in far-off St. Louis, Shaw enjoyed Malta and cities of Germany and France and also visited Cairo and Alexandria in Egypt, St. Petersburg and Moscow in Russia, and Stockholm, Christiana, and Copenhagen in the Baltic lands. Cousin Henry Hoole ceased chiding Shaw about his Continental girlfriends and tried his hand again at matchmaking. He spoke of "Cousin Mary . . . as handsome as ever" and still available. He wondered, "Can she be waiting for Cousin Henry Shaw?"35 But again Shaw eluded the "matrimonial trap."

Sarah wrote regularly all the time he was away. She thought Caroline liked St. Louis better than Rochester.36 She was sorry to hear that he suffered acute rheumatism as Caroline had ten years before.37 He could take courage from the fact that Caroline had ridden fifteen miles on horseback and was not at all fatigued.38 As the day of Henry's return grew imminent, Sarah hoped "that Caroline would not grow priggish again when she returns to Rochester."39

About the same time that Sarah was wondering about her sister, Caroline, already in her early forties, was finding the young man of her life. On 20 January 1846, she bought scythes, hayforks, and a curry comb for use on the Shaw acres from Thomas Meier.40 It may have been on this occasion that she met twenty-five-year-old Julius Morisse, a clerk in Meier's hardware store at the corner of Third and Green.41 A native of north Germany, Julius had come to St. Louis in 1836. In spite of the great differences in their ages, the two took a liking to each other and soon planned to marry.

Henry, too, seemed a little more serious with a friend in France. He treasured letters from a French acquaintance—perhaps the "interesting amiability" Henry Hoole had referred to earlier. Aimée Dupont had wanted to see Henry in early February 1846 but could not arrange a visit for the following Sunday. She felt a great void without him.42 She spoke of their trip together and referred to two letters from him. "You are so generous and loving," she wrote. "No one loves you more than I."43 The correspondence was to continue after Shaw returned to America.

When Shaw reoccupied his suite at the Planters' House on Fourth between Pine and Olive in August 1846, the hotel was "the one fixed point where people met to gossip, discuss politics, talk business . . . the

rendezvous of the Mississippi Valley."[44] In the words of an English visitor who resided in St. Louis for a time, this famous hotel "stood for
wealth, fashion, adventure, ease, romance—all the dreams of the new
life in the great West."[45] He believed that it epitomized "life on the
Mississippi, on the prairies, in the cotton fields, in the cosmopolitan
city. Here North met the South, East met the West."[46] Shaw's hotel fees,
incidentally, averaged about $75 a month.[47]

Before Caroline left St. Louis, she probably told her brother of her
hopes to marry Julius Morisse. On reaching Rochester, she asked
Henry for a business grant to her fiancé and herself, so that they could
marry and enter business in St. Louis.[48]

8.   Loves and Disasters, Houses and Slaves

❖❖

Caroline completely surprised her mother and sister with the news
that she was engaged to young Morisse. Sarah confided in Henry: "Our
sage philosophical sister to be in love with one so much younger than
herself is almost beyond my belief. . . . It must be a mortification to
you."[1] Their mother scarcely knew what to say; she liked the idea of
having a son-in-law, but if he had been a bit older and had owned more
of this world's goods, she would have liked it better. Sarah appealed to
Henry to help Caroline and Julius.[2]

When Julius came to Rochester, Sarah instinctively liked him, but
still thought her sister a fool. "He is not her equal in mind or attain-
ments," Sarah wrote to Henry, "and is awkward and unpolished."[3]
Henry and Sarah agreed with an uncle of Julius who thought a fall wedding a bad idea.[4] Making her own decision, Caroline went ahead with
plans for a wedding in late Lent or soon after Easter.

In the meantime, Sarah heard a rumor that Henry was to marry a
certain Miss Welsh.[5] Whether or not Henry considered Miss Welsh at
this time is unclear, but he did correspond regularly with Aimée
Dupont. "I told myself to have patience," Aimée had written the previous November (1846), "it is only eight months until you return, making fifteen since you left. You are so gentle and loving. . . . My mother
is very ill and I sent her the rest of the money you gave me. You are
always so generous . . . . I send you a thousand kisses from the depth of
my heart."[6] Responding to Henry's generous New Year's gift, she wrote
in January 1847: "This mark of your goodness and generosity is proof of
your attachment to me, and I used it to buy some very necessary
things . . . . Your words give me hope that a more fortunate time will
come. You would never regret having me near you . . . . If you would
send me word I would sell my little store and make arrangements with a
ship . . . . You must be very alone now that your sister has gone to visit
your mother. The season of April or May would be delightful for setting
out upon a voyage."[7] She wrote in April: "I dreamed the other night
that you had come from St. Louis . . . . How I trembled and with what
anxiety I opened the letter from you . . . . You have such good taste

and your conversation has unbelievable charm. If I could only convince you of my lasting and sincere affection."[8] She suggested that she should have followed Shaw to America and would be content to be near him. If she were to make such a trip, she would need expense money for the voyage. He could send it to the place of embarkment. She wondered lastly if it were difficult to learn English.[9]

While Henry and Aimée merely corresponded regularly, Julius and Caroline set a date for their wedding ceremony. Sarah fainted eight times during the nuptials and became ill shortly afterward, but she recovered in time to write to Henry at length about the wedding and her illness.[10]

By midsummer Caroline and Julius were well situated,[11] and a year later they could boast that they were doing well in business.[12] Julius had opened a hardware and cutlery store at 179 North Third Street.[13] Caroline took satisfaction in the success of "Julius Morisse and Co."[14] Their hardware business was to prosper over the years.

Sarah wrote the following spring (1849) that she would cultivate rare plants and flowers in her small garden in Rochester—if she were rich. One would have expected some comment on Henry's garden plans, if he had any; the fact that she made no such reference calls into question an alleged mutual interest in flower gardens that they had shared as children in Sheffield.[15]

In 1849 the leading businessmen of St. Louis were planning to connect that city by rail with the Pacific coast and the Far Eastern trade. Henry Shaw added his name to the distinguished list of Creoles, Celts, and Anglo-Americans who incorporated the Pacific Railroad on 12 March 1849. The list included Louis A. Benoist, Thomas Allen, Bernard Pratte, John Sarpy, Lewis Bogy, James Lucas, Louis A. La Beaume, Pierre Chouteau, Jr., John O'Fallon, Edward Walsh, Robert Campbell, Adolphus Meier, James Yeatman, George Collier, and Wayman Crow.[16]

That same spring, a double disaster struck the city. Undernourished immigrants, weak from hard times in Europe and deprivation on the long voyage across the ocean, did not get to stop and recoup their strength in New Orleans. Immediately transferred to upriver steamboats, they brought the dread cholera to St. Louis. Health procedures at the time were rudimentary: people had limited knowledge of antiseptics and little sense of sanitation; infant mortality stood at high levels; the city had few sewers; the newer unpaved streets had a surface of mud and debris; and lead factories and flour mills sullied Chouteau's Pond, once the choice picnic place of the city. The cholera claimed 21 victims in February, 78 in March, and 126 in April. The city had endured repeated outbursts of the illness before, but this one was to stun the city for six months.

In the midst of the growing contagion, a second disaster struck. A fire broke out on a Missouri River steamboat, the *White Cloud,* moored at the north end of the waterfront on the night of 17 May. The fire jumped to another vessel, the *Edward Bates.* Ordinarily rivermen towed a burning vessel into the channel and let it drift downstream away from the other vessels. This time, to everyone's dismay, an unexpected strong wind from Illinois pushed the *Edward Bates* against one steamboat after another as the current pulled it along. Two boats under power steamed out into the river and escaped the conflagration, but more than twenty others caught fire.

Freight lined the wharf near Locust Street, and wind carried sparks from the burning steamboats. From the levee the fire spread to wooden buildings, giving the volunteer fire companies more than they could handle. Eventually the flames devoured four hundred buildings in fifteen city blocks, with estimated damage at six million dollars.

Although the cholera seemed to pause a bit in the face of this companion disaster, it was only getting its second wind. Three weeks after the fire, on 9 June, it picked up speed, and soon it claimed fifty-seven victims a day and then rose to eighty-six. The city council fled, leaving Mayor James G. Barry to hold the community together. He appointed a Committee of Safety, which helped little, since the committee could think of nothing to do except set aside a day in June for prayer and fasting. Late in July the number of victims decreased, and by the middle of August the disease had almost disappeared. More than one out of every ten residents had died. (Henry's seventy-seven-year-old mother was near death that year, too, but recovered. She was to die within two years.)[17]

The city paused for reflection, then moved directly to prevent any such disaster in the future. It set up a checkpoint for immigrants to quarantine any newcomers with contagious illness. It provided for a municipal fire department, passed a more stringent building code, and drained Chouteau's Pond. The city was to bounce back with surprising speed.

15. Shaw's town house, originally built at Seventh and Locust, shown here after being moved to the Garden.

Henry Shaw had no need to bounce back: the cholera had missed him, and the fire had destroyed none of his properties. In that very year (1849) he commissioned one of the area's few architects, George I. Barnett, a native of Nottingham, England, to design a country house in the Prairie des Noyers property, and a town house at the southwest corner of Seventh and Locust streets. Coming to America in 1839 at age twenty-four after six years in the employ of architect Sir Thomas Hine, Barnett had spent a short time in New York before locating permanently in St. Louis in 1845. He had prepared a perspective sketch of the new courthouse and then worked briefly in the office of Meriwether Lewis Clark before forming the firm of Barnett and Matthews. After 1850, when Barnett would tour Italy and give special attention to Florentine buildings and villas on Lake Como, he began to follow Italian models. But Barnett put touches of the Italianate in Shaw's buildings, especially his country villa, even before his Italian tour. He and Shaw were to become life-long friends.

The town house at Seventh and Locust, usually looked on by Shaw's contemporaries as his winter home[18] and more traditional than its country cousin, contained seventeen rooms, including two kitchens. The three-story rectangular brick building, which faced Seventh Street, had a central door and two windows on the first floor of the wider section and three windows on each of the upper floors. Two windows graced the first and third floors on the side along Locust, while two doors led to small, grill-protected porches on the second floor. Shaw decorated it lavishly with tiles for the front hallway from Stoke-on-Trent in England, carpets from Brussels, elaborate marble mantels from New York, and curtains of silk or worsted, many of them gold in color, also from his native land. A substantial quarters for servants adjoined the side of the building away from the street. Tall pillars stretched from the top of the first floor to the roof in that section.

Many have wondered over the years why Shaw built such an elaborate mansion. A reporter for the *Republic* was to ask that question in 1891 of Mrs. Rebecca Edom, Shaw's housekeeper during most of his last thirty years. "He built it," she stated, "in order that his mother and sister, who were in Rochester, New York, would come to St. Louis, and it

16. Shaw's country residence, Tower Grove House, as it appeared prior to the addition built in 1891.

was a view to their comfort. When it was completed, the mother and sister were afraid to come as they were afraid of the climate."[19] This may have been true, although no letters of Shaw or his sisters mentioned it. But Sarah did write that her mother would never live in a house with slaves.[20]

The country residence, Tower Grove House, lacked the symmetry of its city counterpart. A tall tower surmounted the eastern third of the two-story high-ceilinged main section, with its Italianate flavor. The servants' section, the three-storied, low-ceilinged eastern portion of the house, did not match the western half. Architect Gerhardt Kramer, looking at a photograph of the structure a century later, appropriately spoke of the residence's "split personality."[21] Besides its asymmetrical design, the house had other interesting features. A large oblong window over the front door gave one descending the stairs from the second floor a magnificent view of the area. On the negative side, the residence lacked adequate sanitary arrangements.

Henry Shaw's business papers documented the building of his houses. Up to that time, he had listed twenty to thirty items under building expenses, mainly for upkeep and repair of downtown properties. Now in 1849 he paid eighty-five separate bills for stone, lumber, bricks, iron, copper, cement, and hardware (most of the last from brother-in-law Julius Morisse's store); and wages for a variety of work, including bricklaying, masonry, carpentry, hauling, glazing, fencing, excavating, and taking down and rebuilding two houses. The following year iron-workers and plasterers joined the work force.[22] The names of the skilled craftsmen working on Shaw's houses provide an interesting commentary on the social history of St. Louis. Among others, Pawley and Hawkins were the stonemasons, S. W. Higley the brickmaker, and Sam Robbins the master bricklayer at the town house; W. Johnson was the carpenter and W. O. Strans the master bricklayer at the country house—all Anglo-Americans.[23] A few years later immigrants would move into the building trades.

Even though highly critical of the state's legalizing of slavery shortly after his arrival in St. Louis, Shaw's abhorrence of bondage had obviously lessened over the years. As previously stated, he purchased individual female slaves at different times over the years. In the late fall of 1848, he purchased three slaves, Joseph, Tabitha, and Tabitha's daughter Sarah, from Thomas Purnell,[24] who lived in Benton, a community along upper Mill Creek, to the northwest of Shaw's property. These, as all Shaw's slaves in the years ahead, worked at the town house. The tax assessment for slaves was listed with "clocks, watches and furniture" at the downtown residence.[25]

On 16 October 1850, Shaw paid $600 at an auction at the courthouse for an adult slave named Sarah and her child. The seller was Marshall Brotherton, administrator of the estate of John T. Brown.[26] At the end of the year the circuit court ordered Brotherton to put up for auction at the south front door of the courthouse on 2 January 1851 at twelve noon a thirty-year-old man by the name of Jim who had belonged to the same John T. Brown. On that date Shaw paid $1,010 for Jim.[27]

Shaw had continued to improve his country property in the meantime. Landscapist John Thorburn wrote to Shaw regarding plans for preparing the gardens around his country home.[28] Shaw bought trees from Thorburn, plants from the firm of Scott and Otis and from Nick Riehl at the Gravois Nursery, and trees and seven hundred strawberry plants from the Sigurson Brothers.[29]

In the spring of 1851 Shaw purchased plants from Nicholas Riehl at a cost of $27.50. The order included two black Hamburg grapes, six balsam poplars, two weeping willows, one moss rose, two Japanese anemones, and one *Spiraea tomentosa*—fifty-eight plants in all of twenty-nine different varieties. From the Krypton Nursery in Cincinnati, he purchased thirty-six trees of eleven varieties for $18.00. The shipment included five Scotch pines, two purple birches, and one weeping ash.[30] Shaw placed a $19.25 order for forty-three trees of six varieties, including ten Norway spruce, ten silver fir, and ten red cedar with Mount Hope Garden and Nursery in Rochester, New York.[31]

In March, also, Shaw purchased bluegrass and a "Peoria Plow" from Plant and Salisbury, Agricultural Implements and Machines.[32] Louis Bompart signed an agreement on 19 March that empowered Henry Shaw to lease land in the Prairie des Noyers for three years and granted him an option to renew it for two years more at the same rent.[33] Various business transactions of early 1851 included a balancing of the accounts on Shaw's and Lindell's venture in coal mining ($1,178.90 was due Lindell, and $967.61 was due Shaw);[34] a payment of Dr. A. F. Barnett's medical bill for attendance on "Joe, a woman and a child";[35] a listing of the coupon numbers of Shaw's Paris and London railroad stock;[36] and the purchase of two hundred cabbage plants and one hundred fifty celery plants from John O'Callaghan.[37]

Planning to visit London for the Great Exhibition, the first world's fair, Shaw empowered his brother-in-law Julius Morisse on 7 May 1851 to collect money due in his name but not to sell real estate or endorse any note or bill of exchange.[38] Henry did not, at least at this time, have the same confidence in the business skills of Julius Morisse that he had in those of Julius's wife, Caroline.

Five days later, on 12 May 1851, Henry Shaw made his will, with Robert Campbell as witness. He set aside $2,000 for a lot and vault in Bellefontaine Cemetery for his burial. He gave £200 sterling each to the four children of his uncle William Hoole, to his cousin Henry and Henry's minor son, to his cousin Lucy Miller, and the two daughters of his uncle Richard; £150 sterling to the children of his aunt Wilson; and £100 sterling to the general infirmary at Sheffield. He ordered his stocks under the care of his uncle James Hoole to be sold to take care of this English part of his will.

He gave a lot in St. Louis to each of Cousin Henry Hoole's daughters. He gave Caroline two lots and warehouses in downtown St. Louis and left Sarah one lot downtown and all his property including his slaves in Prairie des Noyers. All his personal items—watches, books, paintings, jewelry, and such—were to go to his two sisters. The property he owned jointly with Peter Lindell was to be sold, and the revenues divided equally. He gave his mother the home she lived in and committed her to the care of his two sisters.

He provided for the care of his slaves. He offered Bridgette and her son Cass freedom at his decease and five arpents of land on Russell Lane in the Prairie des Noyers, along with several domestic animals and a house with a fence around it, providing that Bridgette continued to work for his sister Caroline at an annual salary. Tabitha and her son Joseph were to enjoy the same arrangements on a plot next to Bridgette's on Russell Lane, provided that Tabitha offered her services to his sister Sarah at the going salary. He divided all his other properties equally between his sisters,[39] obviously presuming that Sarah would be moving to St. Louis in the meantime. Shaw did not mention any plans for a botanical garden.

At the end of 1851 Shaw paid $941.90 in state, county, and school taxes on twelve pieces of property west of Grand in southwest St. Louis

County, evaluated at $156,900, and $2,239.65 in taxes on sixteen pieces of property in the city of St. Louis, ranging in value from $2,826.80 to $42,400.50, and amounting to $277,378.99 in total worth.[40]

9.   The Challenge of Chatsworth

❖❖❖

Planning to attend the Great Exhibition in London, Shaw left St. Louis for New York in June 1851. After crossing the Atlantic, he registered at the Royal Hotel in Matlock, England, on 4 July. This village lay about thirty miles southwest of his native Sheffield and was near the ancestral home of the dukes of Devonshire, fabulous Chatsworth with its fountain, cascade, gardens, and conservatory designed by Joseph Paxton. While walking through the grounds of this, the most magnificent private residence in Europe, Shaw began to wonder if he could create his own garden in St. Louis.[1] It was not to prove a passing thought.

After a short visit to northwestern Wales, he took lodging at St. Paul's Hotel in London on 3 August. He attended the Great Exhibition, which marked England's pinnacle as a world power. The creator of the conservatory at Chatsworth, now *Sir* Joseph Paxton, had designed the main feature of the fair, the Crystal Palace, a giant glass-enclosed structure that won universal acclaim. Shaw stayed in London until 16 August. It was probably at this time that he visited the Royal Botanic Gardens at Kew, a visit mentioned later by Joseph Hooker, son of the director, Sir William Hooker.[2] Crossing the Channel, Shaw visited Belgian, German, and French cities. He was in Paris on 24 September.[3] No evidence exists that he saw Aimée Dupont on this trip.

During the month of October he was again in England and purchased suits, trousers, and a shawl from various stores in London, and copperware from his uncle James Hoole's firm at 36 Aldermandy.[4] Returning to America, he stayed at the New York Hotel on 12 November[5] and returned to St. Louis in December. This 1851 journey, incidentally, was to prove his last trip abroad. He would go to Colorado in 1872[6] and to the northern lakes during August in his late years.[7]

Shaw continued to improve his acres in Prairie des Noyers, developing trees and plants. The area would soon be called Tower Grove because of the tower on his house visible throughout the surrounding level upland. With more systematic planning and developing goals, Shaw set aside twenty-five acres for trees of all varieties that grew in the

17. Chatsworth House, as it appeared when Shaw visited in 1851.

region (the arboretum) in the northwest corner of his property, six acres for shrubs and an experimental fruit orchard (the fruticetum) in the northeast corner, and ten acres for herbs and flowers (the Garden) between the fruticetum and Tower Grove House. Shaw subscribed to several horticultural magazines over the years, such as the *Botanical Magazine* and the *Gardeners' Monthly and Horticulturist.* Shaw's Garden was underway.

Henry Shaw did not start the first large-scale garden in the vicinity of St. Louis. Credit for that goes to a resident of Franklin, Missouri, John Hardeman, a man of fine education, tastes, and background. When

18. The Crystal Palace, London, site of the Great Exhibition of 1851.

Shaw came to St. Louis in 1819, the town of Old Franklin was one of the most prosperous in Missouri and one of the two places (the other being Edwardsville, Illinois) that was connected by stage with St. Louis. At that time, steamboats did not yet go up the Missouri River. In 1822 Hardeman had laid out ten acres in an exact square and adorned it with flowers, plants, grapevines, a fruit orchard, and a selection of trees, both native and foreign.[8]

Hardeman had presumed that the Missouri, like the Hudson or the St. Lawrence rivers, would be content with its current riverbed; he did not realize until too late that the Missouri changed its riverbed continually. The river washed away his garden in 1827, but it lived on in the memory of neighbors. A geographical directory of Missouri published in 1874[9] and a history of counties in the region published nine years later would speak of the vanished Hardeman's garden as "a vine clad and rose covered bower, the prototype of the renowned tulip grove of that public benefactor, Henry Shaw of St. Louis."[10]

Shaw had gone to St. Charles, a town about one hundred thirty miles downriver from Franklin, in the early 1820s. Enterprising young man that he was, he may well have taken the stage to the then-prosperous town of Franklin and seen Hardeman's garden. No contemporary evidence supports this, but a tradition among Hardeman's descendants and others in the Franklin area held that he did.[11] Shaw did not mention Hardeman in writing or in talking with friends, either in his early years or when the notices appeared in the *Gazetteer* and the county history.

Shaw had stopped occasionally to admire a local flowerbed during his early days in the city, according to two accounts. "The finest garden in St. Louis then," journalist Thomas Dimmock was to write in a short life of Shaw, "belonged to Madame Rosalie Saugrain; . . . her daughter—the late Mrs. Henry von Phul—remembered how the young Englishman, on his daily afternoon horseback rides into the open country beyond what is now Seventh Street would stop at the garden fence, admire the beautiful flowers, and exchange pleasant words with the accomplished ladies . . . ."[12]

In support of this statement, William Clark Kennerly, nephew of Gen. William Clark and a veteran of the Mexican and Civil wars, recalled in a narrative published many years later, "I can remember how my aunt Rosalie von Phul used to tell me that when Shaw first came to St. Louis he often stopped by Grandmother Saugrain's garden to admire

19. Madame Rosalie Saugrain's French colonial residence was the location of a
flowerbed admired by the young Henry Shaw.

the flowers and to talk . . . ."[13] Kennerly also recalled a feud Shaw had
with a neighbor when he first moved to Tower Grove. "James Russell's
estate, 'Oak Hill' was directly south of Mr. Shaw's country home,"
Kennerly wrote, "but they were not friendly after Mr. Shaw sent him
word to 'cut down his trees' as they obscured his view of the river."[14]
Charles Russell, sculptor and painter of western scenes, grandson of
James, grew up on Oak Hill.

A *Sheffield Antiquary* that presented an interesting account of Henry
Shaw's career saw in his youth an early interest in botany that would
later perpetuate his fame. "He seems to have been a lover of nature from
childhood," this short biography assured its readers, "and with his two
sisters passed many hours in the little garden attached to the family residence, planting and cultivating anemones and ranunculus [buttercups],
as he remembered and told after the lapse of nearly eighty years."[15]

No letter of Caroline's indicates such an interest, and only one of
Sarah's does so, dating from 1847, when she won an award for growing
the greatest variety of roses.[16] Henry himself gave no indication of an
unusual love for nature before his fiftieth birthday.

20. Oak Hill, the residence of the Russell family, nieghbors of Shaw on the south; the artist Charles Marion Russell grew up here.

A St. Louis real estate dealer, Richard Smith Elliott, recalled many years later what he believed to be the first public mention Henry Shaw made of his intention to found a garden. A native of Pennsylvania, Elliott had come west as Indian agent at Council Bluffs before locating in St. Louis and joining Hiram Leffingwell's real estate firm in the spring of 1849. On a summer day in 1853, Henry Shaw had walked into the real estate office carrying a bunch of flowers, as, Elliott recalled, he often did. The real estate man knew Shaw was beautifying his rural home, but knew nothing of any intentions beyond that. Looking at a map on the wall, Shaw "remarked, as if it were a mere commonplace announcement, that he intended to have a Botanical Garden, with proper accessories, free for citizens and strangers to visit."[17] Shaw further intended to give a tract of land to the city for a public park on condition that it be properly improved. "If I recollect rightly," Elliott wrote, "this was the first communication of his intention to anyone."[18]

No one was to challenge Elliott's assertion in the ensuing years. In that same summer of 1853, Shaw's workbooks give a clear indication of his intention to develop a garden, namely the existence of a hothouse on the property.[19] Shaw began to keep careful records of the growth of vegetation and of the weather conditions that affected the plants. On 23 September 1853, the Duchess D'Angouleme pears had matured and the

George IVth peaches had been gathered. In the following year, 26 August was the last day of the violets, and on 6 October 1855 frost killed the dahlias and the cannas. The thermometer ranged from 97 ½ degrees in the parlor of the residence on 30 July 1854 to 16 degrees below zero on 9 January 1856.[20]

Shaw's determination had extraordinary significance on various accounts. The city of St. Louis, less than one hundred years old, stood only three or four hundred miles from the Indian frontier. None of the older cities on the Atlantic seaboard had as yet opened a botanical garden, although there were several smaller ones associated with colleges and universities in New York, in Cambridge, Massachusetts, in Philadelphia, and elsewhere. Congress had set up the U.S. Botanical Garden in Washington in 1820, but it had ceased to function in the early 1840s and was reestablished only later.

Many wealthy families in Europe had set up private gardens. Descendants of their founders later opened these gardens, for various reasons, to the general public. Some American families were to follow this pattern, but Shaw broke the pattern in creating a garden open to the public at the outset.

During these initial years of development at Shaw's estate, workmen continued to come from Ireland. Among them were Patrick and Thomas Meehan, Patrick and Thomas Costan, James and Oliver Dalton, Patrick Dieglan, John Fling, Thomas Dolan, James O'Bryan, Dan Daly, Robert Dempsey, and John Harney.[21] Even though Shaw's will spoke of slaves at Prairie des Noyers, no evidence exists that they ever worked there. Tax assessments, at least, always connected them with the town house on Seventh Street. Nonetheless, when Shaw reached the status of a major slaveowner with eleven slaves in 1853,[22] it would be difficult to envision his keeping that many working all day downtown.

The slave Sarah decided to solve Shaw's problem of keeping slaves employed in her own way—she took her child and escaped in May of that year and fled to Chicago.[23] At this point Shaw entered one of the most distasteful aspects of the slave situation. He paid twenty dollars to a notorious slavedealer, B. M. Lynch of St. Louis,[24] to bring Sarah back under the drastic Fugitive Slave Act of 1850, which required private citizens, under severe penalty, to assist federal officers in retrieving runaways. Lynch, in turn, hired a certain A. Melvin to seek information or to secure the arrest of the runaways.[25] With Sarah missing, the city assessed Shaw for only ten—not eleven—slaves in 1854. Shaw countercharged that he no longer had six of these ten in his possession and received a proportionate diminution of his assessment.[26]

Two days after slavehunter Melvin brought Sarah to Lynch's "slave-pen" on 20 May of the following year (1855), four slaves of Shaw tried the hazardous "underground railway" to freedom.[27] The basement of the home of the late Rev. John Berry Meachum was the "gathering station." (Meachum was the heroic black minister who had taught children on a boat on the Mississippi to evade Missouri's laws restricting the education of blacks. When he had been tardy in repaying a loan from Henry Shaw in the early 1840s, Caroline Shaw had sent the constable after him to collect the money.)[28] Shaw's four slaves fled across the Mississippi River along with five others. Shots were fired as they approached the Illinois shore, and one woman and two children belonging to Shaw were captured, along with two others. Shaw's Esther was among the four who headed for Alton, Chicago, and, hopefully, eventual freedom. Mrs. Meachum was jailed.[29]

Shaw then moved even more deeply into the most distressing aspects of the slave system: he offered Lynch an additional $280 to secure the arrest of Esther and "sell her down South."[30] Within a few days she, like Sarah, was in his slave pen. Two months later Lynch had sold her to John D. Fondren of Vicksburg for $350.[31] Lynch sent an itemized expense account of $41.62 for boarding Sarah and Esther for forty-one and seventy days, respectively; $20 for Melvin for hunting Sarah; and $100 for "arresting" Esther, for a total of $161.62. Subtracting that sum from the $350 he received for the sale of Esther, Lynch returned $188.38 to Shaw.[32] Perhaps Shaw had had his fill of the slave business, for his city tax assessment for the town house in 1856 included watches and furniture but no slaves.[33] They do not appear on the county tax lists either.

The entrance of so many energetic Irish and German immigrants into the St. Louis labor pool at this time rendered slight the need of slaves in the area. During the 1850s more and more St. Louis slaveowners would free their bondsmen. By 1860 only 3,297 of the 160,773 people in St. Louis would be black; and more than half of the blacks, 1,755 in all, would be free, some of them rich men and women.

While St. Louisans were freeing their slaves, parts of outstate Missouri and the rest of the South clung to the "peculiar institution." The series of palliatives at the start of the decade dubbed the Compromise of 1850 merely postponed a national showdown. During the 1850s, the Kansas-Nebraska bill, the Dred Scott decision, John Brown's raid, and the Lincoln-Douglas senatorial debates would keep the slave issue in the foreground.

In the early years of the decade an anti-immigrant secret society, the Know-Nothings, stirred riots in many cities, including St. Louis, especially during election time in 1852 and 1854. These were among the few outbreaks of bigotry in a generally tolerant city.

All the while the city grew, jumping from 16,469 in 1840 to 77,860 in 1850 and then doubling its population in the 1850s with the arrival of thousands of impoverished Irish fleeing the potato famine and of even more Germans, who were generally more prosperous and better skilled than the Irish. Many of the German immigrants in that decade were political refugees who had failed in their efforts in 1848 to build a liberal, unified fatherland. By 1860, these two nationalities would make up nearly 90 percent of the half of the city's population that was foreign-born.

21. The St. Louis Levee in the heyday of steamboating.

St. Louis remained the center of extensive commerce on the Mississippi River and was the transfer point for people boarding the more rugged Missouri River steamboats for the initial stage of their journey to Santa Fe, Oregon, or the mining regions of the West. Railroads reached St. Louis from the East during that decade, and other lines pushed from St. Louis south to Iron Mountain, west toward Jefferson City, and northwest to Macon to connect with the first trans-Missouri railroad from Hannibal to St. Joseph.

Busy with his garden project, and diverted from his previous excessive attention to commercial advance, Shaw did not participate in the business boom of the 1850s except through the rise of real estate values. But many other St. Louisans besides the well-established Charles P. Chouteau, Jr., John O'Fallon, Thomas Allen, and James H. Lucas would rise to power in business during the decade. Between twenty and twenty-five merchants "made a million" during the 1840s. Mining and manufacturing would offer opportunities for others in the 1850s. Among the energetic businessmen rising to prosperity during these years, several were associated in one way or another with Henry Shaw, including James Yeatman, L. A. Benoist, Wayman Crow, Henry Taylor Blow, Edward Walsh, and Shaw's fellow Englishman John Withnell.

Social commentators called St. Louis "a cosmopolitan city" with "an atmosphere of Southern luxury and lethargy, of ease and nonchalance." The St. Louis Agricultural and Mechanical Association began to sponsor an annual exposition at the fairgrounds on North Grand. The Christian Brothers opened a college at Ninth and Cerré streets near McDowell Medical College in 1852. Eliot Seminary, a college for men founded by Rev. William Greenleaf Eliot and incorporated in 1853, took the name Washington University in 1857.

For recreation, southern planters and river pilots gathered at gambling houses. They and other racing fans went to the Abbey Trotting Park or the Laclede Association Track on Page. Two clubs, the Cyclones and the Morning Stars, played a form of baseball in Lafayette Park. Recent young German immigrants gathered at Turner halls for systematic gymnastic exercises, for fellowship, and, before the decade was out, for political harangues that condemned slavery and secession. Unlike earlier German immigrants whose social life centered around their Catholic, Evangelical, or Lutheran churches, the *Turnverein* was the "religion" for these so-called "Forty-Eighters."[34]

City services grew more formalized at this time, too. Fire fighting as an effort of volunteer semiathletic societies gave way to the formation of a city fire department, and policemen began to wear badges indicating their status.

10. Shaw's Mentors: Hooker, Engelmann, Gray

❖❖❖

When Shaw sought guidance for his garden project on 11 February 1856, he went directly to the most qualified man, Sir William Jackson Hooker, director of the Royal Botanic Gardens at Kew, in Richmond, on the south bank of the Thames not far west of London. "I take the liberty of addressing you," Shaw began his letter, "which as a promoter of botanical science, hope you will excuse, even in one who is utterly a stranger—being the proprietor of lands in the vicinity of this town—and having a desire to found and endow a public botanical garden, and in commencing such a considerable undertaking, I wish to obtain such hints and information as may be useful to me."[1]

Shaw went on to state that his knowledge was limited to what he had seen of such institutions in Britain and on the Continent and in the plans and descriptions in *Loudon's Encyclopedia.* He felt that the Glasgow Garden suited the St. Louis scene and came within the limits of his proposed budget. He had set aside about eighteen or twenty acres, three and a half miles by country road from the courthouse or center of the town. Shaw described the area as undulating rather than flat, with a gentle slope rising to the southwest. It stood on a public avenue eighty feet wide to the east of his property. He intended to begin by making a wall on that avenue with an entrance gateway and a small lodge in the center of it. On one side he would erect the curator's house with lecture room and museum, and on the other side, facing south, the plant houses.

He reminded Sir William of the extremes of the American climate at the latitude of 38° 38′ north in the middle of a great continent. It could be severely cold in winter and hot in summer, and thus was less favorable to formal gardens than Britain. Nonetheless it was a rich area in producing maize, hemp, and tobacco. An abundance of fruits—apples, pears, and peaches—flourished, with cherries and plums found more rarely. He hoped to set off a considerable part of the space for an arboretum and a nursery for the fruit trees.[2]

22. Shaw sought the guidance of the eminent botanist Sir William Jackson Hooker, director of the Royal Botanic Gardens at Kew.

Shaw described the governmental policy leading to the land-grant colleges. The Americans had high hopes that these outlays would promote science, but at the time botany as an independent discipline received little attention. It was part of the curriculum of the nation's few flourishing medical schools. The directors of these schools highly approved of Shaw's project and offered him all the assistance possible. One of them was the eminent surgeon Charles Alexander Pope, the dean of the Saint Louis College of Medicine.

Shaw foresaw difficulties in finding gardeners and other persons qualified to manage the institution both at the time and in the immediate future. Since he had some experience in the construction of plant houses—he had several at his country residence—he could undertake the superintendence of that aspect himself; but he needed, above all, plans to reach his goal. He knew only the rudiments of botany as a science and had an amateur's interest in horticulture and arboriculture. He asked Sir William's pardon for intruding on his time, and ended his letter by mentioning that his correspondent in London was James Hoole, Esq., on Grover Street.[3]

If Sir William Jackson Hooker took Shaw's statement as seriously as the Missourian hoped, Hooker's position at the pinnacle of the botanical world as director of the Kew Gardens would have incalculable weight in making the Missouri Botanical Garden a remarkable place. Fortunately, he did take Shaw seriously. But, first, who was Sir William?

A native of Norwich, where he had attended school, Hooker (1785–1865) had journeyed to Iceland on botanical study at age twenty-four. He studied botany on the Continent in 1814, the year before Waterloo. After marriage to Maria Turner in 1815, Hooker began a herbarium at Halesworth in Suffolk that gained world renown. He accepted the Regius Professorship in Botany at the University of Glasgow in 1820. Twenty-one years later, he became first official director of the Royal Botanic Gardens at Kew at the time they became a public garden in 1841.

A tall, erect man, handsome in spite of his long face and large, straight nose, with a dimpled chin and dark bushy hair blown back from a receding hairline, Sir William impressed those who met him. He rose before sunrise, retired late, and went little into society. Charles Darwin spoke of him as remarkably cordial, courteous, and frank in bearing. He produced one hundred volumes dedicated to systematic and economic botany and liberally assisted young botanists. He also corresponded extensively with botanists of various countries.

Sir William sent to Shaw descriptive catalogues of the Kew Gardens and the Economic Museum, strongly urged him to combine beauty and science in his projected garden, and recommended that he confer with St. Louis physician-botanist Dr. George Engelmann. Shaw thanked Sir William for his suggestions and said that he hoped to follow them. He praised Sir William's "magnificent establishment at Kew . . . [as] a wonderful means of promoting a taste for horticultural improvements in the multitudes of people that frequent it."[4] His own effort in St. Louis would be a modest one, something like the gardens at Glasgow or Liverpool. But his property had one major advantage over its counterparts in the British cities: he could lease or rent the adjacent valuable lands, so near the prosperous commercial capitol of a vast area.5

With one of these early letters to Sir William, Shaw sent a map he had drawn of the area bounded by Arsenal Street, Kingshighway, a country road north of Shaw Avenue, and Grand Avenue. It showed three new cottages in the area east of Tower Grove Avenue, two on Arsenal, one on Shaw, and two more on Shaw north of the garden. Central to the sketch, of course, the area just west of Tower Grove Avenue showed a Pleasure Grounds Garden with three summer houses at Magnolia; then moving north, the Shaw mansion, with an egg-shaped grove of trees between it and the Botanical Garden, allegedly the site of Payne's trotting track.

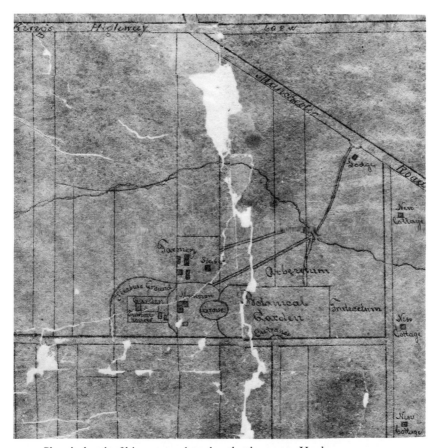

23. Shaw's sketch of his proposed garden that he sent to Hooker.

The Garden entrance looked up Floral Avenue (later known as Flora Place). At the north end of the property stood the fruticetum, the plot for shrubs. The wooded area or arboretum filled the triangle between Shaw Avenue on the north, the lane from the mansion to Old Manchester Road on the southwest, and the Garden and the fruticetum on the east. A creek crossing the west section of the property in a northerly direction swung northeast through the arboretum.[6]

Even before Shaw followed Sir William's advice to get in touch with Engelmann, the St. Louis physician had written about Shaw to Dr. Asa Gray of Harvard, America's premier botanist. Engelmann described Shaw as a "very rich Englishman . . . an old resident and a bachelor, who concluded to devote his whole time and fortune to the founding of a botanic garden and collection, Kew in miniature, I suppose."[7] Engelmann mentioned that Shaw had corresponded with Sir William Hooker at Kew and expressed the hope that something "valuable and permanent" would come of Shaw's efforts.[8] "Bravo Shaw!" Gray responded on 15 April. He saw in Shaw's plans a botanical opening to the American West. "I hope," he went on, "he will get a great many western things growing in his garden."[9]

Shaw had contacted Engelmann by mid-May when the St. Louis physician wrote again to Gray. "I have not yet seen much of Shaw, and am unfortunately not the proper person in address and diplomacy, etc., to work upon him—still I hope for the best; he seems very zealous. Get Hooker to encourage him! He has already a letter from Hooker referring him to me, which has good effects."[10]

Shaw had been fortunate in evoking the interest of Sir William Hooker. He was lucky also in gaining the support of Asa Gray, America's finest botanist, and doubly so of George Engelmann, an outstanding gynecologist by profession and the greatest botanist of the West by avocation, who, as his neighbor in St. Louis, was always close at hand and ready to help. In his recollections years later, Shaw would gratefully recall the contributions and advice of Engelmann.[11] Edgar Anderson, a twentieth-century director of Shaw's enterprise and the holder of the professorship named for Engelmann, would say of the physician-botanist: "There is a possibility that without him there would have been no Missouri Botanical Garden. Almost certainly it would never have become an outstanding scientific effort but for him."[12]

George Engelmann was born in Frankfort-am-Main on 2 February

24. Dr. George Englemann, St. Louis gynecologist and advisor to Shaw on botanical matters.

1809 of German French-Huguenot parentage. His father, an educator, was descended from a long line of ministers; his mother was the daughter of a distinguished portrait painter. The oldest of thirteen children, George received an excellent education at Heidelberg, Berlin, and Würzburg, where he took his doctorate in medicine in 1831. Alienated by the political conditions in the German states, he went to Paris for further medical and scientific studies, including botany, and then crossed the Atlantic. He visited Illinois to take care of business for several uncles who had invested in property in the Mississippi Valley. This responsibility took him into remote areas of Arkansas, Missouri, and southern Illinois. While these trips on horseback did not abet his medical knowledge, they gave him opportunities to pursue a botanical interest. Harvard botanist Elizabeth Shaw stated, "He came to St. Louis with an extremely sophisticated background in botany."[13]

Opening medical practice in the frontier city in autumn 1835, he soon had a busy practice among Anglo-Americans and French-Americans as well as his fellow German immigrants. He gained a great reputation as an obstetrician. In his early years of practice, he had to devote the major portion of his days to medicine. Nonetheless, he had time to begin a herbarium and a botanical library adjacent to his office. He also showed interest in the anatomy of animals, and he began meteorological observations in 1836 and was to take them throughout his life. The study of plants, however, proved his greatest delight, and in this field he was to gain wide fame.

Engelmann was an acute observer, critical in judgment, open in mind, and persevering in his tasks. He drew with facility. Whenever he traveled he observed and sketched. Physically vigorous and strongly built, he had an abounding good nature, an ever-evident enthusiasm, and a kind and considerate way of dealing with others that belied the stern look in his extant portrait.

In June 1840 he visited Germany to marry a distant cousin, Dora Horstmann. They would have one son, George Julius, who would follow in his father's medical chair but not in his botanical hiking boots. On his way back to St. Louis, Engelmann visited Dr. Asa Gray, who had already come to appreciate his botanical findings. The botanist suggested plants Engelmann might find on his way west. Gray's biographer, A. Hunter Dupree, described this meeting: "During 1840 Gray picked up a friend who greatly strengthened botanical science in the west . . . . Engelmann was in a position to be gatekeeper for all scientists going into the wilderness."[14]

The two complemented each other. Engelmann lived at the gateway of the West, from which all military, scientific, or exploratory expeditions set out for the open country. He sought interested plant collectors for all such enterprises. He would number and "ticket" the specimens and send them to Gray, who, in turn, would publish the results.[15] About this time Engelmann began to plant flowers and trees in a small plot at Eighth and Chouteau on the near Southside.[16] In 1852, he published in the *American Journal of Science* the first account of the giant saguaro cactus (now known as *Carnegiea gigantea*) of which he had a sample and a drawing from the Gila River in what is now Arizona. He had not yet had an opportunity to visit the Southwest, but he studied the collections brought in by others and became an expert. His main interests were conifers and cacti, but he studied plants of many groups. Of his researches on cacti, Asa Gray wrote, "Dr. Engelmann's authority is of the very highest."[17] He named and provided the first published descriptions of most of the species of cacti found in the United States. Engelmann also studied North American wild grapes (*Vitis*), recognizing and characterizing a dozen species, which became "of no small importance to grape growers, both in this country and in Europe."[18] He urged the crossing of French and American grapes for durability.

In 1856 Engelmann had helped organize the St. Louis Academy of Science—the first of its kind to be established west of the Alleghenies. At that time, as has been stated, Shaw began to correspond with Sir William Jackson Hooker, who, in turn, referred Shaw to his fellow St. Louisan. Engelmann would eventually join thirty-three scientific societies at home and abroad. He was a charter member and incorporator of the most prestigious of them all, the U.S. National Academy of Sciences, at its founding in 1863. After several years when his work in St. Louis kept him from attending the academy's meetings, he resigned to open the place for a younger and more active scientist. At his death he would leave a mass of notes, drawings, and observations on plants of all kinds, constituting some sixty large volumes. Even more important, he became Shaw's mentor, the contact man with botanical collectors going west, and the ridgepole of a botanical establishment that was formed in the St. Louis area.

Asa Gray called Engelmann "one of the most eminent and venerable cultivators" of science. "Personally one of the most affable and kindly of men, he was as much beloved as respected by those who knew him . . . ."[19] Gray continued, "The name of Engelmann has, by his own researches and authorship, become unalterably associated with the buffalo grass of the plains, the noblest conifers of the Rocky Mountains, the most stately cactus in the world, and with most associated species."[20]

Late in life Engelmann was to travel extensively: in 1877 to Colorado, and in 1880 to Salt Lake City, British Columbia, California, and the Mexican border regions of Arizona, where the giant cactus that he had written about grew. He went through desert areas of the American Southwest looking for plants while many Chiricahua warriors were riding the trails looking for white scalps. In a letter to fellow botanist Christopher C. Parry, he had already written of "a tempting tramp among the Apache (with or without scalps) and yuccas and agaves and cacti."[21] The courageous collector was totally bald by that time.

Asa Gray, the third in the triumvirate of influential men in Shaw's carrying out of his vision, was born in Sauquoit, Oneida County, New

25. Dr. Asa Gray of Harvard University, botanical adviser to Shaw.

York, on 18 November 1810. He was the oldest son of immigrants Moses Gray from northern Ireland and his wife Roxana Howard from Kent in England. Asa's father ran a tannery and a shoe shop. An avid reader and excellent speller from his early years, young Gray began his education at local schools, and continued it at an academy at nearby Clinton. In 1825 he enrolled at Fairfield (New York) Academy. After a year he attended medical lectures at the College of Physicians and Surgeons of the Western District of the State of New York, also located in Fairfield.

At the medical college he came under the influence of James Hadley, a professor typical of the period when many physicians became naturalists. In turning from the study of plants useful for medical purposes to a more general curiosity about botany, Hadley met a most interested and apt student in young Gray. At that time, incidentally, medical colleges provided the only opportunity for serious study in any of the sciences; other colleges concentrated on a classical education.

Before he reached his twenty-first birthday, Gray won his degree of doctor of medicine in January 1831. He practiced medicine at Bridgewater, New York, for a while, and taught botany at Bartlett's School in Utica. Supported by a letter of introduction from Dr. Hadley, he later became assistant to Columbia College professor John Torrey, one of America's foremost botanists. Gray had collected specimens of plants in western New York in 1831, and he began collecting in the Pine Barrens of New Jersey in 1834.

With President Andrew Jackson's support, American scientists were planning an expedition to the South Seas. Gray applied and was accepted for a place on the expedition. Disagreements among both politicians and scientists caused endless delays, however, and Gray resigned from the project on 10 July 1838. In the meantime, the recently admitted state of Michigan had set out to open a state university. The regents of the planned institution appointed Gray professor of botany and zoology seven days after he left the South Sea venture.[22] With a stipend from the university, he visited Europe and purchased books needed in Ann Arbor. Returning to America, he continued his botanical travel, especially in the valley of Virginia and the mountains of North Carolina in 1841. He never taught at Michigan.

On 30 April 1842, Harvard University Corporation offered Gray the Fisher Professorship of Natural History. As the chief subject was to be botany and he would have the care of the seven-acre botanical garden, he accepted the position. In letters to Engelmann at this time, Gray seemed to imply that the need of preparing lectures interfered with his botanical studies. Nonetheless, he still found time—in addition to his duties at Harvard—to teach a Sunday School class for girls.[23]

A contemporary, Professor J. J. Hosmer, spoke of his noticeably unpretentious manner and his vivid, alert personality. Hosmer referred to him as "the first of American botanists."[24] Gray was first both in eminence and in time—no American before him had made a living from botany. (Gray did, though, have to pay the expenses of publishing his first volume in 1847.) A bouncy person, happy in his work, Gray looked on everything in a sprightly manner. Friends remembered him as always on the "half-run" in the street, "lithe in physique," quick and impetuous in manner, and of inexhaustible good nature.[25]

Sir David McNee's crayon sketch of Gray in his thirties shows a clean-shaven, handsome young man with a full head of dark hair and an alert look in his eye. Later photographs showed that McNee had caught the handsome quality of his face, but had underplayed the intensity of his gaze. In the post-Civil War period, Gray would follow the trend of the times and wear a beard.

When he began his collaboration with Engelmann in obtaining botanical specimens in the West, Gray forgot the danger to collectors. Apaches and Comanches threatened all white men traversing their hunting lands in the Southwest. Gray also overlooked the fact that western wagonmasters had little time to wait in a danger-filled canyon while a botanist scaled the heights for an alpine plant.

Gray's correspondence is voluminous. His letters make delightful reading, even if hurriedly scribbled and hard to decipher. His correspondence with Sir William Jackson Hooker and later with Joseph, Hooker's son and successor at Kew, eventually to be knighted too, by itself fills two volumes. One collection contains 626 letters; a second 508. Gray wrote hurriedly and informally at all times, beginning some letters with the simple heading "Dear Hooker."[26]

In his late years, every scientific society of note could claim Gray as an active or honorary member or give him honors. He was to hold the LL.D. degree from Edinburgh, the D.C.L. from Oxford, and the M.A. and LL.D. from Harvard. In 1862 botanist C. C. Parry would give Gray's name to a 14,270 foot peak west of Denver. Gray was to visit St. Louis with Sir Joseph Hooker in 1877, and then, even though in his sixty-seventh year, to climb Blanca Mountain, a 14,345 foot peak in the Sangre de Cristo range of southern Colorado.[27]

Gray's *Manual of Botany,* covering Canada and the northeastern United States, would go into many editions and find its way to the bookshelf of virtually every North American classifier of plants. Like Engelmann, he was a founding member of the National Academy of Sciences. Even more important in the present context, his influence on Henry Shaw, especially through Engelmann, left friends of the Missouri Botanical Garden deeply indebted to him.

II.   Guidance by Correspondence

◆◆◆

Henry Shaw took the occasion of Dr. Engelmann's impending 1856 trip to Germany and other places in Europe to ask the physician to deliver his second letter to Sir William Hooker. "The doctor, as you are aware," he wrote to Hooker, "has a great reputation here as a man of science, a naturalist, and professes a great interest in my projected undertaking."[1] Shaw pointed out that the trees and other plants in the St. Louis area were mostly the same as in Ohio and other midwestern states and had been accurately described by Pursh and Michaux; many of those plants had been long since introduced to Europe.[2]

Engelmann sent Shaw a list of Hooker's botanical writings in October 1856. The number of volumes surprised Shaw. "You might find some others, equally or more suitable to my object," Shaw wrote a week later, "that is to acquire a knowledge of botany and horticulture myself and diffuse a taste for the same among others."[3] Shaw authorized Engelmann to purchase books up to the sum of one hundred dollars, to secure for him a description of the garden in Cambridge, if one existed, and to get all the plans and catalogues available. "My mind is intent on the undertaking, which I am anxious to commence. And by dint of reading and observation am endeavoring to gather up some crumbs of botanical science . . . and am very much flattered at the interest you take in my project and plans."[4]

The following spring Shaw sent another letter to Sir William. He enclosed a few seeds of a pine from New Mexico and a sample of leaves from a unique tree growing near St. Louis, which he believed to be the only one in the area. The pine appeared to be similar to a species from the mountains of southern California that had been described in Loudon's *Arboretum*. Shaw thought it might be a novelty in England.[5]

Shaw then reported on his progress. He had trenched over the ground two feet deep and put in drains, and he hoped to have the wall and entrance completed during the course of 1857 and to condition the soil for planting during the following year.[6] Shaw wrote in his diary during that time that "the Garden had been trenched over two feet deep (at a cost of $1,000) and [was] in fine order for planting anything."[7] He also listed two large tanks with a capacity of 10,000 gallons, and two wells. The drains and tanks cost $2,000. He went on: "Am now building the walls of stone and brick . . . . Two sides cost $6,000 . . . . I shall commence the ornamental planting next spring."[8]

At the same time, Shaw was looking to the future development of the neighborhood, bounded by McRee on the north, Grand on the east, Arsenal on the south, and Kingshighway-Manchester on the west. On 3 June 1857 he entered into an agreement with the other major property owner, Mary L. Tyler, daughter and heir of William Chambers, to establish streets and norms for the coming years. It laid out Shaw Avenue (later called Shaw Boulevard) between Grand and Manchester, Tower Grove between Shaw and Arsenal, and Floral Avenue (later called Flora Place) between Grand and Tower Grove. The two agreed to share equally in the cost of bridges and culverts and to exclude various "nuisances," such as chemical works, slaughterhouses, gas factories, and dram shops.[9]

In a late summer letter, Hooker described the various plans of European gardens and recommended such plans as were consistent with good taste and convenient for study. He had read Shaw's letter to Engelmann, who would know the best way to proceed. The St. Louis physician had seen the finest gardens in Germany, France, Holland, and England. Furthermore, Engelmann visited places "with eyes open" and was "well stored with information."[10]

Hooker contrasted the British government's support of the Kew Gardens with Shaw's approach: "Yours is the gift of a public-spirited private gentleman . . . . Such a gift to one's country, anyone may glory in."[11] Turning from just praise to practical advice, he continued, "Very few appendages to a garden are of more importance for instruction . . . than a library and economic museum; and they will gradually increase like a rolling snowball."[12] He suggested that Shaw purchase books at reduced prices by searching some of the London catalogues. He thanked Shaw for his gift of pine seeds, and wished him well in his venture.

"At last at Kew! The great Mecca of botanists and horticulturists!" Engelmann began his letter to Shaw on 11 August 1857. "And Sir William Hooker, with whom I had no personal acquaintance before, is extremely kind to me."[13] Engelmann received a letter from Shaw the following month that kept him informed of progress at Tower Grove.

Shaw was building the plant houses first; after that, perhaps in 1859, he hoped to open a museum and library. "I intend to have everything substantial and elegant," Shaw wrote in his always clear script, "but on a small scale. All this I am doing according to my ideas gathered from horticultural works of Loudon."[14] Shaw concluded by asking Engelmann to send him a list of botanical books.[15]

In the week before Christmas, Shaw had the leisure to write a thank-you letter to Sir William for his information about the gardens and museum at Kew. He expressed his gratification that in Hooker he and his associates had "an ardent well-wisher and patron to our Botanic Garden,"[16] as Engelmann had again assured him. Since Shaw's previous letter to Hooker, he had begun the four-hundred-foot north wall of brick coped with stone and the one-thousand-foot east wall of stone nine to twelve feet high, at a cost of $8,000.[17] The area at the time, of course, was still open country with its share of smaller wild animals. Shaw planned to proceed with the east or entrenched side in the spring, and to build the gate lodges and plant houses. He pointed out the vast field of investigation in the areas of grapes, plums, and other wild fruits susceptible of improvement over a period of years. He had approved Engelmann's recommendation to purchase immediately the "herbarium of Bernhardi." Perhaps not sure of the German botanist's name, Shaw had scratched over his original effort and rendered the name almost illegible. He concluded with a request for any guidance Hooker might have time to offer on the laying out of the garden in St. Louis and for information on what garden in England (next to Kew) was best fitted to promote the science of botany and horticulture.[18]

Johann Jakob Bernhardi, the German scientist whose herbarium was available for purchase at a small price, had died a short time before. He had been a professor on the medical faculty at the University of Erfurt in his native city. He wrote papers on plant anatomy that established his reputation as a botanist, edited two gardening magazines, and collected by purchase and exchange dried specimens from other parts of the world. Forty-eight collectors sent materials to him, including one from the Missouri-Illinois region, the Belgian-born Jesuit priest and botanist John Baptist Duerinck, who had taken his seminary training in St. Louis County.[19] Bernhardi's herbarium contained sixty thousand specimens of forty thousand diverse species. Engelmann purchased it for $600.[20]

A later Garden director, Dr. Edgar Anderson, would insist that "by this one act, he [Engelmann] did as much for the technical efficiency of the Garden's herbarium as in all his other efforts put together."[21] The Bernhardi Herbarium contained more type specimens—the original specimens on which the names of individual kinds of plants had been based—than any herbarium that anyone could have purchased before or after. "No other herbarium in the New World," Anderson concluded, "has anything to match it."[22]

In a mid-January letter, Hooker thanked Shaw for the kind remarks of his letter of the previous month. Shaw had mentioned the progress of his arboretum and fruticetum and included sketches and lists of trees he had planted. Hooker reminded him that the choice of plant life depended in part on the nature of the soil. He complimented Shaw for doing his countrymen a service, recommended Engelmann as "an excellent coadjutor," and concluded, "Every nobleman has his fine garden."[23] One may well wonder from this remark whether Sir William, who had been knighted himself, saw in Shaw's mind a hope to match the nobles of his native country.

At the same time, Shaw thanked Engelmann for his help. Shaw had selected thirty-four books, most of them on the list that the doctor had suggested, and promised to make more liberal purchases when he had built the library and museum. Further, Shaw had sent his plans to Gray and Hooker for their appraisal. Shaw concluded with a report on progress: "The stone wall on the west side, and the brick wall coped with stone on the north side are finished at a cost of $8,000."[24]

In Florence in May, Engelmann wrote Gray that he had bought a number of the botanical books Shaw selected. Some of these the doctor thought valuable. He had heard that Shaw had sent Gray a plan for his garden, which Engelmann thought "rather stiff and antiquated." He hoped that Gray would encourage Shaw and give him good advice.[25]

Shaw wrote exuberantly to Gray of the spring in St. Louis. Moisture had been abundant and frosts had ceased early in the year. The trees and plants flourished. "I am vigorously at work on the building of the *Hort. Bot. Missouriensis*—everything is being constructed in a durable manner," he wrote.[26]

By the time Engelmann returned to St. Louis in the early fall of 1858, Shaw had built a fine stone wall on three sides of the slightly sloping ten acres and was constructing an impressive entrance and a guardian's lodge near it. He had already put up several small greenhouses and was erecting a much larger one and had set out a rose garden. Engelmann presumed that Shaw was imitating parks in England. True to his classical training at Mill Hill, Shaw wanted to put over the door the superscription *Hort. Bot. Missouriensis.* Engelmann disagreed. Viewing the Latin title as an undue display of learning, he advised Shaw to put the title in simple English: "Missouri Botanical Garden." "You see how trifles occupy him and us!" Engelmann exclaimed in a letter to Gray.[27]

Shaw commissioned George I. Barnett to prepare plans for a museum, library, and herbarium, allegedly according to the Kew plan. Barnett designed a lovely building. "Unfortunately," Engelmann wrote, "he has the plan of the old museum [at Kew] only and worked and planned on that. The rooms, one for library and second for herbarium, are too small and there is no working room in the whole business if it be not the basement."[28] Both Gray and Engelmann took the view that Shaw and his architect Barnett had designed the museum-herbarium after the older plan of the structure at Kew. Comparison of the two shows that while Barnett designed a compact, handsome building expressly as a museum, Kew converted an existing structure, an old fruit-storage building, which became known as Museum No. 2. Kew architects had, back in 1846, drawn up plans for another building; when built, this became Museum No. 1.[29]

Neither before nor after the additions did Museum No. 2 resemble Barnett's external design, nor did the later Museum No. 1. Barnett's design did, however, have great similarities in floor plan to Museum No. 2. Barnett certainly designed a building of beauty, with neoclassical pillars flanking the entrance and a matching pair standing on either side of the rostrum in the main display room. In spite of Engelmann's misgivings, the building possessed, as a later director stated, a "charmingly antique atmosphere."[30]

With his ever-positive attitude, Gray answered Engelmann in October 1858: "I rejoice to hear that Mr. Shaw keeps up his zeal, and will make a creditable establishment. I wish him all prosperity if he will make and keep up a general herbarium; it will save you much time and money."[31] At the end of the same month, Engelmann wrote to Gray that botanical collector Augustus Fendler would make a top-grade curator, with his sense of neatness and order, and could be spared occasionally for excursions into Utah. But he was not sure that Shaw would see the plan. "I must be very cautious in approaching him," Engelmann wrote. "The herbarium to him is a very secondary thing to the garden."[32] Gray seconded the recommendation of Augustus Fendler. If Shaw did not offer Fendler the job as curator, Gray wondered whether Shaw would be willing to pay Fendler a decent sum to collect rare living plants and seeds in the Far West for the Missouri Botanical Garden.[33]

The son of poor East Prussian parents, unschooled but resourceful, Augustus Fendler (1813–1883) traveled much in his youth. He moved from one German city to another, taking employment here and there, usually in tanning. After emigrating to America, he continued his wandering through the Midwest, with St. Louis and its growing German-speaking community gradually becoming his focal point. Learning that he might sell sets of dried plants, he began to collect botanical specimens on his travels. As a result of these collections, he became acquainted with Engelmann, and through him with Gray. The Harvard botanist helped him win appointment as plant collector on a military expedition to Santa Fe.

Fendler returned to St. Louis in the fall of 1847. Two years later he went on another, but less successful, western trip. The Great Fire of 1849 consumed his plant collections in St. Louis, and he went to Panama for several months. After a few years in the lower Arkansas River area, he traveled to Venezuela in 1854 to collect valuable plants. He returned to St. Louis in 1858 and settled on a farm at Allenton, thirty miles west of St. Louis.[34]

"Fendler was a . . . keen observer and an admirable collector," Gray was to write many years later. "He had formed a good literary style in English . . . was excessively diffident... but courteous and most . . . delicately refined."[35] In this description Gray let his imagination prevail over his judgment; he was later to hire Fendler as curator of his herbarium in Cambridge, but for only a short time. Gray's biographer, A. Hunter Dupree, described Fendler as "an undomesticated frontier collector who had acquired neither training nor temperament for sedentary work."[36] Shaw was fastidious in appearance; Fendler was careless. Shaw liked to have people agree with him; Fendler was a maverick. Shaw wanted to welcome visitors to his garden; Fendler, reluctant to shave or dress up, preferred the high mountains or remote forests to civilized conditions. Shaw reflected a long time on hiring Fendler.

On another level of the Garden operation, Shaw during the previous year had secured copies of W. B. Carpenter's *Vegetable Physiology and Systematic Botany* and Robert Bruist's *American Flower Garden Directory.* Now he purchased a copy of the latter's latest book, *The Rose Garden.* 37 Beyond these Shaw was to purchase personally only two other botanical books over the years, so that the Garden library did not begin significant expansion until after his death in 1889. But he would subscribe to magazines of botanical and horticultural interest.

In late February 1859, Engelmann wrote Gray that Shaw was laying the foundation for his library, herbarium, and museum. It would be under one roof and would probably be completed late in the fall. Engelmann praised Shaw's industry.38 He followed the same line in a letter in mid-April: "Shaw is busy; I do not know how he progresses, but he is energetic and businesslike—would that he had more scientific education or taste!"39 Turning to his own situation, Engelmann deplored the fact that his practice left him only a few hours a day to do other things. He did not have the leisure to go out and see Shaw's improvements.40

Engelmann did not mention that the state legislature had chartered the Garden on 14 March 1859. But before the first visitors would arrive for the official opening, Henry Shaw faced a major personal suit. The Garden would have to share his concern for the time with a more immediate matter.

12. Female Friends and Would-Be Wife

◆◆◆

To understand the breach of promise suit filed in the St. Louis Court of Common Pleas against Henry Shaw as he was preparing to open his garden, a look at his social attitudes and interests is imperative. In his sketch of Shaw's life, Thomas Dimmock attributed to historian Frederick L. Billon, a friend of Henry, the remark that Shaw "seemed to avoid making acquaintances among the girls. . . . He intended marrying some English girl."[1] Nowhere in his extant writings, however, did Shaw give such an indication. He never discussed his cousin Henry Hoole's suggestions that he marry "Cousin Mary," and he ignored his sister Sarah's recommendation of several lovely Guernsey girls.

On one occasion, as already stated, Caroline suggested that she, Sarah, and Henry would probably remain "spinsters."[2] And Shaw doubted that his cousin Francis Hoole's impending marriage with Alathea Tattershal would bring him any great happiness. Shaw's remark seemed to transcend Francis's choice of marriage partner and to take a derogatory view of married life in general. While Henry traveled through Europe, on the other hand, he received letters from Demosthenes ("Demo") Simos that spoke of young ladies they had met; and Shaw's cousin Henry Hoole joked about the Missourian's amorous adventures on the Continent. Shaw himself wrote in his journal of the many young ladies he saw on his travels[3] and spoke most warmly of a lovely Caroline he met on his first visit to Vienna.[4]

Among his miscellaneous letters, Shaw kept several from friendly French girls, such as Aimée Dupont, to whom he sent gifts after his return to St. Louis,[5] and some from a St. Louis woman by the name of Honorine Douard, written in 1849. The latter explained in one of her letters that she wrote in English because others were present in the room. French was presumably her native language. She misspelled several words and seemed at times ill at ease with English. She called herself "your little Honorine" and suggested that their relationship was close. She apologized for the deception in not telling him that she was married. "If you wish to aid me, as you promised, [you] will enclose the rest of the money you promised me. . . . My husband is in a situation that he can give me no money now."[6] A short time later, signing herself Honorine Beranger, presumably her married name, she thanked him for the money and for his wishes for her happiness. "My dear friend," she went on, "you say you will see me at Mrs. Harmony's, but if possible I would prefer that you will see me tomorrow at my sister's at two o'clock."[7]

These female relationships were temporary and more or less private. A later one gained national notoriety for Shaw. As Shaw walked in his garden one morning, he saw a young woman whom he later described to a friend as "not only a pretty woman but a fascinating one."[8] After he got acquainted, she came regularly to the garden. When she did not come, she would send him a note (none of which he kept).[9] In early February 1856 this young woman, whose name was Effie Carstang, borrowed $100 from Shaw to be returned on demand.[10] Slightly over a year later, she borrowed another $100.[11] In August 1857, Effie rented from Shaw for one dollar a month a rosewood piano made in Baltimore. She agreed to send it back on recall.[12] Shaw later took the piano back, but that was not the last word on the musical instrument from Miss Carstang.

On 19 July 1858, Effie Carstang sued Henry Shaw in the St. Louis Court of Common Pleas for breach of promise of marriage. She alleged that a friendship had grown between them and that in November 1856 she had promised to marry him and Shaw in turn had promised to marry her. She remained willing to marry the defendant. In the original claim, she asked damages to the amount of $20,000 but then scratched over that figure and wrote $100,000 in the line above with the approval of the court.[13]

In a response three months later, Henry Shaw denied that on any day in November 1856 or on any other day before or since had he ever promised to marry Miss Carstang or asked her to marry him. He denied that she had sustained any damages of any amount whatsoever.[14] Shaw, in fact, had a counterclaim. He held two promissory notes—one of 28 February 1856 and one of 19 May 1857. In each instance Effie had borrowed $100 from him and agreed to pay on demand.[15] Shaw insisted she had not paid.[16] Strangely, Henry never alluded to the rental of the rosewood piano, even though Effie and her sister both mentioned the "gift" of a piano that Shaw took back sometime later.

The *Missouri Democrat* described Effie as a young woman of about thirty, tall and graceful, with dark hair, brilliant eyes, blonde complexion, and "a mouth expressive of great firmness and decision of character."[17] The same edition described Henry Shaw as "about sixty years of age, with hair somewhat grey, rather sharp features, but with an expression of countenance anything but disagreeable. He was a man of great wealth, and his Tower Grove home was one of the finest residences in the neighborhood of St. Louis."[18] The article concluded, "Mr. Shaw is one of our oldest citizens and during a long residence here he has sustained a character hitherto unimpeachable."[19]

Years later, *Reedy's Mirror,* the one St. Louis-based periodical to win a reputation beyond the borders of the United States for pungent literary criticism and the discovery of new authors, described Henry and Effie in an unexcelled way:

> Henry Shaw was a hardware man . . . a nailing good one. By close application to business, attention to judiciously advertising his wares, an incessant working of the scissors in clipping coupons, he amassed a competency which later he invested in St. Louis dirt. Then his eye, 'in a fine frenzy rolling,' turned from the dreary monotony of spikes and mauls to the heavenly ecstasy of flowers . . . and engaged in what Bacon declared the most pleasing occupation of man—gardening. . . . an Englishman, stolid, dogmatic, lettered—a man of strong conviction, few intimate friendships but genial with those who succeeded in getting into his charmed circle. . . . Somewhere and under some strange concatenation of circumstances, Henry Shaw met Effie Carstang. Tall and willowy was Effie. Her entire get-up, her *tout ensemble,* . . . was gorgeous. She possessed a pair of orbs that made diamonds look like cobblestones, cheeks that caused roses to look up . . . a form that set artists to climbing poles, a voice that threw musicians into conniptions, lips—now by the beard of the Prophet—she had lips.[20]

Such were the principals in a stirring court drama. Lawyers for the plaintiff were Maj. Uriel L. Wright, state legislator and spellbinding criminal lawyer, and L. M. Shreve. Judge Edward Bates, John R. Shepley, and Judge James R. Lackland defended Shaw. While the other four were well known locally, Bates, nephew of an early Missouri governor and a national figure, had represented Missouri in the U.S. Congress, served in the state senate, and, after declining a position in the administration of President Millard Fillmore, became judge of the St. Louis Land Court. He had presided at the Whig National Convention in Baltimore in 1856; as one of the Republican candidates in 1860, he would amass almost half as many votes as Abraham Lincoln on the first ballot at the convention in Chicago. The following year Lincoln would name him attorney general of the United States.

On the opening day of the trial, Friday, 27 May 1859, before Judge Sam Reber, the sister of Miss Carstang, Mrs. Marie Seaman, testified in Effie's behalf. She spoke of Shaw's visits and gifts, including the piano and books on botany, and the interpretation she and her sister placed on these favors. On Saturday, 28 May, the second day, the courtroom was crowded during the long testimony, most of it evidence for the plaintiff. The counsel for the defense extensively cross-examined Mrs. Seaman.

The *Missouri Republican* generally gave much less attention to the trial than the *Democrat* did, but on 30 May the *Republican* quoted at length the long speech of Shaw's attorney Shepley. Surprisingly, Shepley admitted the costly gifts that his client had given Effie: valuable jewelry as a token of his affection and the best fruits of his garden in Tower Grove.[21] On

26. An artist for the *New York Illustrated News* sketched the courtroom during the Effie Carstang breach of promise suit.

Wednesday a man by the name of Canese from Charleston, South Carolina, testified that Effie had resided at an establishment frequented by "dashing fellows." But Effie's counsel brought contrary evidence. Especially strong was that of Judge Alexander Hamilton, who said that the sisters were good tenants and prompt in paying rent. From his business associations with them, he knew nothing disagreeable about them. Everything, in fact, indicated the contrary. Another witness, John Brady, also praised Miss Carstang.[22]

On Thursday, 2 June, the sixth day of the case, the huge crowd again assembled. The judge instructed the jury that it was not necessary to have clear evidence of mutual consent of the respective parties; the jurors could infer a promise of marriage from the circumstances of the relationship; no mutual expressions of intention were needed, nor was any third-party witness. The judge also directed them to make any monetary decision not simply on financial values, but to consider any psychological or other difficulties the young woman had endured.[23]

After the judge had instructed the jury, Major Wright introduced testimony for the plaintiff from a man in South Carolina to counter the remarks of Mr. Canese of the day before. This gentleman testified that Effie's character was not tarnished as alleged. Major Wright proposed to introduce a further witness, but Bates and Shepley objected that no new witnesses should be introduced. The judge sustained the objection.[24]

At some time during the trial a letter became public that Effie had allegedly sent to Henry. (Three weeks after the trial, William McHenry, commercial editor of the *Missouri Republican,* stated that during the trial, a counsel for Miss Carstang had pointed to such a letter, wanting the jury to read it, but the court had excluded it.)[25] In this letter Effie stated that Shaw had visited her in her home. He had sent her flowers, fruit, and other presents and seemed to desire that their relationship should be made public. He sent a piano as a gift. She claimed he named a marriage time and then postponed it because of arrangements at the Garden. Then he took the piano back to his own house under the plea of a party to be held there. Finally he ceased to visit her. Presuming he might be sick, she called on him at his house, only to have him insult her with an indecent proposition. Effie concluded her letter, "Had you called me as a gentleman and offered a reasonable excuse or simply asked me to release you from this engagement and assigned a reason, I trust I should have had too much pride not to have complied at once. But your desertion, as it is, deserves whatever punishment the opinion of a just public may visit upon its author."[26]

On the seventh day of the trial, Friday, 3 June, the crowd was larger than ever. Judge Bates "bombarded his hearers," to use the *Missouri Democrat's* words, from 10:15 to 12:15. Following this, Major Wright summarized the case in a speech that lasted two and three-quarters hours. The *Democrat* described it as the most eloquent speech ever made by the distinguished advocate.[27] The crowded courtroom burst continuously into noisy applause. Judge Reber admonished the spectators for this excessive demonstration and ordered the sheriff to arrest disturbers; only then did they grow quiet.

At four o'clock the jury gave its unanimous verdict—for Effie Carstang. The crowd vented its full joy in the rotunda.[28] The *Missouri Democrat* believed that the decision was a popular one.[29] The *Missouri Republican* had little comment on the day of the verdict,[30] but early the next year was to speak favorably of the decision and of the plaintiff.[31] Judge Sam Reber awarded Effie damages of $100,000.[32]

In his diary for 4 June, a day later, Attorney Bates wrote, "This atrocious verdict has excited, as it ought, the indignant denunciation of the public. We have moved for a new trial. . . . Jurors were so stupid or wicked, or both."[33] The evidence, Bates felt, all pointed to a verdict for the defendant. "Yet we were all astonished that a verdict was rendered, after but a few minutes deliberation, for the plaintiff, with an assessment of damages of $100,000."[34] Bates presumed that Judge Reber would want to cleanse his record of so vile a blot upon the administration of justice. "The abominable verdict shocked the moral sense of the community and made most men fear for the safety of property and character."[35]

Perhaps Bates judged the situation properly, perhaps not. To the wealthy people it was a bad verdict; to the average poor person of the city, and of course there were many more of them, the verdict seemed a good one, at least if one may judge from the words of the *Missouri Democrat*.[36] On the same day that Bates wrote those words in his diary, Shepley joined him in asking for a new trial, citing many reasons. They claimed that the verdict was against the law, evidence, truth, and decency. They claimed, on the one hand, that the instructions of the court were not followed; and on the other, that the court admitted improper testimony and excluded proper testimony. They alleged that the jurors were prejudiced against the defendant and reached their decision by bargain and compromise, not by judgment. The Records of the Court of Common Pleas asserted:

> The plaintiff in the progress of the trial was guilty of a gross impropriety and contempt of court in causing to be published in a newspaper, a letter purporting to be from the plaintiff to the defendant, which had been offered in evidence by the plaintiff and ruled out by the court; and the publication of which was well calculated if not designed to bring bias and mislead the jury. The amount of the damages assessed by the jury is excessive—unjustly and preposterously large—unsupported by testimony and, of itself, proof of prejudice, passion and misconduct on the part of the jurors.[37]

On 8 June, Moritz Stienbach, one of the jurors, stated that he did not understand English well, did not believe the verdict righteous, did not understand American practice, and thought he had to go along with the majority.[38] Six days later another original juror, G. W. Chadwick, countered by notifying Wright that Shepley had clearly questioned Stienbach as to his understanding and command of English and was satisfied. And, Chadwick continued, when the jury had retired to the jury room, "All agreed at once to a verdict—except Mr. Stienbach, and he did not object because of any proofs in the case," but because a German newspaper the day before had questioned Effie's conduct in Charleston. After explanation, Stienbach agreed that he was for a verdict of $100,000. Chadwick notarized the letter the same day and submitted it to the attorneys,[39] but the plea for a new trial prevailed.

As soon as the court agreed to a retrial,[40] the attorneys for the beleaguered bachelor set to work. On 6 June, two days after Shaw's lawyers had submitted their appeal, a certain A. H. Smith of Sing Sing, New York, offered to bring proof of Effie's bad character. Fourteen days later he wrote that his wife knew of the sour reputation of both Effie and her sister, Marie Seaman, and offered names of parties for evidence.[41] Many other letters came in June or July of that year that dealt in a negative way with the character, background, or antecedents of Effie Carstang. A New Yorker by the name of J. Nichols stated that some time before her father's death Effie had sued a certain Young Brown for breach of promise. Another resident of New York, Peter Heiler, wrote that Effie had brought suit against an otherwise unidentified Captain Williams. Three letters came from Brooklyn: John Samow claimed that he had facts to set aside the first judgment; John Holdreth accused Effie of improper conduct in church—she had smiled during the sermon (horror of horrors!); and Thomas J. Berry, a Brooklyn sailmaker, listed five men who "spoke lightly" of Effie. An attorney in Cincinnati, R. D. Henry, also claimed that he had facts to set aside the first judgment.[42]

The magnitude of the initial verdict made the case a national concern. The *New York Illustrated News* called it "the largest sum ever awarded in this country in such an action."[43] When the appeal came to court in March 1860, *Harper's Weekly* reminded its readers that this was the great breach of promise case of the previous year that gave a verdict of $100,000 damages for the plaintiff. The article added a few personal items about Effie and Shaw. She was attractive; her father, a widower, Methodist, and businessman, had died ten years before. Effie had met Shaw in 1856, and the alleged promise of marriage had come in November of the following year. Henry Shaw had lived in St. Louis forty-one years; he was a merchant with great wealth, was of medium height, had a hardy complexion with blue eyes, and possessed a great suavity of manners; in fact, he was one of the politest men in St. Louis. His wealth was estimated at between one-and-a-half and two million dollars. He had turned a barren prairie into an Eden.[44]

Marie Seaman testified again that Shaw had begun to visit her sister, who lived with her, two or three times a week in 1856. He gave her jewelry, a piano, gloves, fruit, flowers, and other gifts. Generally he brought a gift at each visit. He brought books about botany, since he wanted Effie to know botany before they married. Shaw told Marie that he intended to marry Effie, and she began to prepare for the wedding in 1857. When she and Effie visited Shaw, she never saw any white person at his residence. Cross-examination avoided Mrs. Seaman's allegations and concentrated on her divorce to cast suspicion on her personally.[45]

At least three different men, Joseph Flavener, Moses Abbott, and Thomas Yostic, said that John Carter, one of the jurors, had publicly stated in their presence that Effie was not a decent woman and that Shaw was unjustly condemned in the first trial. Carter denied having made such a statement.[46]

As counsel for the defendant, Shepley summarized his position in this way: Effie sought Shaw's acquaintance for the purpose of entrapping him. Hence most of the twenty days of the trial consisted of depositions and testimony from men who claimed that Effie had engaged in prostitution in Brooklyn, Cincinnati, and Charleston. Most of them said that they had *heard* she was "a wanton woman." At least one of the men, Steven Birch, was so confused under cross-examination that he testified that Effie was both a good and a bad woman at the same time. The most damaging statement against Effie's character came from James I. Cochran of Cincinnati on the eighteenth day. Cochran had bad things to say about Effie; personally, he had kissed her, but would not admit to having had intercourse with her.[47]

Effie Carstang's counsel had been allowed to take a deposition from John Forbush, a crippled man in Cincinnati who knew Cochran. Forbush stated that Cochran was a perennial liar and known to be such. As to the allegation that Effie was a woman of easy virtue, he had never heard anyone make such a statement. He stated under questioning, "Neither Miss Carstang nor anyone else offered to pay me anything for testifying in this case."[48]

Judge Reber excluded testimony that called into question the veracity of several witnesses for Shaw, and he did not allow the letter from Effie to Shaw to be used. The *Missouri Democrat* felt that the letter's publication in the *Republican* had really formed the basis for successful application for a new trial.[49]

The verdict against Effie came on Saturday, 31 March 1860, the twentieth day of the trial. The *Missouri Democrat* stated flatly that the decision "on the whole surprised the community . . . . Even people in Cincinnati thought she would win and people questioned the impartiality of the jury as others did in earlier decisions. For instance, allegedly the foreman of the jury was seen going to Shaw's house before the verdict. The majority of people seemed to think that Effie should have gotten something, at least court costs."[50] The *Missouri Republican* gave less space to the verdict in the case than to Judge Bates's candidacy for the presidency.[51] It did comment on the throng in the courtroom, and it praised Major Wright for his summary as a "burst of oratory sparkling in wit and humor and sharp edged sarcasms . . . [and] historical allusions."[52]

Effie submitted her request for a new trial on 2 June 1860, basing her petition on the fact that several jurors were prejudiced, among them John Carter and Charles Schuler, who allegedly stated that he had made up his mind and would not change his view no matter what Major Wright or anyone else said.[53]

While the feature writer for the *New York Illustrated News* expected a new trial, he took an ambivalent view on the one just completed. He thought the whole Union should show its appreciation to the jury for its common sense "in the face of lovely women . . . immense legal talent, every possible technicality . . . [and] every known precedent, unlike most juries in his neighborhood that have hitherto been notorious for their liberal donations to female plaintiffs of other people's money."[54] In the same issue, ten pages later, the writer spoke of Shaw's "scandalous means of defense. He ransacked the country to destroy forever the character of a more youthful, humble and poor antagonist."[55] But the writer agreed that Shaw had no alternative under the initial verdict.[56] Shaw was "prompted by a hope of neutralizing the strong feeling the people of St. Louis seemed to entertain toward the plaintiff." The writer saw no real disgrace in proposing marriage and then backing off. He felt that "Shaw was smarting under the heavy verdict in the first trial."[57]

The *St. Louis Times* expressed joy that the case was over and noted the general regret that the plaintiff did not get something. It saw Shaw in a "most unenviable position" and concluded that both lost.[58] Effie appeared as "an *intriguante* and adventurer of the most dangerous type" and Shaw "as a libertine of seventy [*sic*]." The incidents revealed "more meanness than passion."[59]

Shaw's counselor, Edward Bates, had left a vehement denunciation of the first verdict in his diary. That journal—at least in the printed edition—did not even mention the second trial. On the day of the verdict, in fact, Bates wrote highly critical analyses of President James Buchanan's forays into the field of lawmaking.[60]

Judge Bates, who in reality did little at either hearing, received $250 in fees for each of the two trials; Shepley's fees for both suits amounted to $1,425. Disbursement by Judge J. R. Lackland reached $2,079 for travel and expenditures in rounding up testimony. Shaw's entire expenditure on the case totaled $15,358.81 at first counting.[61]

The difference between the fees of Shepley and Bates and the disbursements of Lackland on the one hand and the total expenses on the other leave unaccounted about $10,000. Why this strange discrepancy? *Reedy's Mirror,* many years later, said it went to Charles F. Cady. The article stated:

. . . Charlie Cady . . . one of the legal staff . . . packed his grip and made a bee-line for the city down on the Atlantic seaboard. Better than his education as a lawyer was his experience as a "rounder" on such a mission. He turned Charleston upside down, in and out, secured enough depositions to load a freight car, and sufficient testimony of a damaging character to blacken and blast and smash and utterly annihilate the reputation of all the saints in the calendar. Then he returned to St. Louis, walked into court with a countenance as innocent of guile as a babe's, and began to open up and read document after document of such salaciousness of, and concerning the said Effie Carstang, she and her heirs and assigns forever, as to cause bald heads of that day and generation to clutch at their whiskers, to marvel that doings of the kind described could be carried on in a free and enlightened republic. Effie Carstang didn't get her hands on a cent on account of her suit against Shaw, but Charlie Cady did. He pocketed Ten Thousand in very cool, exceeding cool cash.[62]

Cady did not get the full $10,000, though. He accounted for almost half that much money: $2,526.37 in rounding up testimony, $1,525 in salary for his efforts. The destination of the other six thousand remains one of the few unaccounted outlays in Shaw's account book.[63]

This proved the most sensational, but not the last court case involving Henry Shaw. His business papers show 122 court cases, usually involving minor questions of property. They would begin in 1870 and reach a high of fifteen in 1880, with the second highest number, eight, in 1888, the last full year of Shaw's life.[64]

Effie Carstang and her sister Marie Seaman presumably moved away from St. Louis shortly after the trial. During several previous years the *St. Louis Directory* had listed Mrs. M. Seaman as residing at 123 N. 5th St.[65] Effie resided with her sister in property rented from Judge Alexander Hamilton. After the trial the name of Mrs. M. Seaman no longer appeared in the *St. Louis Directory*.[66]

Though he never married, Shaw did have a true and lasting love, according to the testimony of a man who held the post of head gardener for the last twenty years of Shaw's life. In an interview years later, the gardener told a woman reporter for the *Republic*, "She was an American girl and neither he nor she ever married." One day when they were past seventy, she called on Shaw, and the gardener saw them walking arm in arm through the Garden in the moonlight. The gardener thought they would at last marry. When asked why they had never done so, he responded, "That I know, but I shall never tell you or anyone."[67] The gardener, no doubt, kept his word.

13. The Garden Opens

❖❖

During the eight months that intervened between the trial and the retrial, Shaw had moved forward with his garden plans. Even before the first hearing, the Missouri Legislature had passed on 14 March 1859 an enabling act approving Henry Shaw's intention to convey to trustees about 760 acres of land situated in Prairie des Noyers Common Fields for the development and support of a botanical garden. This land included all real estate owned by Shaw within the following limits: Grand Avenue on the east, Kingshighway on the west, Arsenal Street on the south, and a line on the north that would ultimately correspond with McRee Avenue; a tract on the southeast corner of Kingshighway and Arsenal; land going west from Kingshighway south of Fyler; sections on the south side of Arsenal adjoining Watson Road; and any other real estate Shaw should later decide to convey. "No absolute alienation," the act insisted, "shall be made of such lands or portions of it."[1]

Shaw prepared a guest book and inscribed it as follows: "Visitors to Tower Grove and the Botanical Garden are respectfully requested to write their names."[2] By June 1859 he was ready to open his garden. Many other people in history had opened their gardens to the general public, but usually after a considerable period of family use, or after a generation or two had gone by. Shaw planned his garden as a place of enjoyment for the general public at the outset.

The first to sign the guest book on opening day, 15 June 1859, was E. Leigh of St. Louis, and immediately after, Misses Maggie Barber, S. M. Mills, and Delia M. Grey.[3] State Senator Henry Taylor Blow, businessman and civil servant, brought his wife and daughter to the Garden. While he was United States minister to Brazil in the early 1870s, his wife was to donate a collection of orchids that would start a notable display at the Garden. The daughter, Susan Blow, was to play a distinguished part in educational history by introducing the kindergarten movement into this country. The first out-of-town guests, James P. Fogg of Rochester and Felix Rozier of Ste. Genevieve, signed the guest book on 24 June. John Adams, the son of President John Quincy Adams and

27. Henry Shaw, in a photograph of 1858.

grandson of President John Adams, came with his wife less than a year later.[4]

    Engelmann had written to Gray on 13 May 1859 that Shaw wanted to set up a *magna carta* for his establishment. Shaw's lawyer would soon go east and call on Gray to get his views on the arrangements of the whole enterprise. Engelmann was disappointed in the annual income of Shaw's properties. He felt that for the first twenty years it would not have more than ten thousand dollars annually to pay the curator and the gardeners and to keep up and develop the garden, herbarium, and library. After twenty years things would be better. He hoped that Shaw would live much longer so as to expend larger sums on the arrangement of the garden and the enrichment of the museum, herbarium, and library.[5]

In a response on 18 May, Gray stated that he would not disdain ten thousand dollars—he wished they had half as much at Harvard. Turning to another item of Engelmann's message, Gray would gladly confer with Shaw's lawyer when he came. "If Shaw will be liberal in his establishment," he suggested to Engelmann, "why not turn over to him your general herbarium? If I had one I could have free access to always, I would not take the expense and trouble of keeping up and increasing one myself."[6] "Shaw is liberal enough, to be sure," Engelmann admitted two weeks later, "but then with an income of seventy-five thousand dollars (it is said) and no family, he might do more than give ten thousand annually for his botanical garden."[7] He believed that until Shaw finished his museum, then up to its first story, he would avoid decisions on such matters as buying Fendler's plants or hiring Fendler to take charge of the herbarium and the library.[8]

Gray countered that Shaw was quite liberal to give ten thousand dollars out of an income of seventy-five thousand. Perhaps he would do more when he got his project underway. Gray agreed that Shaw ought to hire Fendler as his curator. For the present, Engelmann should keep his herbarium, but arrange the specimens on the same size paper as used in Shaw's herbarium and look to an eventual combination, either in Shaw's lifetime or soon after. Gray urged Engelmann to heed any reasonable proposal that Shaw made; such might be an offer to take Engelmann's herbarium, provide for maintenance and development, and when ready, make the physician director of the entire operation. When he does that, Gray went on, "with a decent salary, you could reside up there, throw physic to the dogs, or only take a share in consultations, and have time to do yourself justice in botany."[9] In summary, Gray wanted his friend Engelmann to have "the best of two worlds." And Shaw would profit, too, from the physician's botanical knowledge. Not surprisingly, in a letter nine days later Engelmann seconded everything Gray had said. He believed that when builders finished the museum, Shaw would unpack his herbarium, put up his library, and find it necessary to employ a curator. In the meantime the two botanists had to keep quiet but be ready.[10]

Shaw's effort "cannot be called a garden yet," Engelmann wrote in early August,[11] but valuable hothouse plants had come from Germany. Engelmann wanted to make some botanical studies at Shaw's place, but foresaw little leisure time. Further, though he got along well with Shaw personally, the doctor admitted he was perhaps too blunt in his dealings with the successful businessman.[12] In the meantime, Shaw had written Gray, and the latter had shown great interest in Shaw's plans and offered to help, should Shaw wish. Gray enclosed Shaw's letter in his next message to Engelmann.[13]

While the two expert botanists were wondering about the sometimes-amateurish efforts of Henry Shaw, a Boston-based correspondent visited the Garden, then "assuming definite form and shape."[14] He lavished praise on Shaw and his project. *The Magazine of Horticulture* carried an account of his September 1859 visit to St. Louis. The writer began by praising the men of the West for answering the great challenges of the wide land. Among the many achievements he could mention, he chose "one of the most magnificent projects in this or any other country: to wit, the establishment and endowment, by private individual munificence, of a Public Garden, on a broad and liberal plan, at Tower Grove,"[15] the country residence of a St. Louis businessman. The Garden comprised ten acres of the richest soil, amply sufficient for its purposes. The approach was along Floral Avenue, as it was then known, a mile in length, sixty feet wide, bordered by shade trees.

Shaw had been working quietly and unostentatiously for several years, the correspondent pointed out. The already completed entrance gate of cut stone combined architectural beauty and solid workmanship. The gateway included rooms for the keeper and "retiring rooms" for the visitors. The high stone fence surrounding the garden on three sides protected it from wintry winds. The garden had to be well fenced for another reason also: to keep out the many wild animals in that area beyond the city limits, rabbits, muskrats, raccoons, opossums, foxes, and an occasional deer; and later from foraging horses, cows, and mules; and from boys of the neighborhood who looked longingly at the ripe fruit in the orchard. The carefully constructed walkways, rivaling

28. The entrance gate to the Garden.

the Roman roads, consisted of five layers: the first of coal slack, the second of broken stone, another of coal slack, a fourth of cinders, and a top layer of "fine Merrimac [*sic*] gravel."[16]

The extensive greenhouse had an unusual glass roof, so patterned as to reflect no rays of the sun but to receive them all. An adjacent building housed the furnaces. To the north of the Garden, two arched openings afforded entrance into the walled fruticetum. Eight walks radiated from the center of this six-acre plat, with a winding way encircling the outer limits. The two upper stories of an attractively planned building going up at the time would soon house the books and the forty thousand specimens purchased for Shaw by Engelmann. The high and spacious basement would provide classroom space. On the west of the Garden the arboretum was already underway with many varieties of American trees, as well as cedars from Lebanon and a "pine" from Australia.

Shaw planned to hire a curator "of highly scientific and practical ability" and offer him the "present elegant residence."[17] To find such a

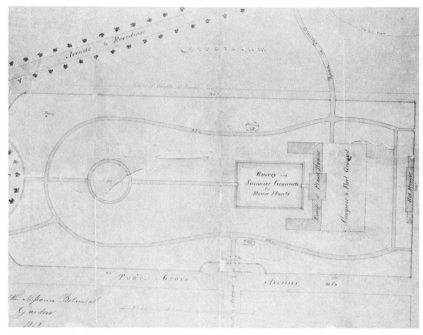

29. A rough sketch of the Garden dating from 1858.

person other than Engelmann in the Midwest at the time, even with Shaw's country home as a bonus, would not prove to be an easy task. Shaw told the correspondent of his intention to begin a row of planthouses near the middle of the Garden during the following year. Together these buildings would be the main feature of the Garden. The largest, eighty by forty feet, to be called the "Pavilion," would be "constructed of glass and iron columns on stone arches, somewhat after the style of the famous conservatory at Chatsworth, or the Crystal Palace."[18] This was the first reference to Chatsworth in any extant newspaper account or magazine article or in any of Shaw's correspondence.

"All honor to Henry Shaw!" the correspondent concluded. "May his life be long spared to superintend and develop his grand and difficult undertaking."[19] Editor C. M. Hovey reacted eloquently: "The whole history of our country, with all the numerous bequests and endowments of its wealthy men for charitable, educational and religious objects, does not furnish an instance of such private munificence as this, nor, indeed, one calculated to confer a greater benefit upon mankind."[20]

Engelmann had expressed dissatisfaction with Shaw's approach in a letter to Gray during the summer. Now in the fall, in spite of the praise

30. The arbor in the fruticetum.

that came to Shaw for the article in the Boston-based journal, and the obvious joy of the visitors at Shaw's generosity, Engelmann criticized him even more sharply: "Shaw is busy," the doctor wrote, ". . . he continues zealous, but unfortunately does not know enough and is in many things a little narrow-minded."[21] But by the time of his next letter, the busy physician must have had time to reflect, for he did an about-face. He told Gray that he believed Shaw would be a far better head of operations than the trustees, since he moved more energetically and would have more resources at his disposal.[22] Perhaps Engelmann had heard that Shaw was naming the Episcopal bishop of Missouri and the chancellor of Washington University to the board of trustees; Engelmann might with fairness question the business experience of the two. All the while, Engelmann saw limited botanical possibilities for himself. His medical work grew but provided just enough revenue to live on. He foresaw little possibility of working at the Garden full time.[23]

Further public recognition of the Garden came soon. In the forty-page report of the Chamber of Commerce for the year 1859, Secretary W. B. Baker devoted one-and-a-half pages to the Garden. He called it "the equal, if not the superior of any establishment in the United States," estimated Shaw's gift at one million dollars, and described the prospect leading to it as "a broad avenue (already designated Floral Avenue) one mile in extent and 60 feet in width . . . lined on either side with ornamental trees."[24]

The museum that the correspondent from *The Magazine of Horticulture* had described as going up the previous September[25] was completed during 1860 at a cost of $25,000. Much of the work that year consisted in carpentry, according to Shaw's papers.[26] He intended the arboretum and fruticetum to foster all the trees and shrubs that grew in the climate of Missouri. During this time, Gray and Engelmann continued their interest in, and their correspondence on, Shaw's project. Gray wondered if he should urge Shaw to employ Augustus Fendler and then send him out to California to collect specimens for a year or two before becoming curator of the herbarium.[27]

On 10 April 1860, Engelmann wrote of Shaw, "He is as tough as any

31. The museum at the Garden, completed in 1860.

Scotsman, and I fear for the present he won't buy any more books."[28] He would speak to Shaw about Fendler, but was not hopeful. When he had advised Shaw to set aside $1,000 annually for the library and $500 for the herbarium, Shaw had only laughed at what he thought a preposterous suggestion. His museum had cost him $25,000, and he had nothing yet to fill it. Engelmann felt that he made no headway with Shaw. He didn't understand the "soft-soaping" so common in the West. "A man who had no real scientific zeal or knowledge who must be got to do things by diplomacy," the doctor stated, "I cannot do much with."[29]

In June 1860, Engelmann wrote again that Shaw was working hard at his project but that he did not see much of him. "We are very good friends but I am afraid would not hitch well together. Scientific botany is secondary or tertiary with him, while I cannot get up an enthusiasm for what interests him most."[30] By October, Engelmann saw that the museum was almost ready and that Shaw would then have proper space for the specimens from the Bernhardi herbarium. The doctor felt that Shaw would then give Fendler a place in his operation; and Fendler, in turn, would put everything in order.[31]

With a more favorable view of proceedings at Tower Grove, Engelmann wrote on 1 November 1860 (while most other Americans were concentrating on the national election of the century), "Shaw has the ornamental as much at heart as the scientific, which I think is very well to popularize his establishment."[32] Shaw had put up a small memorial obelisk in honor of Thomas Nuttall, pioneer botanist in the American West, who had traveled up the Missouri River in 1810. Engelmann wanted Shaw to put up a bust of Nuttall and so asked Gray if there were a bust or portrait in existence. Eventually, he believed, Shaw would also get busts of Sir William Hooker and of Robert Brown,[33] the world-famous botanist who had been keeper of the Botany Department at the British Museum. Gray wrote back the following summer that he had a fine cast of a bust of Brown and a splendid one of Hooker. Gray hoped that Shaw would want to secure both if possible for the library at his garden.[34] Shaw chose not to do so.

Shaw finally succumbed to the repeated urgings of Engelmann and Gray and hired Augustus Fendler late in 1860.[35] A migratory bird by nature, Fendler stayed only one year. His name no longer appears in Shaw's ledgers after 20 December 1861.[36] "Fendler arranged the first botanical specimens in the herbarium which was just being started by

Henry Shaw for his botanical garden," botanical historian Perley Spaulding was to write.[37] Unfortunately, no one was to look after the nearly sixty thousand specimens of the herbaria of Johann Bernhardi and local collector Nicholas Riehl for thirty years after Fendler left.

Alsatian-born Riehl had sold to Shaw many of the early trees in the garden. His nursery on Gravois Road in Carondelet, begun in 1836, was the oldest in St. Louis County and one of the oldest in the state. Riehl began collecting dried specimens of plants—herbarium specimens—before he permanently left his native town of Colmar in Alsace in 1835. He continued to do so after reaching America, trading American specimens for European ones and amassing a good collection. Since Riehl died in 1852 at the age of forty-four and Shaw was not looking for herbaria until some years later, it may have been that someone else, perhaps Riehl's friend Engelmann, kept an eye on the 3,356 specimens in the Riehl collection until Shaw was ready to pick them up at the time he began his garden.[38]

During the 1860s Shaw recorded weather conditions and the progress of flowers, trees, and shrubs on his acres with the same care that he had previously given to cutlery sales and would continue to give to his rental properties.[39]

By November 1861, Shaw had to face the necessity of changing his will, which in its present form gave the Tower Grove area to his sister Sarah at his decease and divided the bulk of his rental properties between Sarah and Caroline. He was to annul the document with John Shepley as witness on 18 November 1861.[40] On the same day, Shaw's mother died in Rochester at the age of eighty-nine.[41] While one would presume that Caroline and Henry went east for the funeral, there is no evidence one way or another. No correspondence between Henry and Sarah after 1851 is extant, and there are no receipts for Rochester hotel bills. If Caroline and Henry did attend the funeral, they obviously stayed at the family residence. Further, Shaw was not as yet sufficiently known nationally to merit for his mother an extensive obituary notice in the local newspaper.

14.   Civil War Comes to Missouri

◆◆◆

Until the Mexican War of 1846–1848, outstate Missouri had reflected
the southern attitudes of people in the upper tier of slave states, Maryland, Virginia, North Carolina, Tennessee, and Kentucky, the places of
origin of its settlers. These slaveowners had concentrated in counties
along the Mississippi in northeast and southeast Missouri and along the
Missouri River in west-central Missouri. Many men in this latter area
had taken part in the Kansas border wars of the 1850s. Ten of Missouri's
first fifteen governors, further, came from this "Little Dixie" area. But
in the 1850s many antislavery men made their way to Missouri. Sons of
farmers from Ohio, Indiana, and Illinois moved into the fertile lands
along the Iowa border, Unionists from the Carolinas chose areas in the
Ozark highlands, and German farmers settled along the southern bank
of the Missouri River below Jefferson City, the state capital. By 1860
only one out of every nine individuals in Missouri was a slave—a striking contrast with South Carolina's more than one out of two. Slave labor
had ceased to be a major economic factor. The one railroad that crossed
the state ran between Hannibal and St. Joseph, roughly fifty miles from
the Iowa border, through land tilled predominantly by farmers of strong
Union sympathy. Three railroads, slightly over one hundred miles long
each, spoked out from St. Louis to Macon in north-central Missouri, to
Sedalia in the west-central part of the state, and to Pilot Knob, a mining
area south of St. Louis.

St. Louis, the Missouri metropolis, had its own background and varied attitudes toward the slave question. Francis Grierson, an English
visitor who had resided in St. Louis for a time before the Civil War,
described St. Louis in 1859 as conventional and contented, like someone
long used to fixed modes and habits. There was no hurrying or bustling,
thanks to the southern atmosphere of ease and nonchalance into which
so many upper-class St. Louisans had been born. "In the commercial
world, the Yankees ruled," Grierson pointed out, "but the old, slow,
languid, proud, hospitable forefathers of St. Louis who had been its
social leaders, were the owners of slaves."[1] While the casual visitor
hardly noticed slavery in the city, many of the city's political and eco-

nomic leaders accepted the institution as part of the city's life. The extremism of the abolitionists offended many St. Louisans.

The number of free blacks had risen in the previous ten years, but still the total black population was negligible. In 1850 it had been 4,054, a third of them free, in a total population of 77,860. The 1860 census takers found 3,297 blacks, over half of them (1,755) free, in a total population of 160,773 St. Louisans.

In the presidential campaign of 1860, states of the deep South bolted the national Democratic ticket and rejected its candidate, Sen. Stephen Douglas, in favor of Vice-Pres. John C. Breckenridge of Kentucky. Missouri remained firmly in the Democratic camp, becoming the only state to give all its electoral votes to Douglas in November 1860. Abraham Lincoln won few votes in the state outside of St. Louis, and those he won in the city were chiefly cast by people of German background. Between Lincoln's election in November and his inaugural in March, seven states seceded from the Union in spite of Senator Douglas's efforts for unity. Four states of the upper South broke away after the firing on Fort Sumter in April 1861.

In response to this challenge, President Lincoln called for volunteers from the states. In Missouri, newly elected Gov. Claiborne Fox Jackson refused to honor the president's call. Instead he ordered the militia into training encampments throughout the state. One of these, called Camp Jackson in honor of the governor, was located at the west-central edge of St. Louis in Lindell Grove, property that took its name from Shaw's partner and friend Peter Lindell and Lindell's brother, Jesse. Northern-born Gen. Daniel Frost, who had served with distinction in the Mexican War and then married a granddaughter of St. Louis philanthropist John Mullanphy, headed the encampment. Actually the muster resembled a homecoming more than a menace, with parades and colorful uniforms that gave the young ladies of the city a chance to admire their young men friends, and gave the oldsters, such as Prof. Elihu Shepard of St. Louis College, an opportunity to visit former students. Unfortunately for the southern sympathizers, Governor Jackson sent to the encampment military stores pirated from the federal arsenal at Baton Rouge, Louisiana. Further, streets at Camp Jackson bore the names of the two men most responsible for the firing on the flag at Fort Sumter, Jefferson Davis and Gen. Gustave T. Beauregard.

Under pressure from Cong. Frank Blair of St. Louis, the federal government had, in the meantime, removed conciliatory Gen. William Harney, whose wife was an aunt of General Frost's wife. An unconditional New England Unionist, Capt. Nathaniel Lyon, took charge of the Federal Arsenal on the south side of the city. The bulk of the military stores once held there had already been taken across the river to the free state of Illinois. Learning that Camp Jackson contained the contraband war material from Baton Rouge, Lyon called into service between four and five thousand men, mostly members of the German gymnastic societies (*Turnvereine*), to add to his few regulars, and they surrounded the encampment on Friday, 10 May 1861. Since Frost did not have the manpower or firepower to resist, he surrendered.

Instead of moving the captured forces by a back road to the Arsenal, Lyon marched them conspicuously through rows of hostile spectators. Someone fired at one of the immigrant officers. Lyon's men returned the fire, and the ensuing melee brought death to twenty-eight and injuries to more. Rioting swept the city that night. Many westside residents thought the "Dutch" were going to burn the city. Local authorities joined with federal officers to keep the peace.

Early in June, Governor Jackson and Gen. Sterling Price, head of the state militia and former governor, called upon Lyon, now a brigadier general, with plans to keep the state "neutral." Lyon threatened dire consequences for Jackson, Price, and every other Missourian siding with them and gave the two leaders one hour to get out of the city. They complied. War followed, and Missouri suffered far more than most states. Within its boundaries the conflict was truly a neighbors' war, in some instances a brothers' war, with all its attendant bitterness.

The Camp Jackson affair and the almost-brutal manner of General Lyon pushed many St. Louisans off the fence into the secessionist camp. Among these were General Frost and many of the state militiamen from Camp Jackson, once they were released in an exchange of prisoners. Among Confederate officers were Col. Meriwether L. Clark, son of the explorer, Maj. William Clark Kennerly, who had been an occasional guest of Henry Shaw, and Maj. Uriel Wright, who had defended Effie Carstang in the trial. Ultimately an estimated five thousand St. Louisans fought under the Stars and Bars. Far more Unionists answered Lincoln's call, so many volunteers in fact that the federal government never drafted a man from St. Louis.

Lyon marched out of the city at the head of the Federal forces. Abetted by troops from Kansas, in August he met the Missouri and Arkansas Confederates under Generals Price and McCulloch at Wilson's Creek near Springfield in southwest Missouri. The Confederates won after heavy losses on both sides; Lyon was mortally wounded. Rumors spread that the way to St. Louis was open for the Confederates. Town-talk centered on the possibility that St. Louis would be in the West what Washington was in the East—the great prize to be fought for; and many in the city seemed to think that the botanical garden, situated in a prominent place on a large elevated plain, with substantial buildings and long and solid walls surrounding it, would be the principal battlefield.[2] With the same fatuity that Washingtonians displayed in driving their carriages to Bull Run "to see the show," some St. Louisans thought of the honor that would come to the Garden should Union Gen. John Charles Frémont try to halt Gen. Sterling Price's Missouri Confederates there as they came in from the southwest on the Old Manchester Road.[3]

But the expected battle for St. Louis never came about. Unsupported by the states'-rights-oriented Arkansas militia, General Price could not advance and threaten the city. The federal government, in turn, set up ten forts and three outposts to protect St. Louis, all well east of the Garden. St. Louis relaxed in relative security from invasion.

With St. Louis safely in Union hands, the traditional river communication between the strongly pro-Southern area of west-central Missouri and the deep South was cut. Wagon roads to Arkansas and cattle trails to Texas formed the only paths connecting the Missouri Confederates with their co-secessionists to the South. Moderates ousted Governor Jackson and chose Hamilton R. Gamble as provisional governor, and the state government remained in Union hands. Even though the Confederacy put a star in its flag for Missouri, the pro-Confederate members of the state legislature, meeting in Neosho, could supply no money, equipment, or even uniforms for its men who fought for the South. In spite of this, numbers of Confederate sympathizers stole quietly out of St. Louis to join the Southern ranks. In response the federal government began to introduce some elements of a "police state" in the city.

Henry Shaw's mentors, Asa Gray and George Engelmann, differed sharply on the war. The Harvard botanist, reflecting the extreme views of so many New Englanders, wrote Engelmann: "I believe in capital

punishments. The life of a rebel is duly and justly forfeit."⁴ If such drastic views had rocked St. Louis moderates when a professional soldier
(General Lyon) had expressed them, one should not be surprised that
Engelmann was shocked. "I did not think you so bloody-minded,
harsh, and one-sided," he wrote, "but, I suppose, hearing and seeing
only one phase, one aspect, and being far removed . . . from the scenes
and sorrows of fraternal war, you (I mean all your people) can well
afford to indulge in this way of thinking."⁵ Fortunately, the two did not
completely break over the issue of secession and war. But their views,
typical of the time, make the reticence of Shaw to declare himself on the
issues that much more amazing.

Shaw generally kept his politics to himself. Practical man of commerce that he was, he no doubt recognized the dilemma that Missouri, a
peninsula of slavery extending into free soil, would have faced in secession: if the North won, the state would have become a conquered
province; if the South won, Missouri would have been a landlocked area
of commerce and manufacturing, ruled by a planter-oriented Confederate government. While a few St. Louis politicians and lawyers supported the Confederate cause, Shaw stood with most local businessmen
who did not let sentiment, or anger at the drastic measures of Frank
Blair, Nathaniel Lyon, and the German Unionists in 1861, cloud their
good judgment.

During the second year of the war, several Confederate officers, pris-
oners-of-war, signed the Garden's guest book, among them Capt. H. L.
May and Capt. William Davis. Other soldiers also came, including
Lucas Sherry, paymaster, U.S.A.; Brig. Gen. J. M. Schofield, former
math instructor at Washington University; and Capt. Richard S.
Shelley of the British Army.

Robert Campbell, a prominent St. Louis merchant-trader, visited
the Garden on 3 April 1862, as did Professor Beresford of Kazan University in Russia. Frederick Law Olmsted, urban designer, came exactly a
year later. Col. John O'Fallon and his son-in-law, Dr. Charles Alexander Pope, both men of distinction, the one in business, the other in
science, came on 5 May 1862. Mrs. Thomas O'Flaherty, widow of a
prominent businessman killed in the Gasconade Railroad Bridge disaster, visited the Garden on 29 May, as did David Ranken, founder of
Ranken Trade School in St. Louis.

During that same spring, two young ladies clearly indicated their opposing loyalties. Yvette Pratte listed herself as "a rebel," and Miss Frankie Cheney indicated her loyalty to the Union cause.[6] This juxtaposition of names and allegiances spoke eloquently of a lasting value of Shaw's legacy. Here within the high walls of the Garden lay undisturbed peace and tranquillity, while in the northwest corner of Arkansas, less than three hundred miles away, young friends of Yvette Pratte and of Frankie Cheney, once neighbors in St. Louis, had just faced each other in the bloodiest battle of the Civil War fought west of the Mississippi.

During those same early months of 1862, Union Admiral David I. Farragut captured New Orleans, the Confederacy's only large city, and Gen. U. S. Grant took Confederate Fort Henry on the Tennessee River and Fort Donelson on the Cumberland, with the aid of gunboats made in Carondelet by St. Louis engineer James B. Eads. Grant then began his great campaign that would sever the Confederacy with the fall of Vicksburg and Union control of the Mississippi the following summer. The cause of the Union looked bright in the West, but the Confederates still held on the Virginia battlefields, and the seemingly interminable war would drag on for many months.

Toward the end of the Civil War, Shaw became aware of a young woman walking in the Garden—in much the same way as he had met Effie Carstang several years before. Her name was Rebecca Edom. Talking with a friend, Shaw mentioned that he "liked her face" and wanted to hire her as housekeeper. Hearing of his statement, Rebecca called at his town house a few days later and applied for the position. Shaw warned her that she would find it lonesome, "as there would be no one around but Negroes." Undeterred, she accepted the position and was to hold it throughout the rest of Shaw's life.[7] When asked, after Shaw's death, if he had ever proposed marriage, she was to remark that he often spoke about it in an obviously jesting way, but never seriously. She stated that Shaw also joked much in other situations[8]—an allegation surprising in view of Shaw's usual seriousness. He was to commission R. A. Clifford to make a portrait of Rebecca at the same time as one of Asa Gray some years later.[9]

Many wondered over the years about Shaw's views on marriage. By this time his sister Sarah no longer recommended lovely Guernseys, and Frederick Billon no doubt had concluded that Shaw did not intend to marry an English girl. Even though Shaw had come from the business class and made his own fortune, perhaps he saw himself in the image of the typical English country gentleman of the lower nobility, who, untrammeled by responsibilities to wife and children and the resultant social obligations attendant upon wealth and position, wished, after years of travel in the warmer cities of the Mediterranean, to return to his homeland and spend his autumnal years cultivating his ancestral acres.

Before the Civil War, Shaw had held many indentures and mortgages on property. By the beginning of the war, more and more people had begun to rent property from him. He hired the firm of Webb and Kaime and later that of J. E. Kaime and Brothers to collect his rents. He had 11 renters in 1862, 15 in 1863, 56 in 1870 and 1871, 80 in 1875, 90 in 1877, and, after going up to 107 in 1879, would have 100 renters in the last year of his life. Ultimately, 481 individuals or firms would rent from Shaw. These renters stretched from individuals to big stores like Scruggs, Vandervoort and Barney, and also included the United States Government.[10]

Architect-engineer Francis Tunica drew a sketch of the Garden area dated 1865 (see figure 46 below). He must have added to it later, since several of the buildings were built after that time. Earlier, Old Manchester Road had given access to the property along a road running roughly southeast to Shaw's residence. By the end of the Civil War, Tower Grove Avenue ran along the east end of the Garden, and the street along the north side was named Shaw Avenue. Patterned flower beds filled the area just south of the fruticetum, and behind Shaw's residence were a large vegetable garden and associated buildings.[11]

Regional maps published in midcentury, such as one by Julius Hutawa (1862),[12] often contained the names of original owners, usually Creole French, with the names of the later owners in larger script, and the current owners in block letters. Maj. William Christy had gained a large section of the land in Prairie des Noyers in early American days. He sold much of it to William Chambers in 1816. Even though Chambers had willed a good portion of his property to his daughter Mary Tyler earlier, his name covered the area in Hutawa's map. Shaw owned much of the remainder, as well as property just west of Kingshighway a few blocks south of Arsenal and a large section on the south side of Arsenal, east and west of Watson Road.[13] The one built-up section in the vicinity at the time, McRee City, lay north of the Garden along the Missouri Pacific Railroad.[14]

When the well-known philanthropist and businessman John

O'Fallon died in December 1865, Henry Shaw was one of the honorary pallbearers, along with former mayor John Darby and Shaw's fellow merchant-trader Robert Campbell.[15] Shaw had known O'Fallon from his early days in St. Louis when Shaw had hardware to sell and O'Fallon was sutler to the troops going up the Missouri.

The one time in his middle years when Shaw seemed to display his political leanings came on the fifth anniversary of the capture of the state militia at Camp Jackson by federal troops and German immigrants under Lyon. Supporters of Lyon felt this action saved Missouri for the Union; hence the celebration of the fifth anniversary. Shaw hosted the jubilants, who included Governors Richard J. Oglesby of Illinois and Thomas C. Fletcher of Missouri, at the Garden. Missouri historian William Parrish saw the Radical Republican campaign of vindictiveness against Confederate sympathizers as getting underway at this rally. "Unfortunately," Parrish wrote, "Governor Oglesby became indisposed during his talk, perhaps because of the elaborate refreshments served earlier at the Tower Grove Estate of Henry Shaw."[16]

The guest book at Tower Grove carried the names of a large number of Republican political figures on that day, including both governors.[17] Interestingly, the name of Charles Drake, the real leader of the Radical Republicans in Missouri, does not appear. He had led those men the previous year in writing a vindictive constitution for Missouri—the "Drake Constitution"—that took the vote away from all Confederate sympathizers and called into question the loyalty of clergy, teachers, and lawyers. The following year those Missourians still allowed to vote were to elect Drake to the United States Senate.

On the same day that the Radical Republicans visited the Garden, four youngsters with names of prominence among St. Louis French signed the guest book: Samuel Auguste Chouteau and his sister, Marie Isabelle Chouteau, and Jane and F. Desloge.[18]

While Drake and his friends were trying to pattern future Missouri history to their own prejudices, a group of citizens with more long-range views decided to celebrate St. Louis's past. The Civil War had prevented any celebrations in 1864, the anniversary of the founding of the city. These men agreed to commemorate the centenary of the first grant of land in the city on 1 August 1866. Henry Shaw signed this resolution, along with several prominent citizens of French descent, his friends Charles P. Chouteau and Louis Benoist, and his fellow native of England, John P. Withnell. This was the first act of what came to be the Missouri Historical Society.[19] Shaw was one of the many vice-presidents, although some historians have questioned whether Shaw took part in the proceedings or simply gave his verbal support. In 1872 his name would appear on the certificate of incorporation of the Historical Society, along with such other famous St. Louis names as James Lucas, Elihu Shepard, William G. Eliot, Silas Bent, Charles Chouteau, Albert Todd, Wilson Primm, and John Darby.[20]

In 1867, Shaw hired a fellow Englishman, James Gurney, as head gardener. A native of Buckinghamshire, Gurney had gained experience in botanical work in his native England and was to participate in the establishment of the giant *Victoria* water lilies in St. Louis. He never claimed the title of botanist, but he knew flowers. A prayerful, Bible-reading, family man, he came in later years to resemble Gen. Robert E. Lee, with his white hair, his beard style, and his clear, intent eyes. A conciliatory man, Gurney early learned how to deal with his fellow Englishman, who did not readily brook disagreement. At Shaw's death years later, Gurney was to remark, "In twenty-three years I never heard him speak a harsh or irritable word."[21]

Gurney's name first appears on the staff list in 1867. His two younger sons, George and James, Jr., who had accompanied him to America, worked with their father at the Garden during the summer months.[22] At that time, the position of head gardener covered every conceivable task. He was timekeeper, label writer, tree planter, floral expert, and vine-grower. When Shaw began Tower Grove Park, as will be seen in the next chapter, he called on Gurney continually. Gurney was to stay with Shaw until his death and was later to become superintendent of the park.

The Garden was beginning to gain wide recognition by this time. With plenty of time to write to friends while her colorful cavalry-officer husband was stationed at Fort Riley in Kansas, Mrs. George Custer wrote to a friend about her "elegant time in St. Louis. We went to the famous 'Missouri Botanical Gardens' [*sic*] . . . the most superb gardens in America."[23] She found everything in excellent taste when she visited there with other members of President Andrew Johnson's party. The general had been traveling with the president at the time.[24]

During the year of Gurney's arrival, the first edition of *Stranger's Guide to St. Louis,* which told what to see and how to see it in and around the

32. James Gurney relaxes on one of the ornamental iron benches in the Garden.

city, devoted two pages to the Garden. It quoted Elizur Wright in the *Boston Commonwealth* as saying, "Would that Boston had such a Shaw!"25

In 1868 Shaw built a main display greenhouse, which came to be called "the Old Conservatory," with additional wings for moist and temperate conditions. Thomas Meehan, editor of *The Gardener's*

33. The first greenhouse in the Garden, later called the Old Conservatory. The statue of Juno still stands in the Garden.

Monthly, told the story of the Garden that same year, concluding, "The name of Shaw, Engelmann and the Botanic Garden will go down in history together."[26]

During the war, a four-year-old orphan, Joseph Tarrigan Monell, had become a ward of Shaw. He was the son of the Archer and Hester (Tarrigan) Monell; Hester had worked for Shaw for a short time in early 1859.[27] Both she and her husband had died in the meantime, and young Joseph was living at the Episcopal Orphans' Home at Eleventh and Market. When in early 1867 the Episcopal Ladies Society began to raise money for a new home for the sixty youngsters, Shaw gave them land at De Tonty and Grand,[28] where the new orphanage was built. Every year after the building was completed,[29] Shaw sent a Christmas tree for the orphans, and he occasionally spent Christmas afternoon with them.

When Joseph reached school age, Shaw sent him to the school that bore Shaw's name on Manchester Road ten blocks west of the orphanage. By the age of ten Joseph could translate Latin and French and showed an early interest in nature, especially the study of flowers and insects. But nothing in Shaw's extant papers refers to the young man until 1869, when Shaw began to pay Monell's tuition at Smith Academy, the preparatory school for Washington University.[30] Shaw continued paying for Monell's tuition on the secondary, collegiate, and graduate levels. Monell's successful career justified Shaw's generosity.[31]

Shaw also gave a strip of land for Mount Calvary Episcopal Church. On the west side of Grand, it faced east down Lafayette Avenue, which dead-ended there. When the city wanted to cut Lafayette through to the west later on, the church relocated on property behind the orphanage. Whether or not Shaw worshipped occasionally at this church when he spent his summers at Tower Grove is uncertain.

Even though less than ten years had passed since he had opened the Garden, and a terrible war had convulsed the nation during the first half of that period, Shaw could look back with intense satisfaction on what he had achieved. A prestigious botanical journal in Philadelphia had asserted that his botanical garden had no equal in the United States and, indeed, few anywhere in the world.[32]

15. Tower Grove Park through Two Decades, 1867–1889

❖❖

With the Garden moving along well, Shaw began to look to his tree-less acres lying south and east of the botanical area. At that time, the city of St. Louis had eight small parks, but not a single sizable park commensurate with its progress and character as the representative metropolis of the Mississippi Valley.[1] It would open Forest, O'Fallon, Carondelet, and Fairgrounds parks in the mid-1870s.

In previous centuries European parks had been the grants of royal lands for the enjoyment of the people; but by mid-nineteenth century the cities of western Europe and America were beginning to reserve space for this purpose. New York City had purchased the acres in 1857 that would become Central Park. During the Civil War, Chicago had set aside eighty acres that eventually became part of Lincoln Park and an area along Lake Michigan destined to become Grant Park.

Mayor Chauncey I. Filley of St. Louis planned a park during the Civil War also. On 5 February 1864, he named Henry Shaw one of the commissioners, along with James B. Eads, the boat-builder, and two others, of a projected park. The demands of wartime, the resignation of the mayor because of ill health, and the rejection of the proposal by the citizenry doomed the project. In 1867 Shaw decided to move on his own initiative to open a large park. He approached Mayor James S. Thomas (1864–1868) and offered to turn the broad area into a park. In return the city would float a bond issue to develop the land along the lines of Shaw's thinking and set aside a yearly sum for its upkeep. Both mayor and benefactor faced one technical problem: most of the area Shaw intended to set aside for Tower Grove Park, the rectangle bounded by Grand on the east, Arsenal on the south, Kingshighway on the west, and Magnolia, widened the year before to fifty feet, on the north, lay outside the city limits. Under the existing charter, the city could not accept or develop the tract. The state of Missouri alone had such authority.

On appeal, the Missouri legislature passed an act on 9 March 1867 setting up Tower Grove Park according to the following arrangement: a board of not less than five nor more than seven commissioners controlled the park; Shaw would be one of these members for life; the rest would receive their appointment from the state supreme court. This brilliant and unique legal structure secured the park from tampering by politicians and faddists. The initial board consisted of Shaw, Mayor Thomas, businessman Adolphus Meier, Judge William P. Ferguson, and Shaw's friend Charles P. Chouteau. When Thomas died, Robert A. Barnes stepped in.[2] Upon the death of Shaw, the director of the Missouri Botanical Garden would, by law, take his place.

On 20 October of the following year (1868), Shaw gave the oblong tract of 276.76 acres, 7,676 feet long and 1,550 feet wide, to the city. St. Louis passed a special bond issue that brought $360,000 to the commissioners of the park. The city would contribute at least $25,000 annually to development. Unlike the Garden, where Shaw's money and not city taxes supported the operation, the city would take care of the original development and subsequent improvements. Besides giving the land, Shaw also used his energy and imagination in its development.

To provide support for the Garden, Shaw planned a row of "villas" along a two-hundred-foot strip around the perimeter of the park—a pattern found in England. He presumed that many St. Louisans would want to live in such lovely surroundings and would rent the ground under long-term leases. They would build impressive residences along the lines of the villa that he was building for the caretaker of the Garden. In this way the rent would continually support the Garden during the succeeding years.

Shaw had seen the best parks in Europe, among them Hampton Court near London and the Bois de Boulogne in the suburbs of Paris, and had studied reports of parks in American cities. He wanted recreation for all, not for the wealthy alone, with broad drives, shady walks, benches, ponds, space for games, music stands, and evergreen circles. While Shaw remained the chief designer and supervisor of the planning and development of the park without the liability of ownership, he had the able assistance of head gardener James Gurney. In the tradition of their native England, they saw the area as a place of tranquillity and ordered beauty, a place to enjoy as well as to view. "A beautiful prospect," a writer on the history of the park later wrote, "delights the soul as much as a demonstration, and a description of Homer has charmed more readers than a chapter of Aristotle."[3] Shaw laid out the acres both as a strolling park with lots of walkways and as a driving park with broad carriage roads, bordered by neat stone gutters.

Four elaborate gates provided access for carriages. The Grand Avenue entrance led to a broad avenue that ran straight west, looping around two circles that would later welcome statues of great men. Shaw secured entrance columns for the north gate from the dome of the Old Courthouse in downtown St. Louis at the time of the remodeling of that building, and built that gate between 1868 and 1870. The firm of Shickle and Harrison of St. Louis did the ironwork on the east (the Grand Avenue) gate in 1870. Griffins, a mythological combination of lions and eagles, stood atop the piers on that entrance. Lions adorned some piers, while stags, designed in Berlin, adorned others. Each entrance had an attractive gatehouse. Pauley and Brothers did the ironwork on the south and north gates. During the 1870s Shaw contracted for twelve "wellhouses"—shelters for wells.

Under Shaw's general direction, Gurney and his helpers would plant an estimated twenty thousand trees over the years. They chose 103 deciduous varieties (those that lose their leaves every year) and 35 types of evergreens. Gurney spaced the trees five feet apart, each in a

34. Looking out the west gate of Tower Grove Park.

pit three feet deep, and staked and tied them to insure proper growth.4

Former mayor John Darby donated six trees from North Carolina—tulip, cypress, hornbeam, linden, holly, and pine—which Gurney planted at the east end of the park. But Shaw did not stop with domestic stock; he brought in the finest foreign trees adapted to local soil and climate. Most came from northern Europe, a few from Siberia, China, and Japan. Norway maples, German lindens, European larches, and oriental ginkgos matched the native oaks, maples, hickories, walnuts, sycamores, honey locusts, Osage orange, mulberry, redbud, persimmon, catalpa, and many other broadleafed trees. Evergreens of other areas—juniper, spruce, fir, and pine—grew alongside Missouri's own "red cedars" (native junipers). Few parks anywhere in the nation could claim the variety of trees that soon flourished in Tower Grove. The tree planters used stock established in the arboretum in the Garden that the local writer and publicist David MacAdam called "the most complete and extensive collection of forest trees in the United States."5 Shaw discussed with Gurney and friends his failures as well as his successes with exotic varieties of trees: the failures included cedars of Lebanon, the eucalyptus, the Indian cedars, and certain California evergreens.6

As a special feature, Shaw plotted a maze, consisting of hemlock, spruce, and cedar hedges surrounded by a row of Osage orange. In the center stood an ornamental structure with balcony and tower to be climbed by all who could find their way through the maze. Gurney and staff also planted evergreen circles of spruce, cedar, and pine, and many thick groves in various areas. They left an open meadow to the west of the main circle.

In a short time, bird watchers noted that many species flocked to Tower Grove Park: robins, swallows, cardinals, catbirds, mockingbirds, swifts, purple martins, yellow warblers, woodpeckers, thrushes, wrens, orioles, sparrows, doves, bluejays, blackbirds, and hummingbirds.

In the Second Annual Report of the park, issued in January 1871, Henry Shaw as comptroller furnished an inventory of property and gave estimates for the coming year. The inventory listed stables and sheds for horses and vehicles, tools, towers, stone, piers, entrances, and bridges and a house for the foreman and stablemen.7 Shaw reported that the nursery had 12,753 trees of 202 varieties, with 1,670 white maples and

1,204 Norway spruce, the most common varieties, and 2 pin oaks and 2 ashes, the least common. He described the area as 200 acres of gently rolling prairie land, without sinkholes, requiring little labor in grading and filling, with the surrounding strip obviating the necessity of a costly enclosure.

Shaw discussed the current objections to large parks, such as Central Park in New York with its 707 acres, and noted that park roads in New York cost $100,000 per mile, while at Tower Grove the costs did not go above $60,000. In short, he thought Tower Grove Park the right size and suggested that the north side of town needed a park also.[8]

In his developing plans for the park, Shaw began to recall his first return trip to his native land. The variously designed gazebos—shelters or pavilions so common at the time—had fascinated him: the Chinese temple at Kew, the Tudor summerhouses, the medieval structures of Windsor and Hampton Court. He had seen the temple gazebos of the Petit Trianon at Versailles in France, the garden teahouses in Holland, and the various gothic gazebos of Germany, Spain, and Italy. When he designed his ornamental pleasure gardens in Tower Grove Park, he built ten gazebos, adaptations of those he had seen on his travels, designed to afford shelter from showers and sunshine and to provide places for a drink of refreshing well water. The large dovecot gazebo

35. Tower Grove Park, pedestrian's walk, with one of Shaw's ten gazebos.

near the Arsenal Street entrance, with its gradually narrowing cupola, begun in 1871 as a home for doves and pigeons, became a rendezvous for citizens. Near the east gate, the largest of the shelters, which had a tin roof and was entirely supported by wooden columns, became the rendezvous of older persons and won the nickname "Sons of Rest Shelter." Fierce dragon heads looked down from the roof of the Chinese pagoda.

"Had Henry Shaw chosen to direct his many-faceted talents to architecture," architectural historian Gerhardt Kramer was to write over a century later, "he might have done creditably in that profession."[9] Shaw seemed well-versed in the disciplines of architecture and landscape planning; he certainly knew what he wanted in applying these skills to planning and developing his park. As he planned it, Tower Grove Park was to encompass beauty in all its forms, with works of art and music used to enhance its natural beauty. He commissioned an octagonal building with a curved cupola in 1872 for the music stand. White marble busts of Shaw's favorite composers on pedestals of polished granite would eventually encircle the music stand.

Neighbors in the area, not yet part of the city, would come for the first concert in 1873. Summer concerts came to be held every Sunday. Shaw's enjoyment of music became well known among his friends, and on one occasion the local papers carried an account of Prof. August F. Herwig's band serenading Shaw at his downtown residence.[10]

Shaw realized that no English park was complete without a pond for children to sail their boats, but to create a pond away from a stream had never been easy. Unlike Kew on the Thames and Chatsworth on the Derwent, Tower Grove lacked a stream of any size. Three drainage runs crossed the property in a northwardly direction, uniting beyond the Shaw properties and forming a branch of Mill Creek; these carried water only during the rainy seasons. Shaw built stone culverts to bring carriageways over them.[11] Stone and pipe drains connected with these runs handled even unusual rainfalls.

In 1872, fortunately, the county court was putting in a pipeline to the Asylum for the Insane three blocks beyond the southwest corner of the park. Shaw was able to tap into this line for water to irrigate the land, control dust in summertime, and form a small lake.[12] Shaw chose a site for his pond just east of the north-south carriageway, midway between the east-west mall and Magnolia Avenue. Grassy banks bound the pond on three sides. An artistic arrangement of stone blocks from the old

36. The fountain and the "ruins" in Tower Grove Park.

Lindell Hotel, destroyed by fire in 1867, lined the north bank. The casual placing of this "ruins"—a practice popular in Victorian times—suggested antiquity. The central fountain did not match the Emperor's Fountain at Chatsworth, but it had few rivals in midwestern America in the 1870s and 1880s. Whenever an orchestra took its place in the music stand nearby, James Gurney opened the valve, and the sound of water blended with the strains of Rossini or Mozart.

Shaw worked with four different architects during his lifetime. The closest was his fellow Englishman George I. Barnett, who had already designed his town house and his country residence. Barnett undertook the south gate and gatehouse, and pedestals for the statues in the park. The other three architects were Francis Tunica, Eugene L. Greenleaf, and Henry Thiele. Tunica worked as engineer and architect of the park from 1868 to 1871, designing and supervising the building of the first "villa" in the two-hundred-foot perimeter strip. Under Shaw's direction he also worked on the north gate and gatehouse, the east gate and its original gatehouse, the west gate, the gatehouse stable, the stone house near the stable, and six bridges. Eugene L. Greenleaf designed the park pavilions erected in 1871 and 1872, the children's playground shelter, the ornamental wellhouses, the music stand, the "Sons of Rest Shelter," the Turkish pavilion, and the lily pond summerhouse. Henry Thiele apparently drew maps and other plans for the park and designed the Chinese summerhouse and other summerhouses and wells.

Busts of composers did not satisfy the sculptural interests of Henry Shaw. He wanted several colossal statues, the first of William Shakespeare. Baron Ferdinand von Miller of Munich, who had already finished the busts of Beethoven and Wagner, designed and completed the statue of Shakespeare. The square stance and challenging gaze that the Bard of Avon assumes in this statue seem more appropriate for an empire-builder or victorious general, a Champlain or a Wellington, than for a poet—even one of Shakespeare's stature. The more realistic bronze bas-reliefs on the pedestal depict fat-bellied Falstaff, the horror-haunted Lady Macbeth, dignified Queen Katherine, and Hamlet talking to the grave digger. Barnett designed the base and fifteen-foot pedestal of Missouri red granite. The redbuds that James Gurney had planted in Tower Grove Park were about to burst out in their spring glory when Shaw formally unveiled the statue on 23 April 1878 and presented it to acting mayor John Lightner, who in the absence of Mayor Henry Overstolz accepted the gift on behalf of the citizens of St. Louis. Capt. James McDonough praised Shaw for this benefaction and recited a portion of one of Hamlet's soliloquies.

A few years later, a famous Shakespearean actress, Adelaide Neilson, came to see the statue and promised to send a mulberry slip from Stratford-on-Avon when she returned to England. Unfortunately she died within a month, before she returned to the British Isles. Another actor, N. M. Ludlow, accompanied by poet Thomas Garrett and writer Thomas Dimmock,[13] planted a mulberry tree from Shaw's arboretum in her honor.

Only the oaks still held their then-brown leaves when five *Turnvereine*, thirteen German singing societies, and six other fraternal, cultural, or religious organizations took part in the unveiling of von Miller's second bronze statue of Alexander von Humboldt, German naturalist and South American explorer, on 24 November 1878. The reflective posture of Humboldt emphasized his scientific achievement rather than his ventures into the South American jungle or his assault on the heights of

Mount Chimborazo, a 20,561 foot peak in Ecuador. Below the statue, the viewer could see the majestic mountain in the bas-relief on one side, the Orinoco Valley on the other, a likeness of Henry Shaw on the back, and the name of the explorer-scientist on the front.

Even though the glory of Indian summer had departed, the German-American community came in force. A seemingly endless procession of visitors rolled through the park. A cascade of oratory, more fitting for the political stump during an election year, poured forth at the unveiling. William Torrey Harris, superintendent of St. Louis public schools and later to be United States commissioner of education, gave the main address, which concerned Humboldt's travels in Latin America. The statue, he believed, could well bear the legend ". . . There is Mexico, there is Central America, there is South America, and the Isles of the Sea"—in short, the new frontiers of the hemisphere.[14] Less than two months later, a grand-niece of the explorer, Matilde von Humboldt, wrote Shaw from Germany, conveying the family's joy that Henry had dedicated the monument to their famous relative.[15]

The column-like poplars reached to a height of eighty feet in the park[16] by 11 June 1882, when Shaw presented St. Louisan Howard Kretchmar's busts of Mozart and Rossini to the "Future Great City"—as publicists then called St. Louis. The St. Louis Grand Orchestra opened with selections from Mozart's *Don Giovanni.* Shaw escorted the popular pianist Lena Anton to the statues to unveil them. Postlewaite's band and forty singers of the *Liederkranz* participated in the entertainment.[17]

Shaw spoke of meeting the Italian composer Gioacchino Antonio Rossini, composer of the *Barber of Seville* and other operas, at Bologna and later at Paris during his European travels. "Rossini had a smile for everyone," Shaw stated, "and was the picture of good nature, politeness and affability."[18] Judge J. Gabriel Woerner gave the main address. His closing words had a lilt: "Where music is heard, there is the land of Rossini; where song is cherished, there is Mozart enshrined in the hearts of the people."[19] At the urging of the Board of Park Commissioners the following year, Shaw commissioned David MacAdam, park publicist and factotum for Shaw's enterprises, to publish a 119-page book, *Tower Grove Park,* that increased public interest.

With the busts of composers beginning to encircle the bandstand, Shaw turned again to his plans for major sculpture, commissioning Baron von Miller to create a statue of the discoverer of America,

Christopher Columbus. Early in the planning the baron sent Shaw a photograph of a portrait of a bearded Columbus done by a fellow artist of Munich, which Shaw liked. Even though the baron later found other portraits of Columbus without a beard and discovered that Genoese sailors were usually clean-shaven in the late fifteenth century, Shaw had decided on a bearded mariner.[20] He chose a location for the first bronze figure of the "Admiral of the Ocean Sea" facing west just inside the Grand Avenue entrance to the park. The ever-thrifty Shaw described the statue "as a work of art that cannot fail to meet general approbation—luckily works of art for public pleasure grounds are duty free—and pay no tax to vested interests . . . ."[21] David MacAdam served as secretary of the Committee of Arrangements for the unveiling on Columbus Day, 12 October 1886.

Over the years many people came to wonder who first suggested the park idea to Henry Shaw. Shortly after Shaw's death, a writer for the *Republic* was to credit Shaw's friend and personal physician,[22] Dr. Thomas O'Reilly, with having first suggested to the merchant-capitalist the gift of a park to the city. When the two dined at Shaw's mansion, his host allegedly asked O'Reilly how best one might help his city. The doctor responded unhesitatingly: "By the gift to the city of grounds for a public park."[23] Shaw reflected but held his opinion. O'Reilly went on to speak of refreshing shade, pure air, artistic surroundings, and all the advantages available in a park for those whose lives were spent in squalid and smoke-filled streets. A few days later, according to the *Republic* article, Shaw unfolded to O'Reilly his plans to give Tower Grove Park to the city.[24] Shaw himself did not leave any clue as to what led to the park's founding, and the only other reference to O'Reilly's recommending this munificent gesture would come in the biography of the physician in Hyde and Conard's *Encyclopedia of the History of St. Louis* (1899).[25] However, no one else, including David MacAdam, historian of Tower Grove Park, was to dispute this claim.

Shaw had made a munificent gift to the people of the city. With the help of James Gurney and the tree-planting crew, he had developed the treeless acres into a reserve of beauty in what as the city expanded would be a residential area of an industrial city. A board of commissioners appointed by the state supreme court would guide the park in the years ahead.

37. Dr. Thomas O'Reilly, Shaw's friend and personal physician, who allegedly first suggested Tower Grove Park.

16. Progress at the Garden, 1869–1889

◆◆

During the years immediately after the Civil War, the Garden wel-
comed a surprising number of illustrious names: Civil War officers,
such as Gustave T. Beauregard, Confederate commander at First Bull
Run, and Union generals William T. Sherman and Philip Sheridan;
the actor Edwin Booth; publisher James Harper; scientist Louis
Agassiz; editor Horace Greeley; auxiliary bishop Patrick Ryan of St.
Louis, later archbishop of Philadelphia; Gov. Frederick Smyth of New
Hampshire; and young John Hay, who had been personal secretary to
President Lincoln and would be one of America's greatest secretaries of
state.[1]

When the spring flowers began to bloom in 1869, Shaw could look
back on a rich half-century in the history of the nation, of the city, and of
his own life. When he arrived, steamboats had only recently reached St.
Louis and would not yet hazard the wide and wild Missouri for almost
ten years. Indians still felt at home in St. Louis, coming down the river
to visit old French fur-trading friends or Gen. William Clark, their
"Great White Father." Politicians from the "Little Dixie" area of the
state were seeking Missouri's admission to the Union as a slave state.

Now, in the spring of 1869, the driving of the "Golden Spike" in Utah
would unite the Atlantic with the Pacific by rail via Chicago. Rails
would tie St. Louis with California only later. Cheyenne and Arapahoe
warriors, who had once welcomed the French mountain men and the
Anglo-Americans from St. Louis, now faced an irresistible tide of hostile white men. As to slavery, the Missouri legislature had abolished it
four years before.

To celebrate the fiftieth anniversary of his arrival, Shaw invited
friends to the Garden on 4 May 1869. Hundreds came, according to an
article in the *Missouri Republican*. "There is not a person in St. Louis, we
venture to say," the writer began, "who is not familiar with Tower
Grove. It is the place all strangers visit when they come to St. Louis; and
they carry away a remembrance of beauty, and its fame had gone
abroad far and wide."[2] The principal charm of the Garden, the news-

38. Horse-drawn wagons brought visitors from the streetcar to the Garden.

paper writer went on, lay in its simple beauty of arrangement. The most attractive spot of all was the conservatory.[3]

One hundred and seventy-five individuals signed the guest book that day, many of the oldtimers noting the year of their arrival. The earliest, merchant Henry von Phul, had come to St. Louis in 1811; John Daggett, mayor during 1841, had arrived in 1817. Other guests of prominence were Prof. Elihu Shepard, publisher John Knapp, and businessmen Robert Barnes, Robert Campbell, and James Lucas.[4]

Shaw reminisced about St. Louis at the time of his coming, mentioning explicitly two of his friends: publisher Joseph Charless, Sr., and Judge J. B. C. Lucas, whom President Jefferson had sent west as arbiter of land claims. He recalled that a few of the city's founders still lived at his arrival and followed the old Creole custom of calling St. Louis *Le Village* and New Orleans *La Ville* (the city).[5] He talked of the grass in Prairie des Noyers and the white water-lilies that grew near Auguste Chouteau's pond.[6]

Former United States senator (and soon to be Missouri governor) Benjamin Gratz Brown responded in the name of the citizens of St. Louis. He felt gratified in being able to participate in the celebration. It was rare, he said, for one man to have had such a varied experience as the founder of the Garden had. Brown wished him many pleasant years ahead.[7]

The Shaw properties had long been in open country, but in 1871 real estate dealers began selling lots beyond the Garden, west of Kingshighway and north of Arsenal. The new subdivision lay just south of Fairmount Heights, the high ground later known as "the Hill," where Italians would reside when they began working in the clay pits in the vicinity.

Shaw took part in the twenty-fifth anniversary celebration of the Mercantile Library on 13 January 1871, along with Dr. Engelmann, Bishop Charles F. Robertson, Mayor Nathan Cole, Col. George Knapp, Wayman Crow, Silas Bent, and others.[8]

Shaw traveled to Colorado in June 1872, presumably on the two-year-old Kansas Pacific. He stayed at the Holmes House in Colorado City (later Colorado Springs) and rented a carriage for touring the lovely countryside.[9] While in the West he chanced to meet Prof. Sylvester Waterhouse of Washington University, who would later ask Shaw to begin a school of botany at the university.[10] Shaw left no journal of this trip through the lands of the Cheyennes, whose fierce "dog soldiers" raided far and wide seeking revenge for Custer's massacre of a peaceful band of their people at Washita four years before. This was Shaw's only recorded trip west. In his later years he would vacation in the northern lakes region of Wisconsin or in upper Michigan during the hot days of August.

While Shaw breathed the thin, clear air rolling down from Pike's Peak, his contractor was building an interesting structure in the southeast corner of the Garden facing Tower Grove Avenue. Dubbed the "Casino," this building was to house a lecture hall, dormitory, and restaurant over the years. While the Tower Grove House reflected an Italian villa, the Casino seemed a refugee from Coney Island. It combined a Mansard-style roof with dormer windows, and French colonial patterns with galleries all around the second floor. The railings on the gallery and the cornices had a tinny appearance. Outside steps led to the second floor on the front, the east or Tower Grove Avenue side. During its use as an eating place, a conspicuous sign reading *Restaurant* crowned the front of the structure, and a second identification, *Casino Restaurant,* caught the eye of riders or cyclists on Magnolia.

39. The Casino at the northwest corner of Magnolia and Tower Grove avenues served successively as a restaurant and a dormitory for gardening students.

The greatest tribute to the Garden in its early years came from the most prominent overseas guest to visit the Garden, the celebrated Englishman Charles Kingsley, Regius Professor of Modern History at Cambridge, tutor of the prince of Wales, and writer of best-selling novels. Kingsley visited St. Louis in 1874. A local clergyman, Rev. Montgomery Schuyler, invited Kingsley to the Garden on 20 July of that year.[11] While there, the much-traveled historian stated with finality: "With the exception of Kew Gardens, I have seen nothing in any part of the world that compares with the rarity and variety of the collection here."[12]

Local writers could not appraise the Garden with the background and experience of the canon of Westminster, but they did write in glowing terms in the guides to the city that came out in the late 1870s and early 1880s. An 1874 visitor from Indiana called it "the Pride of St. Louis."[13] *Compton's Pictorial St. Louis,* published the following year, made this claim: "The Missouri Botanical Garden may with truthfulness be called the finest floral garden in the United States. . . . The flower garden contains almost every plant and flower . . . from every corner of the globe. The large conservatories on the north side contain the tropical plants, and all the flowers of rare quality."[14] In one of these hothouses a visitor could see hundreds of cacti and other desert plants; in another an almost endless variety of geraniums, ferns, heliotropes, fuchsias, and dahlias, besides palm trees, fig trees, India rubber trees, and bamboos. Compton stated that every kind of tree known to the American climate could be found in the arboretum, with proper labels, and planted in such graceful irregularity as to suggest that they were all indigenous. He wrote of "Shaw's summer residence in the southern end of the enclosure, and near it the museum, a neat, fireproof building, containing many rare and beautiful things, . . . and a botanical library, . . . open to those who wish to examine it, on application to Mr. Shaw."[15]

Artist Camille Dry sketched the Garden area, with treeless country and cornfields all around. He showed the plan of the Garden as Shaw had sketched it in the map he sent to Sir William Jackson Hooker almost twenty years before. Except for a few trees along the watercourse to the west, the only trees were planted ones in the Garden and along Tower Grove Avenue, Flora Boulevard, and Arsenal Street. A row of Osage oranges paralleled the roadway from Shaw's home northwest to Old Manchester Road; some of these were to endure for more than a century.

The central location of the city of St. Louis made it a favorite site for national conventions. The Garden added to the pleasure of a visit to the city. Shaw was a delighted host. When the Millers' National Association, for instance, held its convention at the Southern Hotel in May 1875, the members and their ladies came to Tower Grove and drank to their host's health "with some of his oldest wine of a rare vintage."[16]

If Charles Kingsley was the most prominent foreign writer to come to the Garden, botanist Joseph Hooker (1817–1911), who visited in 1877, was the most famous scientist to tour it, native or foreign. Director of the Royal Botanic Gardens at Kew, son and successor of Sir William Hooker, who had guided Shaw at the outset of his project, the younger Hooker was to accomplish even more in botany than his father and was to be knighted in 1878.

Twelve years before, at his father's death, Hooker had sent a biographical sketch of his father to Dr. Engelmann. The St. Louis physician congratulated Joseph on his new position and recalled visits with Joseph's father and the kindness and liberality the "departed Nestor among botanists" had shown him almost a quarter of a century before. "To the encouragement then given," he wrote, "more than to anything else I believe is due whatever I have done in botany ever since."[17]

Though in youth thought less talented than an older brother, Joseph had moved steadily through his classical and medical courses at the University of Glasgow, receiving his M.D. degree in 1839 when he was twenty-two years old, going on an extended expedition to the Antarctic, and returning five years later with five thousand specimens of plants, which he described in a work called *Flora Antarctica.* He traced the relationships of temperate plants from the far southern reaches of South America to those of Australia and New Zealand for the first time, setting the terms of the scientific riddle that was to puzzle students of geography for many decades.

In 1855 he had joined his father at Kew as assistant director. A portrait taken that year, when he was thirty-eight, showed a handsome man, with straight nose, dimpled chin, a full head of hair parted on the left, and sideburns. He had the kind of face that made middle-aged women want him for a son-in-law. Occasionally he donned wire-framed spectacles. A close friend of Charles Darwin, he had urged Darwin to publish his paper proposing natural selection as the mechanism for evolution. Joseph had corresponded regularly with Engelmann, exchanging plants and seeds with him, and had continued his father's interest in Henry Shaw's project. In 1873 Engelmann had asked Hooker to send him, "or rather Mr. Henry Shaw in St. Louis, living forms of well-known forms of yucca."[18]

On his visit to America in 1877, Hooker came to St. Louis in mid-July. He praised the Eads Bridge, the Lindell Hotel, the lager beer, the blackberries, and the plums. The sight of the *Grand Republic,* the most luxurious steamboat on the river, thrilled him. On 16 July he visited Tower Grove Park, which he described in his journal as "most beautifully kept." He noted the "magnificent garden and arboretum and fruticetum . . . with museum, library and herbarium attached."[19] Hooker also wrote in the journal of Shaw's early years in England, his business success, his acquisition of land about four miles from downtown St. Louis, his purchase of the Bernhardi Herbarium, his visit to Kew, and his correspondence with Sir William.[20]

Hooker then pushed on to the Rocky Mountains with Gray, Parry, and others to study American plants. Two years later a correspondent would write of him, "Sixty-two years of age, he seems to possess all the activity and vigor of a young man . . . ."[21] Shaw records this quote in a sketch of Sir Joseph Hooker that he wrote but never published.[22]

40. The Hooker botanical expedition camping in the Rockies. Asa Gray is seated on the ground to the left, and Joseph Hooker, wearing a rumpled hat, is seated at his right.

In December 1878, the Merchants' Exchange of St. Louis thanked Shaw for developing Tower Grove Park and the Garden. Other St. Louisans had amassed greater fortunes, but none outranked him in civic spirit. Among the distinguished citizens taking part in the acknowledgment of Shaw's generosity were Henry Overstolz, the first St. Louis mayor of Germanic ancestry, Shaw's long-time friend Charles P. Chouteau, Albert Todd, Wayman Crow, James E. Yeatman, and publisher George Knapp. Five months later, on the sixtieth anniversary of Shaw's arrival in St. Louis, Albert Todd gave the formal greeting of a grateful citizenry to Shaw. Todd seemed especially appreciative of the fact that the Garden was available "for the free enjoyment of all, without distinction or discrimination."[23]

In response, Shaw recalled once again that he had first seen the area when he arrived in St. Louis in his nineteenth year. Open country stretched in every direction, including north, where the Missouri Pacific Station stood at the time of Shaw's remarks. The almost-octogenarian next reminisced about a man whom he had never previously mentioned. "My slight knowledge of French," Shaw began, "acquired at school, enabled me to converse with a few of the old people. I so formed the acquaintance of Mon. Tibet, a venerable Canadian of four score years, who was at Fort Duquesne before the British took it. He came to Cahokia before St. Louis was established and he traded with the Mandan Indians."[24]

"Every large city possesses its one object of supreme interest," J. A. Dacus and James W. Buel stated in their *Tour of St. Louis,* published that year. "In the Old World it is either some ruined castle of feudal times, some wonderful church or old abbey . . . ."[25] In St. Louis, the authors believed, it was Shaw's Garden. They saw it as a college of botany, as well as a place of floral beauty, "an enduring monument, nobler than battlefields, sweeter than any man-made creed, and holier than any relic of dead saints."[26]

Richard Smith Elliot, a local real estate developer, also penned a glowing tribute. "Tower Grove Park," he wrote, "with its three hundred acres . . . its roads, walks, trees and flowers, is the creation and gift of Henry Shaw to the people of St. Louis. . . . The Botanical Garden and its attached Library and Herbarium, with its plant houses . . . a museum of living vegetation representing nearly all climes . . . its . . . innumerable dried specimens, classified and arranged, . . . all the literature worth noting of Botany and Horticulture . . . [and] the opportunity afforded for the study of these allied sciences, are unequaled in the western hemisphere."[27]

The bombastic promoter Phineas T. Barnum visited the Garden the following year and dissented strongly with Shaw's lack of an entrance fee. He predicted that the Garden would not win the general public "because it was free. The American people," he insisted, "like to be humbugged."[28] Henry Shaw disagreed and kept the gates of his Garden open.

A short list of special guests at the Garden, incidentally, included Shaw's close friends Dr. Thomas O'Reilly, George I. Barnett, and Charles P. Chouteau.[29] The ordinary visitors included individuals from all areas of life: botanists, writers, clergymen, generals, farmers, ranchers, skilled and unskilled workmen, teachers, housewives, society matrons, men and women, native-born and immigrant, young and old, dull and brilliant. Many of them appreciated the uniqueness of the placement of such a Garden in the American Midwest; some, however, came to the Garden and looked fondly at the gingkos, the flower beds, and the lily ponds with little awareness of the amazing fact that such a botanical

41. A formal garden in the Missouri Botanical Garden.

enterprise had developed at what had been the far extremity of the civilized world; just as a Mandan chieftain, coming to St. Louis to see the explorer William Clark, might have wandered into the cathedral near the waterfront and gaped in awe at the size of the structure and the colorful paintings on the walls, with no understanding of the meaning of the building.

During the summer of 1879, a young black man by the name of John Feugh knocked at the door of Shaw's office-residence at Seventh and Locust. He had come from Georgia the day before and needed work; and even more immediately, he had to have money to pay his landlady, who had told him to ask Shaw for a job. Shaw asked him if he could read and write. Surprisingly for a Georgia-reared black in those days so recently in bondage, John answered yes. Shaw told him to get a sponge and chamois and begin washing the windows. Feugh knew what windows were but had no idea what either of those tools might look like. He was ready to look somewhere else for a job when one of the servant girls brought him a sponge, chamois, and bucket and showed him what to do. He stayed. He worked as a messenger for Shaw at his downtown residence, taking money to the bank, mailing letters, and running errands. When Shaw moved to his country place, Feugh went with him.

He hauled young trees from local nurseries and from the depot down-town. He picked up the mail at the post office and distributed it to the proper person on the garden staff. For a time he served as farm foreman. He had his own place and reared his family there in later years.[30]

After Shaw's death Feugh was to remain as caretaker of the grounds, and later worked as doorkeeper of the office building that had originally been Shaw's town house and was rebuilt at the Garden in the meantime. Two little girls who lived on the property, Marguerite Irish, daughter of Superintendent H. C. Irish, and Marian Smalley, daughter of the director's housekeeper, were to remember him "almost as a celebrity." "He was our friend," Marguerite wrote, "always ready with stories and endless patience."[31]

Feugh was still at his post in October 1932, when Walter J. Monaghan, feature writer of the *Globe-Democrat,* told his story in that paper's Sunday magazine. Monaghan singled out his "fastidious attire" and "flowing white mustache." Feugh remarked that Shaw had said how gratified he was that the caretaker of the Garden took such excellent care of his own appearance. As he showed Monaghan around the Garden, Feugh said, "A great many of these big trees you see here, I hauled in my wagon behind a pair of Mr. Shaw's frisky bays from the depot to the places where they were to be set out."[32] Feugh had an almost reverential respect for Henry Shaw, whom he rated along with Washington and Lincoln as the three great Americans. Feugh was always ready to talk of the methods and qualities of Shaw, Monaghan wrote, as long as the questioner did "not touch too deeply the purely personal side of his life, which is a sacred trust, as it were, reposed in the fealty and loyalty of a grateful employee."[33]

Friends regularly visited Henry Shaw at the Garden on his birthday. In the 1880s they did not wait for an invitation, knowing that he was glad to see them. "Mr. Shaw is as genial a host as he is entertaining as a companion," a writer for the *Missouri Republican,* most likely Thomas Dimmock, wrote on Shaw's eighty-first birthday.[34] Shaw had illumi-nated his home with Japanese lanterns, and in front of the door he placed a sign made of red flowers on a green-grass background that carried the Latin welcome *Salve!* Postlewaite's band provided back-ground music.[35]

During 1882, George I. Barnett designed a greenhouse to provide display place for the camellias and winter storage for the potted palm

42. The main gate as seen from inside the Garden.

collection. Completed that year and named for Carl Linnaeus, the Swedish botanist, the long rectangular brick structure stretched east and west, with its back to the wall of the fruticetum in the northeast section of the Garden. A continuous skylight with a few ventilators covered about a third of the north and south slopes of the roof. Sixteen windows opened on the south. Over the door, the builders placed busts of Linnaeus, Nuttall, and Gray, the work of Howard S. Kretchmar.

Shaw attended the theater regularly, preferring comedy to tragedy. He felt there was enough suffering in the world without becoming involved with it theatrically. In support of this attitude, friends pointed out that Falstaff was the most conspicuous character he placed on the

43. The Linnean House, designed in 1882 by George I. Barnett.

bas-relief of the Shakespeare statue in Tower Grove Park. The incomparable Missouri writer Mark Twain, who had introduced Tom Sawyer to a grateful public a few years before and would offer the unforgettable Huck Finn a year later, published his *Life on the Mississippi* in 1883. In it he praised the parks of St. Louis, "notably Tower Grove and the Botanical Gardens [*sic*]."[36] Then he praised the city for interesting "herself in such improvements at an earlier day than most cities."[37]

With the Democrats, led by Grover Cleveland, advocating sectional reconciliation in 1884, Shaw contributed to the National Democratic Fund.[38] This was one of only a few indications of his political preference.

During the fall of 1885 several interesting visitors came to the Garden. Rev. Alfred Gurney of St. Barnabas Parsonage, London, who came on 15 October 1885, probably toured the Garden with his distant cousin James Gurney, Garden superintendent. Ten days later, Col. Patrick Sarsfield Gilmore, unmatched leader of the "Matchless Band," signed the guest book. No doubt Shaw invited him to return and bring his entire band, which Gilmore would do three years later. On 2 November elder statesman Benjamin Gratz Brown of Kirkwood, Missouri, visited the Garden. Although of Southern ancestry, Brown had come out early for the Union after the attack on Fort Sumter and had commanded a brigade in several battles before being elected to the United States Senate. He had given the main speech at the Garden in 1869 on the fiftieth

44. The cactus display at the Garden.

anniversary of Shaw's arrival in St. Louis.[39] Later he became governor of Missouri and a nominee for the vice-presidency on the Democratic ticket in 1872.[40]

Shaw usually welcomed important guests such as Brown with a glass of claret wine. Then he would have invited the senator to a vantage on the stairs of Tower Grove House, where an unusually large window gave a direct prospect through the grove of trees north to the floral area. Shaw would have pointed first to the two-story pagoda and probably told the interesting story of the place. The second-floor observation area gave such an enchanting view of the gorgeous flower beds that many young men chose the place to propose marriage to their sweethearts. Many of them did not know, however, that the building had unusual acoustics: even whispers could be heard downstairs. Sometimes the eavesdroppers below applauded these impassioned pleas of love.

Shaw would then indicate the parterre beyond the pagoda, a large sunken square of carefully planted and tended flower beds, filled with urns and pedestals. Beyond the parterre to the north, the main conser-

45. A young lady strikes an ethereal pose in the lily pond in front of the Linnean House.

vatory, a tall, large building, facing south, with a hip roof and windows on the front and sides, dominated the entire area, hiding the lily pond and Linnean House. Shaw may well have praised this latter structure, which George I. Barnett had designed three years before, as much as the impressive main conservatory. In the far northeast corner of the Garden, surrounded by walls on the south, east, and north and a fence on the west side, the fruticetum abounded in shrubs and fruit trees.

The octogenarian Shaw would probably not have had the energy to walk around the Garden with the fifty-nine-year-old ex-governor. But he would have pointed out the two-and-a-half-story museum, with its books and display cases of plants on the first floor and the stuffed birds and animals on the balcony. He may have alluded to the collection of dried plant specimens, mostly kept in the basement. Most likely he offered Brown a ride in his Victoria, the open four-wheeled carriage, along the lane fringed by Osage orange trees. Shaw had long driven the Victoria himself, but by that time friends had prevailed on him to hire a coachman. As the carriage moved along, Shaw would have pointed first to the tract of North American trees in a rough square to the west of Tower Grove House, then, on their left, the pasture land, where city

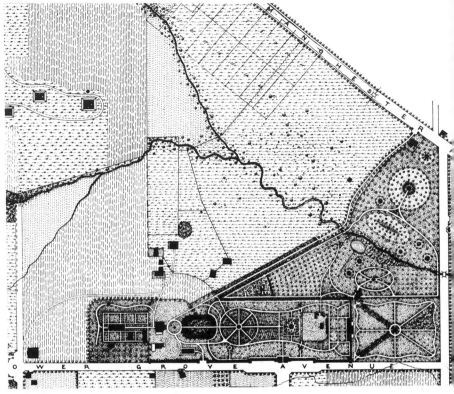

46. The central portion of an 1865 map surveyed and drawn by F. Tunica of St. Louis, showing the garden area bounded by Tower Grove Ave., Shaw Ave., Old Manchester Road, and Magnolia Ave. Buildings, summer houses, statues, and brick and stone walls are shown in solid black; fences are single lines. At the top left is farmland, and at the top right is Shaw's arboretum. At the lower right is the fruticetum; continuing to the left of the fruticetum are the Linnean House, the Conservatory, the square Parterre, the Formal Gardens (above the "E" in *Grove*), the Grove, with the Museum in front of it (above the "O" in *Grove*), Tower Grove House (above the "R") with its private garden and outbuildings, and, at the far left, the Casino.

fire, water, and police departments pastured their horses—at a fair rent, of course. Some prominent citizens, including woodenware magnate Samuel Cupples, also pastured horses there.

Shaw might have indulged a minor irritation at that time, especially if he saw any cows grazing on his property. He regularly ordered his workmen to chase out interloping milk cows that belonged to immigrants who worked in the clay pits to the west.[41] Then, relaxing into a smile, Shaw would have called Brown's attention to a building Shaw had erected beyond the pasture at Kingshighway and Old Manchester

Road. He had built it for school purposes and then given it to the Board of Education, which had named it Shaw School.

As the coachman moved the Victoria slowly along, Shaw would have then directed Brown's attention to the arboretum on their right. It covered the triangle formed by the west fence of the Garden, Shaw Avenue ahead, and the lane along which they rode. Shaw would have been especially enthusiastic in pointing out the shapely English purple beech that he had planted a quarter of a century before, a tree rarely seen in Missouri. He would have indicated maidenhair trees from the Orient, bald cypresses from the swamps of the South, and trees of the region: hollies and wild cherries, silver and sugar maples, hickories and ashes, many varieties of oaks, including a large pin oak, and stately evergreens—pines, hemlocks, cedars, and spruce. How few areas of the West could boast so many varieties of trees!

Long before this, Henry Shaw had indicated that he recognized his own mortality. He had asked his architect-friend Barnett in 1862 to

47. Henry Shaw takes two ladies for a ride in his Victoria.

48. This granite mausoleum, designed by George I. Barnett in 1885 for Shaw, is located in the Garden just north of Tower Grove House. Photograph taken in 1895 by John W. Dunn.

design a mausoleum of Missouri limestone for him in the grove of trees directly in front of his country house. In 1885, Shaw changed his plans, wanting a granite resting place. He had the limestone building moved, and to grace it ordered a marble statue of the symbol of victory from Ross C. Adams of Italy. When Adams's creation arrived, Shaw placed it in the old limestone mausoleum, which he moved to a new location farther north. Shaw asked Barnett to design an octagonal structure for an area abounding in sassafras trees just north of the Tower Grove House. The tomb, with a domed roof of copper and a cross on top, bears a scriptural quotation: "How manifold are Thy works; in wisdom Thou hast made them all; the earth is full of Thy riches." Baron Ferdinand von Miller carved a marble statue of Shaw in repose for the tomb.

While Shaw was generally reticent in conversation and talked little about himself and less about what he had done, he did like people to express their appreciation of his work. When he saw the finished mausoleum, he asked a friend, "Does this do me justice?"[42] On the other hand, a short time later when Judge Charles F. Cady told Shaw that he intended to urge the city to erect a monument to Shaw in Tower Grove Park, the philanthropist said, "Don't do it. How would I look compared to such men as Humboldt, Columbus, and others with statues there?"[43]

According to Shaw's will, no one else was to be buried in the Garden.

17. Prolific Writer and School Founder

If a man is an acute observer, a regular reader of good literature, a fluent penman in correspondence, a tenacious applicant to the task at hand, and an enthusiastic student of a given subject, one would readily expect that man to leave in writing his views on that field. Henry Shaw was all of these, and he does not disappoint us. With the help of James Gurney, he published a twenty-nine-page booklet in 1879, entitled *The Rose,* with historical and descriptive sections.[1] It covers the history of the rose from Homer, who put roses on the shield of Achilles and on the helmet of Hector, through the poet Anacreon, who called it "the most beautiful of flowers," and Charlemagne, who recommended its cultivation in his *Capitularies,* down to the modern popes who conferred the "Golden Rose," a valued papal honor, on Henry VIII and other dignitaries.

In 1884 Shaw published *The Vine and Civilization,* a seventy-one-page treatise, which he distributed among his friends. Beginning the story well before Homer's time, Shaw opened with Noah's first planting after the Flood. The vine always followed the footsteps of civilized man, and men joyfully received this blessing. The grape was among fruits what the wheat was among cereals and the potato among root crops.

With a far more fluid style than in his letters of twenty years before, Shaw advanced a novel philosophy of history. "Historically and physiologically," he asserted, "the use of good wine produced those great and luminous developments of the human mind which at diverse epochs and always progressively have drawn the world to regions of a better civilization."[2] Wine spurred all human progress. He pointed to the countries of western Europe. "France received as a legacy from Greece and Italy the plants of her vineyards," he wrote, "and with them their intellectual supremacy in the world."[3] While wine brought greatness, with the use of tobacco "laziness overcame intellect. . . . Wants remained without the necessary activity to satisfy them."[4] Shaw attributed Britain's nineteenth-century supremacy to the consumption of the finest of French wines by the nobles and the middle-class parliamentarians.[5] Spain had taken an opposite course: the decline in wine production, the Inquisition, and the Jesuits brought Spain to its low ebb. With the Inquisition abolished and the Jesuits expelled in 1867, it would seem that all Spain had to do to regain her former place among leading nations was to restore her vineyards.[6]

On the subject of religion, Shaw stated, "The vine is as inseparable from Christianity as from civilization."[7] He criticized the Roman Church for offering "communion with one kind," the priest alone consuming the cup. "Protestantism," he pointed out, "admits all the faithful to full communion under two kinds, such indeed as was ordained by Jesus Christ."[8]

As to the production of wine in the United States, Shaw wrote at length about California wines.[9] He gave only one sentence to his own state even though it ranked third in wine production. In spite of its late, cold springs and its dampness, he pointed out that Missouri produced good wine.[10]

All the while Shaw had been jotting down his views on trees and gardens, but he published none of these writings. They make no contribution to botanical science, but do show his concern for preservation, the extent of his knowledge of horticulture, and the goals he had in mind for Tower Grove Park and the Garden. They support David MacAdam's claim in his book *Tower Grove Park* that Shaw "had made arboriculture a special study."[11] The amateur dendrologist recognized that his botanical gifts would prove helpful to the general public in many fields: medicine, agriculture, commerce, horticulture, and various forms of manufacture.

The first of his two main treatises dealt with trees; he presumably planned it as a guide to the arboretum. But, except for the first sentence and last paragraphs, in the main it discussed intelligently the danger of excessive tree-cutting and the need of programs of reforestation.[12] "The tree department is a large division of the Garden," he began.[13] Commenced in 1860, the arboretum occupied about twenty-five acres with a collection of such trees, native and foreign, as grew in the St. Louis climate. He then spoke of trees' grandeur, beauty, and usefulness and of the concern of great men about them. Shaw pitied the man who had no interest in trees: "He is robbing himself of one of the greatest sources of enjoyment that nature has placed within the reach of human kind."[14] All nations have needed trees, but it was not until the sixteenth century that men in Europe began to realize that they might exhaust the supply

49. Octogenarian Shaw and two ladies in the Garden's arboretum.

and began to plant trees as a matter of necessity. Germany and France made the care of forests a governmental concern, and even India became conscious of the need for reforestation. Shaw concluded, "A scarcity of timber . . . will be a national calamity."[15]

In his treatise on gardens, a much more formal presentation, he began by discussing systematically the various branches of gardening: landscape gardening, to lay out grounds to the best advantage; vegetable gardening, to obtain an abundant supply of vegetables for all seasons of the year; and lastly flower gardening, with its three subdivisions, floral gardens for the sake of flowers, nursery gardens for the sale of plants and trees, and botanical gardens, devoted to the culture of plants and study of the science of botany.[16] Shaw defined botany as the branch of natural history that related to the vegetable kingdom, included the naming and classification of plants, their external form, their anatomical structure, their functions, their distribution over the globe, and their uses. This science demanded careful, minute investigations and great powers of observation and research. Shaw saw the goals of gardens as the collection and cultivation of all species and varieties of plants that thrive in a given climate with or without the aid of glass.

Besides being a scene of beauty and attraction in itself, a botanical garden should stimulate the residents in the neighborhood to plant ornamental trees and shrubs, both those native to the area and those not generally found in the vicinity. All gardens and pleasure grounds should thus take their tone from this central institution. Gardens too were a source of great help to medical schools in the development of pharmaceuticals.

Shaw saw seven constituents of a botanic garden: (1) a systematic arrangement of classified plants; (2) a general arboretum; (3) the American garden (to use the term employed by the horticulturists of Europe), a collection of flowering shrubs native to this continent; (4) a fruticetum, for the growth of shrubbery and fruit trees where one can learn the art of grafting, building, layering—everything pertaining to the growth and management of vines and fruit trees; (5) plant houses properly glazed and supplied with heating apparatus, and, especially in this area, a palm house with stoves, fernery, greenhouses, and propagation pits; (6) a botanical museum; and (7) a library of books on botany and natural history and especially books of the great masters of natural science.

This last item gave Shaw a chance to discuss botany in his native land: "Great Britain and its colonies yield a most interesting and useful exhibition of this kind. The museum in the Royal Botanical Gardens of Kew is the object of national patronage, and is rapidly increasing in magnificence and importance and the admiration of every American traveler visiting London."[17] Shaw also saw a botanical garden as being a way of introducing new or otherwise desirable plants to the notice of the professional botanist, the agriculturist, the gardener, the amateur botanist, and the everyday citizen.[18] It was, finally, "one of the greatest of temporal blessings that can be enjoyed by a people . . . alike an object of interest, of instruction and amusement."[19]

While Shaw's writings on trees were mainly analytic, he wrote poetically on birds and showed a far greater knowledge of swifts and swallows than he did of oaks or hickories. He devoted twenty-two pages to ornithology, dividing his treatise as follows: two pages of flowery introduction, eight pages to various species of birds, one page to John James Audubon, the bird-painter, and the rest to ornithologist Alexander Wilson.[20] He described some of the birds from his personal observation during thirty years at Tower Grove; with others he leaned heavily on writings of Wilson.

Shaw penned descriptions of thirty-five different birds, giving the greatest space to one of the most colorless of birds. The crow remained in the area all winter, coming in the morning to feed in Tower Grove Park and then leaving in the evening to nest in the tall trees of the bottomland east of the river or on Arsenal Island. Shaw pointed out the bird's good and bad qualities and thought the former outweighed the latter.

About twenty swifts chose the chimney of the museum for their resting place, leaving in the early morning and returning at twilight. St. Louis was the winter home of the snowbird, which arrived at Tower Grove House during the first cold days of October from his summer nesting woods in the vicinity of Hudson's Bay. When a blizzard hit Missouri, the snowbirds approached Tower Grove House and picked up crumbs Shaw or Rebecca Edom threw to them. Shaw devoted an equal number of lines to the bluejay, but had a mixed impression of the bird's worth.

Henry Shaw's appraisal of the English sparrow left the final decision on that "pugnacious intruder" to posterity. But he spoke enthusiastically about the bluebird, the "harbinger of spring" that came to the Garden during the first days of March; the cardinal, "the lively red-plumaged songster"; and the American nightingale, the mockingbird. "We are almost sure," Shaw wrote, "to hear the notes of . . . the Mocker in his nuptial bower, running over the modulations of his matchless song, as if he were fearful that an April night would be too short for him to utter forth his love chant and disburden his full soul of all its music!"[21] One can only wonder if Shaw had been fortunate enough to hear the "falling song" of the mockingbird, generally acclaimed the most beautiful musical notes of any American bird. Only the poet Henry Wadsworth Longfellow had written more beautifully of the marvelous white, black, and gray mockingbird.

"Dogwoods and Redbuds may bloom, and shrubs deck themselves in softest green," Shaw wrote, "but not until the swallows have come, do we feel that it is really spring."[22] When they finally come, they dart "through the balmy air of spring in their never-ending chase for insects, turning, twisting, coursing and chasing each other with a joyousness of heart; now swooping the cool bosom of river or pond, dipping in the water, and dashing the spray aside but not for a moment ceasing in their aerial flight."[23] This description of the swallow's flight would apply perfectly to that of its cousin the purple martin, but Shaw mentioned that he had seldom seen any at Tower Grove.

Shaw praised the birds especially because of their preservation of trees by devouring caterpillars, grasshoppers, beetles intent on ravaging the foliage, and worms burrowing on the trunks and branches. With his usual business exactitude, he gave exact figures on the insects per acre taken care of by the thrush family alone.[24]

The fifth area of writing that challenged Shaw was the history of French colonial achievements in the Mississippi Valley. He stated his intention to publish this 373-page manuscript.[25] Shaw relied heavily on the writings of colonial missionaries Francis Xavier Charlevoix and Jacques Gravier, on his own contemporaries John Gilmary Shea and Francis Parkman,[26] and on two lesser-known historians of the Louisiana Territory, Benjamin Franklin French[27] and Francis Xavier Martin.[28]

The quality of Shaw's penmanship places this writing at the latest in the early 1880s, and probably before that. By 1885 his letters would no longer have the smooth flow of earlier correspondence. His history was written in a graceful style, easy to read, with accurate grammar and few misspellings. He still preferred dashes to periods. His sentences were lengthy; often a paragraph contained successive sentences of fifty to a hundred words, but they did not lose or confound his readers. His meaning was always clear. He employed parenthetical phrases—for instance, "as Parkman says"—to substantiate a historical view or to relate an historical event or place with the present. In locating a site in colonial Texas, he wrote "where Houston now stands." Sometimes to gain immediacy he moved into the present tense at the start of a new paragraph. He did this in describing what the French called the Battle of the Monongahela (1755) and the British referred to as "Braddock's Defeat." He used concrete expressions but few figures of speech.

"My design, kind reader," Shaw began his history of the discovery and settlement of the Louisiana Territory, "is to publish . . . a collection of what I have found interesting and instructive in the early history of the Mississippi Valley, especially Illinois and Missouri."[29] When he placed the word *interesting* before *instructive* in the foreword, he pointed to a telling facet of his treatise. He rated highly stories of human interest as well as those of historic significance. He began with the Portuguese and Spanish explorations and extolled Columbus, as one would expect of a writer who was to erect a statue in honor of the "Admiral of the Ocean Sea." He devoted five pages to the adventures of Cabeza de Vaca and a few to Coronado, who headed toward Missouri from the Southwest. Shaw wrote of the Christian missionaries of the Southwest, the Jesuits in lower California and southern Arizona, and the Franciscans in California. He quoted two travelers who rightly praised the mission of San Xavier del Bac near Tucson that came to be called "The White Dove of the Desert."[30]

Shaw wrote even more exuberantly when he told of the great French explorers of the central Mississippi: both missionaries like Marquette, Hennepin, and Gravier, and military officers like Joliet, LaSalle, De Tonty, Du Tisne, and Bourgemont. He called Captain Du Tisne "one of the most esteemed and efficient French officers of Upper Louisiana."[31] He told with relish the story of Du Tisne's great bluff of hostile warriors who planned to scalp him: understanding their intentions, Du Tisne dramatically pulled his wig off his head and threw it at their feet. Then to their astonishment, he threatened to burn their rivers and forests; and to indicate that he might do just that, he threw a little brandy on the edge of a lake and set it on fire. From then on, the tribesmen respected his "medicine."[32] As mentioned earlier, this was Shaw's one public expression of humor.

Shaw had great skill in penning short descriptions of other heroes. "De Tonty was a man of capacity, courage and resolution . . . (who) in all his actions sustained the character of a brave and intelligent man."[33] Ignatius Loyola, the founder of the Jesuits, was "a Biscayan military gentleman of a zealous and ambitious spirit."[34] "Ferdinand De Soto was . . . a person of good address, polished manners and of an age and constitution well fitted to endure hardships."35 In LaSalle, Shaw noted a "reputation of excellent acquirements and unimpeachable morals. . . . Intense longing for action and achievement subdued in him all other passions; and in his faults, the love of pleasure had no part."36

Shaw described Jacques Marquette as the first to explore the upper Mississippi and first to attempt to civilize the Indians in the Great West. Shaw had a local interest in Jacques Gravier (1651–1708), a successor to Marquette, who founded the first mission in the area in 1700 among the Kaskaskia Indians at the mouth of the River des Peres. In Gravier's account Shaw found the first reference to the lead deposits in Missouri and the initial mention of the Meramec River. Shaw showed his narrative skill in his account of the French attack at Fort Ticonderoga on Lake Champlain and the subsequent massacre of the surrendered English by General Montcalm's Indian allies, and in his description of the final battle between the French and English on the Plains of Abraham before the walls of Quebec.

Had he wanted to excel as a historian, Shaw had the necessary qualifications: exactness, tenacity, ability to work steadily at a desk, imagination, balanced judgment, a good feel for the humanly interesting, and a lively style of writing. He obviously would have done well. He had stated his intention to publish his history and certainly devoted considerable time and energy to its completion. Why, then, did he put the manuscript back in his files? A newspaper article at the time of his death was to state that he "finally abandoned the plan to publish on the grounds that the field had been so thoroughly covered as to leave nothing new."37 Francis Parkman, for one, was publishing accurate and fluent histories at the time.

Shaw's venture into the field of education took a more public form than his literary efforts: in the mid-1880s he was to add a school of botany to his previous public gifts of a garden and a park. But that school was born only after a long gestation period. When Eliot Seminary, chartered in 1853, had become Washington University in 1857, William Greenleaf Eliot, president of the university's Board of Directors, had announced the appointment of Dr. George Engelmann to the chair of botany and natural history in the university's scientific department.38 Years had gone by with little happening. But in a letter to Shaw of early February 1879, Sylvester Waterhouse, professor of Greek at Washington University, had suggested possible close ties between the Garden and his university. Waterhouse recalled an earlier conversation he had had with Shaw in Colorado in 1872. At that time, he had suggested that Shaw set up a botanical division at the university and that ultimately he give the Garden to the university. Shaw presumably had received the suggestions with an open mind; now Waterhouse repeated his appeal, asserting confidently, "The foundations of Washington University are broad and catholic. No institution in all the world rests upon a more comprehensive philosophical basis."[39] Science students would flock to the Tower Grove for research and study, Waterhouse argued, and the Garden would enjoy the university's tax-exempt status.

Shaw reflected before answering, insisting that prudent old age deliberated slowly. Men set up botanical gardens, he pointed out, to promote botany and horticulture. All British colonies established such gardens. America failed to follow this good example, so that it did not have a single institution of the kind worthy of the name. Yet America produced and was producing fine botanists. "Gray and Engelmann," Shaw pointed out, "are among the first in our day, and Nuttall, Torrey and others are names that will be known for all time."[40] After careful consideration, Shaw concluded that the study of the vegetable kingdom was of sufficient importance to support itself and would probably interfere with the routine of the studies practiced by universities. To close the question, he pointed out that the botanical gardens in London, Paris, Edinburgh, and Berlin remained free of university connections. He would seriously consider, however, the endowing of a department of botany at Washington University.[41]

Waterhouse failed to see that the battle was over. He came back again with an even longer letter.[42] Had he adverted to Shaw's bent for rating with caution all business propositions, Waterhouse would have come to realize that Shaw wanted no outside person, individual or corporative, controlling his Garden. Sensing this attitude of Shaw, Chancellor William Greenleaf Eliot moved on the more acceptable alternative in 1883. He suggested to the Board of Trustees of the university an endowed school of botany in relationship with the Missouri Botanical Garden. Chancellor Eliot invited Shaw to attend a gathering in honor of General Sherman in January 1884. The old gentleman had already begun to curtail his activities, especially in wintertime. When the dry west wind did not bring the "January thaw" as it usually did in St. Louis, Shaw had "to forego the pleasure," mentioning that "the evening was too stormy for an octogenarian."[43] As to the school, Shaw wanted to get a botanist's view of what he should do both on the projected school and the Garden.

Around the time of Engelmann's death early in 1884, Shaw consulted Charles Christopher Parry, an associate of the St. Louis physician and of Asa Gray in botanical research and writing. Parry had accompanied Hooker and Gray to the Rockies. Like Shaw, he had been born in England and come to America at an early age. As with Engelmann and Gray, he had finished medical studies. Like the latter, he devoted his time almost exclusively to botany; like the former, he moved into the Mississippi Valley, making his home base in Davenport. This quiet and diffident but knowledgeable man researched extensively in the Rockies, where a thirteen-thousand-foot peak near Berthoud Pass on the Continental Divide west of Denver came to bear his name.

In early April 1884, with the increasing crowds indicating the Garden's growing popularity,[44] Parry pointed out that it was as important to have a competent curator as to have a general director. Parry suggested a committee of three men, Asa Gray of Cambridge, Spencer Baird, secretary of the Smithsonian Institution, and a third man of their choice, to advise Shaw on the hiring of a curator and a director. Then, pursuing another interest, Parry went on, "If you accept the Engelmann herbarium . . . this would at once place the botanical collection of the Garden in the first rank, second only in this country to that at Cambridge, Mass."[45] A few years before his death, Dr. Engelmann had set aside a substantial fund to maintain his herbarium,[46] and had hired Heinrich Eggert, a self-made man and a collector in his own right, to supervise it.[47] When Parry visited him, Engelmann and he had discussed the herbarium and had agreed that only the Missouri Botanical Garden could take care of the collection.[48] Two months after Engelmann died on 4 February 1884, Parry wrote to Gray that he was willing to be curator for a few years.[49] But he was not able to come.

Dr. George Julius Engelmann, son of the botanist-obstetrician, was willing to deposit his father's specimens, books, and papers in the Garden, but only if Parry accepted the task would he feel that his father's legacy was in sure hands. He felt that Shaw looked upon the Engelmann herbarium as "simply a greater mass of bundles than he already has."[50] Since Shaw thought of asking Parry to help in putting the materials in order,[51] young Engelmann authorized the transfer. In early June, James

50. Head Gardener James Gurney (at front center) with his forty assistants, mostly Bohemian immigrants or their sons.

Gurney and his assistants were tying up and delivering several hundred packages of plant materials.[52] Dr. Parry, however, had made his offer out of deference to the senior Engelmann and really wished to go to California.[53]

The Engelmann legacy was only one of the many matters Shaw had to decide at this time. The two main ones were these: should he follow Waterhouse's suggestion that he give the Garden to Washington University, or incorporate the Garden under its own independent trustees with its own distinct purposes; and, should he set up a school of botany at Washington University?

In April 1884, civic leader James Yeatman repeated Professor Waterhouse's recommendation that Shaw turn his Garden over to Washington University.[54] But Asa Gray cautioned Shaw about giving the Garden to the university. He knew the tendencies of schools to absorb or redirect the legacies of benefactors. He urged Shaw to incorporate his Garden, setting down a clear concern for botany, agriculture, and horticulture. He liked Shaw's idea of a few ex officio members on the board, such as the mayor, but negated the governor, who resided too far away and would immerse the Garden in politics. Lastly, he urged him to set up a chair of botany at Washington University.[55]

In late 1884 Shaw wrote to Joseph Hooker, recalling the pleasure of

51. James Yeatman, civic leader and member of the original group of Garden trustees.

Hooker's visit in the previous decade and telling him of Engelmann's great help, of the work of the head gardener, James Gurney, and of his own contacts with Asa Gray. Gray had shared his valuable experience and had suggested that Shaw endow a school of botany. The Missouri merchant intended to do this in conjunction with Washington University in St. Louis.[56]

52. William Trelease in his office at the Garden.

Hooker thanked Shaw for sending plants and wrote that Gray had told him of the fine work Shaw had done in keeping botany alive in his city. He concluded, "I do hope you live to see the realization of your hopes."[57] Shaw answered a month later. He spoke again of his projected school of botany and gave the opinion that its success would depend on the selection of a professor or director who combined scientific knowledge with the ability to make the study of science popular.[58] At this juncture Gray recommended as director of the projected school Dr. William Trelease, who had received his doctorate in science from Harvard the previous year and had risen to the rank of professor of the newly founded Department of Botany at the University of Wisconsin. When Shaw wrote to a friend at Wisconsin, Prof. James Butler, for an appraisal of young Trelease, Butler enthusiastically approved the choice.[59]

At the same time, Eliot wrote to Prof. Edward S. Holder at the Washburn Observatory in Madison for a similar reason. Holder praised Trelease without stint on three counts, as a scientist, as an administrator, and as a person of worth. ". . . Trelease is exactly the man for your place. Scientifically he is the very best of the younger men . . . extremely capable of administering a school . . . a fine fellow and an agreeable man. We should all be sorry to lose him."[60]

While in St. Louis on a visit in May, Gray wrote to Trelease of Shaw's intention to set up a school of botany at the local Washington University.[61] Shortly after Gray left the city, Shaw wrote to Trelease, inviting him to be his guest at the Garden during his hoped-for visit to St. Louis. He told him that he spent Wednesdays and Saturdays at his in-town residence at Seventh and Locust, and the other days at the Garden.[62]

Gray also told Eliot of Trelease's fine qualities as an instructor of basics as well as an advanced scientist. Eliot notified Shaw of Gray's views and of the fact that the Board of Trustees of Washington University had elected Shaw a member at its meeting on 28 May 1885.[63] Shaw was now ready to set in motion his plans for a school of botany; he still had to make final arrangements with the university and with Trelease. But before he could do so, Chancellor Eliot moved arbitrarily, writing to Trelease in June about his nomination to the position of "Asa Gray Professor" at a salary of $2,500 to start on 17 September of that year (1885).[64]

A meeting of the Washington University Board of Trustees on 8 June 1885 took up the proposal of its newest member that called for the establishment of a school of botany as a special department of the university, with the title "The Henry Shaw School of Botany," and a professorship of botany named for Dr. Engelmann. The trustees decided to invite Trelease to fill this position at the beginning of the next academic year, and to place the school under the special care of an advisory committee of five members, two from the board itself and two from outside, with the chancellor an ex officio member.[65] The original members were William G. Eliot, Henry Shaw, Asa Gray, Judge John H. Lightner, and Dr. George Julius Engelmann, the botanist's son, a gynecologist of growing reputation.[66]

On 19 June, Eliot assured Trelease that $2,500 would be available for purchase of books, apparatus, and supplies.[67] But fifteen days later he authorized Trelease to spend only one thousand dollars.[68] No wonder a later Garden director called him "a mesmerizing wangler" and a "wangling parson."[69]

To finance the institution, Shaw designated certain improved properties that yielded an annual revenue of $5,400. In any year that the property did not bring in that amount, Shaw set down in his will that "the Trustees of the Garden shall pay over to the said University such sums of money as may be required to make the annual income equivalent to $3,500 per annum."[70] During his regular August visit to Wisconsin, Shaw took advantage of his proximity to Madison to spend a day there, staying at the Park Hotel[71] and presumably talking with Trelease.

Twenty-eight-year-old William Trelease proved a happy choice as first Engelmann professor. Besides teaching at Madison, he had accepted invitations to lecture at Harvard and Johns Hopkins and was fast gaining recognition as an outstanding young botanist. The son of a Long Island blacksmith, William had attended high schools in Brooklyn and Connecticut and then worked as a helper in his father's shop to earn money for college.[72] He had received a B.S. degree from Cornell University in 1880.

While an undergraduate at Cornell, he published in the *Bulletin of the Torrey Botanical Club* and in *The American Naturalist* for 1879. He served as special agent for the United States Department of Agriculture, analyzing insects, an interest that led over the years to nearly a score of publications on insects as agents of pollination in plants. He undertook graduate work at Harvard, where he received his Doctor in Science degree in 1884, and while there came under the influence of Asa Gray. In the meantime, he had engaged both in fieldwork and in teaching botany in Madison from 1881 to 1883. He rose to the rank of professor and head of the Department of Botany the following year. In the summers of 1883 and 1884 he directed the botanical program at Harvard and during 1884 lectured at Johns Hopkins. He would show throughout his life the same radiant interest in his students as his professors had taken in him; and he remained a valuable counselor to students and younger botanists.

Dr. Trelease had a fine sense of humor and could enliven solemn scientific discussions with an occasional quip. His children long after his death were to cherish a silver loving cup presented to him by a round table of fellow scientists. The cup bore the inscription: "To one whose minutes kept us roaring with laughter."[73] Washington University was lucky to secure his services.

Besides his regular classes at the university during the first fall term, Trelease offered a special class for the study of grasses on Saturdays between nine in the morning and one in the afternoon. Seventeen young ladies, most of them teachers, signed up for the course. The professor's wife also attended the lectures.

In his inaugural address in Memorial Hall on 6 November 1885, Dr. Trelease spoke of "the hope of its founder to advance the science of botany . . ." and "prove useful in the pursuit of practical life, to which that science can be made to contribute."[74] He saw, among other goals, the development of a love for the beauty of nature and a recognition of the interdependence of plants and certain animals, especially the human animal. The school would foster pharmaceutical education, he said, since so many medicines had vegetable origin.[75]

The following summer, Trelease added to his classwork a botanical expedition to the Clear Creek country of Colorado, not far west of Denver. He would regularly combine his teaching with field expeditions, going to the Azores, to the West Indies, and to Madeira. In 1887 he began to write a series of "Contributions from the Shaw School of Botany." This would include six papers between 1887 and 1890. In the spring term of 1886–1887 Trelease taught twenty-two women and two men; in the fall term of 1887-1888 he taught fifteen women and five men. Louis H. Pammel was his assistant.[76]

18. Sunset at Tower Grove

While religion played only a minor part in Shaw's life, he had often attended Mass in Catholic churches during his travels in Austria and Italy, usually preferring those churches with excellent choirs. In his short treatise on *The Vine,* he had noted that only the Protestant churches had retained the custom of giving the cup to the congregation at Communion time. Over the years he had purchased several books of religious history for his library,[1] and he had shown great interest in the work of French Jesuit missionaries among Indians in colonial times. Now in his eighties he bought a prayer book and hymnal of the Protestant Episcopal Church.

While he lived simply and frugally and concentrated most of his resources on the Garden, he contributed to various charitable enterprises of that church. Among these donations Shaw had given the property on the northeast corner of Twentieth and Washington as the new site for St. Luke's Hospital, and spurred the fund drive with a gift of $5,000, almost one-eighth of the total cost of the building.[2] When the hospital was underway, he paid for the painting of several rooms and donated two works of art, *A Gift of the Magi* and *Madonna and Child,* for the chapel. He also contributed to the Hebrew Free School of St. Louis, the Lafayette Guard uniform fund, the Compton Hill Mission, the Good Shepherd Fund, and the Humane Society of St. Louis.[3]

In the one charity besides the Garden and Tower Grove Park that brought wide acclaim, Shaw responded to the urging of Secretary Julius Walsh and other officers of the Missouri Historical Society to purchase for that association the library of the late Bishop Charles F. Robertson of the Episcopal Diocese of Missouri. Francis Marion Cockrell, general of the First Missouri Confederate Brigade during the Civil War, a friend and correspondent of the bishop, and at the time United States senator, congratulated Shaw in a letter of 11 January 1887. He mentioned how often the bishop had written him about government documents of historical interest.[4]

As gratifying as was this letter from the distinguished war hero and statesman, Shaw was at least equally proud of two letters he received from historians praising his purchase of the bishop's library. John Gilmary Shea, leading church historian among American Catholics, had already shown his interest in Shaw's activities with a letter at the time of the unveiling of the Columbus monument a few months before. Now he felt so much a beneficiary of Shaw's donation that he presumed to express his gratitude. "As a scholar," Shea wrote on 4 January 1887, "I appreciate perhaps more than many what your act really means and effects . . . Bishop Robertson's Library I have long known by reputation."5 While Shea was widely known only among church historians and members of the American Catholic community, Francis Parkman had attained national fame as one of America's two premier historians for his profound scholarship joined with consummate literary ability. This Herodotus of the French colonial empire and the American West praised Shaw for an important service to historical research in the Midwest. The library consisted, he believed, almost entirely of works on America, and chiefly on the West. But since "the interests of the mind are not sectional but universal," Shaw should receive "an expression of appreciation from the East."6

Even though Shaw centered his interest on flowers and trees, he had few books on botany among the more than six hundred volumes on his personal shelves. His three main reading interests were history, with England, France, ancient Rome, and the French colonies in the Mississippi Valley his chief areas of concentration; travel, especially on the European continent; and literature, with books of the ancient classic authors, Homer, Cicero, and Livy, of French philosophers such as Michel Montaigne and Jean Jacques Rousseau, and of all the great poets of England, including Chaucer, Shakespeare, Milton, Goldsmith, Pope, Dryden, Gray, Burns, and Scott, many of the lesser poets prominent in his day, and of romantic novelists, French and English. He had more books on religion and religious history than he did on botany. His wide tastes reflected the Renaissance man.

Shaw had many associates and acquaintances, but few close friends. Skeptical of people and things, like the French essayist Michel Montaigne whom he admired, he tested every individual and every thing before he gave his trust. A business associate remarked that he had dealings with Shaw for two years before the acquaintance warmed into friendship, and three more years went by before Shaw invited him to his residence.7 "It is doubtful," Dimmock was to write, "whether Mr.

Shaw ever had, at any time, what is called a 'bosom friend' . . . . The nearest of them felt that they could come just so near, and no nearer."[8]

One of his close relationships was with Joseph Tarrigan Monell, his ward. Shaw financed his education at Washington University from preparatory classes through graduate school. Monell earned a Master's degree in mining engineering in 1881 and married Nellie Gifhorn that same fall. They were to have five children.[9] Several letters of the young man to his patron remain, all of which Monell begins, "Dear Pa." One of these he wrote in early February 1887 from Cooney, a mining town in southwestern New Mexico, where he hoped to straighten out the process of silver mining for the Sheridan Company of St. Louis. "If I could have made this trip six months before," Monell wrote, "I could have saved half a million dollars for a few of the mining-crazy folk of St. Louis."[10] On 18 May 1887, back in Missouri, Monell wrote from Mine La Motte, where he was in charge of smelting operations: "Dear Pa. Sunday afternoon a brand new little girl arrived at our house, weight six pounds. Mother and little one are doing well. Your little namesake is doing finely and is improving wonderfully in this country air. Yours affectionately, Joe."[11]

Between this and Monell's next letter, Shaw remembered Professor Trelease at the School of Botany with a small but highly valued gift, a membership in the Mercantile Library,[12] and supported Trelease and Gray's publication of the *Botanical Works of George Engelmann* (1887). "Great" was the tribute botanic historian Andrew Denny Rodgers gave to this memorial volume.[13] Gray had originally intended to recognize the "auspices" of Henry Shaw on the title page, but Shaw thought this too pretentious a term and suggested instead "collected for Henry Shaw" as being nearer the truth. But he left the final decision to Gray's "superior judgment."[14] Gray acceded to Shaw's suggestion; the title page bears the words "Collected for Henry Shaw, Esq."[15] In the more personal section of the letter to Gray, Shaw mentioned that he dreaded "asthma, bronchitis, pneumonia, gout and rheumatism." He contrasted his life situation with that of the Harvard botanist, who had "a life-long, loving helpmate and companion," to whom Shaw wished Gray to present his "most respectful regards."[16]

When Shaw received two hundred copies of the book, he expressed his delight. He commented on the expensive printing and on the weight of the book, ten pounds, which made mailing difficult.[17] In spite of the cost, however, Shaw saw to it that the book had wide distribution. He sent a number of his copies to strategic botanical centers, such as the Herbarium and Botanical Library of Johns Hopkins University in Baltimore.[18] Shaw closed his letter to Gray with a boast that the Garden had welcomed forty thousand visitors in the previous forty days.[19]

When Shaw sent Joe Monell one of these two hundred copies, the young man wrote another "Dear Pa" letter: "The *Engelmannia* arrived today. It is a truly magnificent volume and worthy of your name. I have pursued my youthful hobby of entomology rather than botany simply because the carrying about of an extensive herbarium was impossible. I also have to keep up-to-date with progress in chemistry and metallurgy. I have just received 'Specimens of the *Monelia carvae*' which a well known entomologist has named after poor me. I shall have an interesting time studying them, but still I rather wish the new genus was not named after me, as considering my youth, it seems a little ironical. P.S. Your little namesake is getting to be a fine bright little fellow."[20] Shaw was to remember Monell in his will with a piece of property in downtown St. Louis. Monell's scientific career was a credit to his patron.

Flowers lined the Garden walks when Charles Dudley Warner, co-editor of *Harper's Magazine* and a popular writer on the American South and West, visited on 14 May 1888. Warner was well known in Missouri for having co-authored *The Gilded Age* with Mark Twain fifteen years before.[21] Later that month, on 28 May, several men already designated as trustees of the Garden in Shaw's will visited Tower Grove: civic leader James Yeatman, Judge George A. Madill, and Maj. Henry Hitchcock. Judge J. H. Lightner, William L. Huse, and woodenware magnate Samuel Cupples accompanied them.[22]

The following month the Democrats, converging on St. Louis for the party convention, renominated President Grover Cleveland. Twenty members of the South Carolina delegation, led by Congressman William Elliott, took the opportunity to visit the Garden on 5 June.[23]

Shaw enjoyed good music. He had heard or met some of the outstanding composers of his day during his European tours, and he sponsored Sunday concerts in the music stand in Tower Grove Park. He attended those concerts regularly, happy that others could enjoy things he provided. Joseph Postlewaite's Band provided most of the music during the 1880s.

Few musical programs pleased Shaw more than the concert of

Gilmore's Band at the Garden on an Indian summer morning, 7 October 1888. The sumacs, sassafras, and flowering dogwoods had begun to turn when the sixty-five members of the famous orchestra opened their program. Col. Patrick Sarsfield Gilmore had become famous during the Civil War as director of a military band by composing the popular song, "When Johnny Comes Marching Home." Now his "Matchless Band" was on a nationwide tour and was playing in Exposition Hall in downtown St. Louis for three weeks. The *Post-Dispatch* called him the "most lovable of men and best of bandmasters . . . a master of his calling" who "won critical approval and the heart of his public" with his "rare and subtle gift of personal magnetism."[24] Gilmore presented varied programs during his three weeks in St. Louis, with "Familiar Music," "All New Music," "Flower Night," "Scots Night," "Ladies Request Night," "German Music Night" (when the *Liederkranz* Cultural Society with a thousand voices joined the band), and "Children's Day" (when twelve hundred people of St. Louis sang with the musicians). Even the temperature provoked raves from a *Post-Dispatch* writer. "Such weather as this could not be improved," the newspaper began. "Splendid as the climate of St. Louis is, its delightful autumn weather . . . makes a stay in St. Louis so enjoyable."[25]

In the midst of all Shaw's successes in life, only one plan did not work out. He had planned to build and lease a number of villas along the periphery of Tower Grove Park, the revenue from which would help to support the Garden. He built the first villa, which later became the residence of Park Director James Gurney, at the southeast corner of Magnolia and Tower Grove, adjacent to the north entrance of the park. But Shaw built no others. Americans, and particularly St. Louisans, did not favor this idea of long-term rental that might have succeeded in places in England. They preferred outright ownership, and so did not avail themselves of what was otherwise a grand opportunity of living in a parklike area that would never lose its value or charm. The idea itself did not die, however; eventually, houses adjacent to golf courses would enjoy the Shaw vision. And the model subdivision of Radburn in Paterson, New Jersey, would employ features both of Shaw's unrealized plan and of the "private places" so popular in St. Louis.

In his property bounded by Grand Boulevard and Shaw, McRee, and Cabanne (later Spring) avenues, Shaw commissioned Surveyor Julius Pitzman to try again a plan the surveyor had used in Benton

Place, north of Lafayette Park shortly after the Civil War. Pitzman laid out an oval drive surrounding a parkway, with gates on both ends—unlike Benton Place, which had no gate on the north end, away from the park. Shaw called on George I. Barnett to design ten brick Victorian houses, to go up within two years, with high windows and white painted front porches. Shaw intended to rent these residences.

This private place proved successful, unlike Shaw's earlier plan to lease property for villas along the outer rim of Tower Grove Park. When Shaw realized that American families hesitated to lease residences, he offered to give the 250-foot strip to the city, provided the city fathers agreed to put up an iron fence around Tower Grove as it had done at Lafayette Park. But the aldermen had other priorities for their available funds.[26]

During Shaw's declining years the Garden was in good hands. It employed a dedicated staff of thirty workers at this time, about a third of them of Bohemian ancestry. James Gurney, the head gardener, W. Huxley, foreman, carpenter, and general utility man, C. Strobee, foreman in charge of one range of plant houses, and M. Zardili, foreman in charge of the fruticetum and one plant house, had homes on the grounds, close at hand during any emergency.[27] Little seemed to be done at the herbarium at that time.

One after another, the pioneers who had lived in the area when Shaw arrived passed away: Pierre Chouteau, Jr., William Clark, Thomas Brady, John O'Fallon, William Carr Lane, John Darby, Bishop Joseph Rosati, Bryan Mullanphy, James Lucas, Peter Lindell, and many others. But Shaw lived on, a remnant of an earlier and more robust day, enduring beyond his time, like the lone cottonwood standing defiant on the otherwise treeless Prairie des Noyers that watched a wealth of newer growth take root, mature, and die while it continued to lift its rugged branches to the sky.

Henry Shaw had long been accustomed to visit the city twice a week: on a Wednesday business trip with Mrs. Edom, his housekeeper, accompanying him; and for a Saturday night dinner party with a few friends at his Locust Street residence. These dinner parties became irregular as time went on. He gave up the use of claret, his favorite wine, which he had used in moderation all his life. He became subject to colds and other disturbances, and lack of exercise further impaired his health.[28] He would go with friends and associates to Pewaukee, Wisconsin, to escape the heat of late July and August, but even these trips to a cooler climate did not bring back his strength for long.

He seemed to suffer depression in those late years, and in the summer of 1888, acting on the advice of his physician, he went to Mackinac Island, Michigan. Mrs. Edom accompanied him, as did his sister Caroline and her husband, Julius Morisse; Miss Hannent, a niece of Mrs. Edom; J. E. and D. F. Kaime, the collectors of his rents; and a few others. A heat wave gripped St. Louis when he departed. Even though he traveled in a special sleeping car, he found the trip fatiguing. The drastic change from near-ninety-degree weather in Missouri to the fifty-degree breezes off the Straits would have staggered anyone, but especially a weakening octogenarian. The vacation did not renew his strength.

During that same summer of 1888, Shaw's neighbor Mary Tyler sold her property to a developer. At that time the streets Flad, Shenandoah, and Russell, for instance, had not yet pushed west of Grand into the Shaw area.[29] But later in that year they did, and the realtors began to sell residential sites in "Tyler Place." That designation included most of the area between Grand and Tower Grove and between Magnolia and Shaw avenues, except Shaw's strip on the north side of Flora. The first street north of Magnolia was named Tyler, but later became Botanical Avenue; eventually only Tyler Place United Presbyterian Church would recall the Tyler name. Lovely homes soon began to go up along the south side of Flora Place, but Shaw's side would remain untouched until after the turn of the century.

During the winter of 1888–1889, friends of Shaw saw no signs that his strength was returning, but his manner was serene and his mind was clear. A friend, David MacAdam, recalled, by way of instance, an evening when Shaw claimed that he could name every man doing business on Main Street at his arrival in 1819. Challenged to try, he succeeded in dictating the entire list, interspersing each name with personal recollections and historic incidents. On New Year's Day, a great number of friends and acquaintances stopped by at Seventh and Locust: his brother-in-law Julius Morisse, old friend Charles P. Chouteau, architect George I. Barnett, writer Thomas Dimmock, Dr. P. S. O'Reilly, his collectors the Kaime brothers, civic leader James Yeatman, Judges Cady and Normile, and an otherwise unidentified person by the name of Napoleon.[30]

A few months later, M. M. Yeakle presented to Henry Shaw a copy of his new book *The City of Saint Louis of Today,* which surveyed the history, government, resources, population, schools, parks, commerce, manufacturing, and markets of the city. The author devoted four pages to Tower Grove Park and the Garden. He called the park "a gem of sparkling beauty—in spring and summer with its bowers and vine clad houses; its artistic bridges, pagodas, lakes, fountains and flowing freshwater springs; while through all are set, by nature and art, beautiful evergreen and deciduous trees, shrubs and flowers."[31] Yeakle then turned to the Garden: "If the Park . . . be a gem, then the Gardens are sapphires—in clusters of brilliants and flowers . . . and resplendent with selections from nature's choicest beauty."[32]

Yeakle ended this chapter of his book with a personal tribute to Henry Shaw, "munificent in his gifts . . . whose . . . liberality . . . shall carry his name down to posterity with a sweet savor."[33] The author spoke of Shaw's good health and his clear and active brain in spite of being near his ninetieth birthday. Yeakle hoped that Shaw might lead a life of peace and tranquillity for many years.[34] This proved to be the final public tribute during Shaw's life.

When even the cacti in the conservatory were feeling the early August heat, many of Shaw's associates scattered for the summer. He read less and would fall into a period of seeming stupor. He grew inattentive to questions and speech became difficult. A fever hit him in late August. Shortly after midnight on 25 August 1889, Dr. Thomas O'Reilly visited him. Shaw died at 3:25 that morning. Many were at his bedside: his sister Caroline, his housekeeper Rebecca Edom, physician William Porter, his supervisor of collections D. F. Kaime, associate David F. MacAdam, and the superintendent of the Garden, James Gurney. Joseph Monell would arrive a short time later.

A writer for the *Republic* tried to reach his imaginative best for the occasion: "The ending of this good man," he wrote, "was as peaceful and serene as the closing of a morning glory's leaves at sundown."[35] Mayor E. A. Noonan ordered a period of mourning in the city, with the flags to be flown at half-staff until after the funeral.

Shaw had wanted a private ceremony at the Garden, but Shaw's sister Caroline and Mrs. Edom would not insist on that in view of the wide concern at the event. They left arrangements to a committee that included Mayor Noonan, Judge John Lightner, Charles P. Chouteau,

George I. Barnett, James Gurney, Dr. Thomas O'Reilly, D. H. Mac-Adam, Charles A. Cox, president of the Merchants' Exchange, and newspaperman Thomas Dimmock,[36] who would, a short time later, write a life of Henry Shaw. The committee for the funeral would have included Robert A. Barnes, one of the park commissioners, but omitted his name because of his ill health.

Shaw's body lay in state for several days at the museum, surrounded by palms fifteen feet tall. Visitors entered the north door and left by the south. The coffin was of cedar, covered with black velvet. The honorary pallbearers included many distinguished men of various cultural, ethnic, and denominational backgrounds who escorted the coffin to the Christ Church Cathedral. The actual pallbearers were employees of the Garden under the leadership of James Gurney. Bishop Daniel Tuttle and Rev. Dr. Montgomery Schuyler of Christ Church Cathedral officiated. After the obsequies, the pallbearers escorted the bier back to the gate of Shaw's property on the Old Manchester Road. Employees of the Garden brought it between the rows of Osage oranges to the mausoleum.

Newspaper articles during the next few days estimated the worth of Shaw's wealth and leaseholds at more than $2,000,000. They hesitated to assess the value of his stocks and bonds. Among distinct pieces of downtown property, his winter residence at Seventh and Locust, valued at $65,250, led the rest.[37] Thirty-nine properties rented for a total of $88,515 annually.[38]

William Marion Reedy, a local writer rapidly gaining a reputation as a literary critic throughout the English-speaking world, penned a short tribute to Henry Shaw that is appropriate: "In his later days he won our hearts by his generosity, his hospitality, his kindliness, his consideration for our comfort and happiness. In his declining years we walked with him through miles of his beautiful garden, and listened with rapture to his talks about his pets."[39] More than anyone else, botanist Dr. George T. Moore, later to be director of the Garden, epitomized Shaw's place in history: "During his lifetime the institution he founded was the only one of its kind in the United States."[40]

Shaw's will, admitted to probate on 2 September 1889, consisted of four main clauses. The first dealt with the property to go to the Garden trustees. This consisted principally of two large areas in southwest St. Louis: large sections in the general Tower Grove area, bounded on the

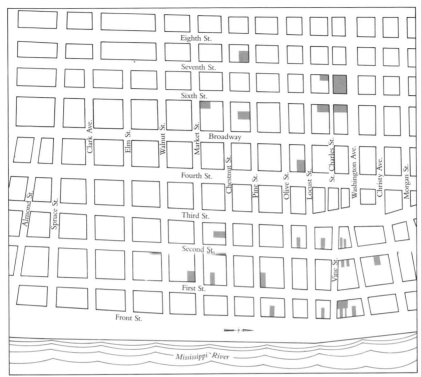

53. Shaw's rental properties in downtown St. Louis in 1889.

east by Grand, on the south by Magnolia, on the west by Kingshighway and Old Manchester Road, and on the north by McRee; and tract 2037, owned in common with Peter Lindell, bounded on the north by Fyler, on the south by Pernod, on the east by Kingshighway, and on the west by a property line not designated as yet by a through street but approximately where Sublette would later run. The second clause dealt with the valuable property in block 27 of the City of St. Louis, bounded by Main and Second, Washington and Christy. It would go to Washington University to finance the School of Botany and other efforts for horticultural education. The third clause contained a large number of lots in downtown St. Louis that would go to support the Garden.

The fourth clause included a number of personal items: first some property to Caroline Morisse, who was to outlive her brother by four years, dying in late December 1893; a lot on Poplar between Twelfth and Thirteenth to Rebecca Edom, housekeeper, as well as an outright grant of $5,000 and a lot and dwelling, the northwestern of ten houses erected by Shaw on Shaw Place between DeTonty and Mercy; and property in a block in downtown St. Louis to Joseph Monell, who was then employed at the Desloge Lead Works in St. Francois County, Missouri. A number of grants went to various cousins, both the Shaws in New York and the Hooles in England, including £100 sterling to cousin Henry Hoole, who had corresponded regularly with him during their middle years, and to lovely cousin Mary, still unmarried, whom Henry Hoole had strongly recommended as a wife for Shaw; and to one or two other individuals in Sheffield or who had come from Sheffield to St. Louis. He gave $1,000 each to these institutions: the Good Samaritan Hospital, the Academy of Sciences of St. Louis, the Missouri Historical Society, the Protestant Orphan Asylum, the Home of the Friendless, the Memorial Home, the Little Sisters of the Poor, the St. George Society, and the Caledonia Society. To architect Barnett, he left a clock, an oil painting, and a bottle of sherry; to David MacAdam, a watch and wine; to James Gurney, $300; and to all other workers of five years or more seniority $75 each.[41] Shaw did not mention his sister Sarah, who still lived in Rochester and would outlive him by two years, dying on 9 September 1891 at age 87.[42] Back in 1884, however, Henry had listed stocks and bonds that totaled $17,498.72 to be handled by J. A. Eastman for his sister Sarah.[43]

The *Post-Dispatch* estimated his estate at $2,000,000, exclusive of stocks and bonds.[44] The *Chicago Tribune* calculated his total wealth as $2,500,000.[45] The *Republic* concentrated on the fortune in his wine cellar, listing 2,246 bottles of the choicest vintages.[46] A writer for this last paper also noted, "The library in the museum was found to contain 1,007 volumes."[47] Presumably this figure included books in Shaw's personal collection and those of Engelmann, which had been at the Garden since his death in 1884.

19. The Three Legacies of Henry Shaw: Garden, Park, and School of Botany

❖❖

Henry Shaw provided in his will that the Garden should be accessible to the general public and be "forever kept up and maintained for the cultivation and propagation of plants, flowers, fruit and forest trees; . . . and a museum and library connected therewith, and devoted to the same, and to the science of Botany, Horticulture and allied objects . . . ."[1] He left most of his estate to the trustees of the Garden to administer. When the property came under their charge, the trustees saw clearly a botanical center unrivaled in the American Midwest. But they also found a country home built forty years before that required refurbishing and updating for new residents and a well-planned and kept-up garden that needed minor improvements here and there in grounds, walkways, and greenhouses.

The trustees had first to organize themselves into a functioning body. A group of them called for a meeting to be held at Boatmen's Bank on Tuesday, 7 September 1889. One of the board, David F. Kaime, notified Mayor Edward Noonan, an ex officio member. The mayor acknowledged the invitation on 6 September, the day before the scheduled meeting, and suggested instead that they meet at his office.[2] Maj. Henry Hitchcock responded for the other trustees that it was too late to make a change, but he had no doubt that they would have the pleasure of the mayor's presence.[3]

The mayor no doubt would have made his presence felt on the board; whether it would have given that formal body "pleasure" remained a matter of conjecture. A Pennsylvanian by birth and a lawyer by profession, the newly elected mayor was at the time encouraging the building of a new terminal for all the trains, a new City Hall, and a new waterworks along the Mississippi River at the Chain of Rocks north of the city. He was a man of action. Marion Reedy, that astute observer of the local scene as well as the national literary map, spoke of Noonan's "gleams of splendid humor and dazzling genius"[4] and called him "the embodiment of the unexpected."[5]

54. William G. Pettus, St. Louis banker and first secretary of the Trustees of the Garden.

Those who met at Boatmen's Bank in early September, less than a month after Shaw's death, included Boatmen's Bank president Rufus Lackland; journalist-attorney and first dean of the Washington University Law School, Maj. Henry Hitchcock; Dr. John B. Johnson; Judge George A. Madill; manufacturer Joseph W. Branch; Shaw business associate David F. Kaime; banker William H. H. Pettus; school board president Frederick N. Judson; and Rev. Daniel Tuttle, bishop of the Protestant Episcopal Diocese of Missouri. They elected Lackland chairman and Pettus secretary. The place of meeting, an article in the *Post-Dispatch* alleged, "had been selected for the convenience of R. J. Lackland,"[6] president of the bank for many decades. Three men failed to attend the first meeting. Civic leader James Yeatman was bedridden in Philadelphia, but if he were home and healthy, he would have come.[7] Episcopalian Bishop Charles F. Robertson, designated an ex officio member in Shaw's will, had died in the meantime. Mayor Noonan notified the board that, as representative of the people of St. Louis, to whom Shaw had given the Garden, he should have called the meeting and presided. Further, the group should have gathered at the City Hall, not at the Boatmen's Bank.[8]

The trustees met again on 10 September, this time at the Garden, and designated Bishop Daniel Tuttle, Robertson's successor as bishop, to succeed him on the board.[9] They chose as director of the Garden Dr. William Trelease, Engelmann Professor of Botany at Washington University, and set his salary at $2,500 annually. Even Mayor Noonan would have approved that choice, both from the botanical and the personal side. Young Dr. Trelease had excelled in botanical studies, had organized the School of Botany at Washington University, and taught effectively there. He had known Shaw and won his approval. He knew what Shaw had wanted and inherited a good staff at the Garden to carry out Shaw's wishes. When the secretary of the trustees notified Trelease, he immediately set about his added tasks. The trustees next commissioned the firm of J. E. Kaime and Brother to oversee the repair of the varied properties under their care.[10]

At a meeting on 30 September, the trustees considered a possible donation of Dr. George Julius Engelmann, son of the botanist-physician. The younger Dr. Engelmann offered his father's herbarium, then temporarily kept at the Garden, but without provision to house the collection permanently. He would gladly also grant to the Garden his father's library, should the trustees see fit to provide space. The board accepted these two valuable additions and thanked Engelmann.[11]

During the following month, the trustees met again to set rules and regulations for the operation of the Garden. They forbade smoking and the use of intoxicants and, among other things, asked visitors to check their picnic baskets at the Garden door.[12] If visitors wanted to picnic, they could go do so in Tower Grove Park. The trustees themselves were to meet monthly except during summer months.

The *Post-Dispatch* did not let the dispute between Mayor Noonan and the trustees of the Garden die quietly. It recalled late in 1889 the mayor's insistence that the trustees could not order him to come to Boatmen's Bank, or to Shaw's residence, the site of the second meeting. The mayor repeated that, as representative of all the people, he should have presided. A reporter for the *Post-Dispatch* interviewed Shaw's housekeeper, Rebecca Edom, who concurred with the mayor's views. She recalled that Dr. Asa Gray had asked Shaw who would preside. "The Mayor, of course," Shaw had answered. As natural representative of the people, Shaw had stated, the mayor could even make appointments. But at the same time, Mrs. Edom insisted that Shaw did not want politics to enter into the Garden operation. When Mrs. Edom had spoken privately with Shaw a few days after his conversation with Gray and wondered if the other trustees would regard the mayor's position, Shaw had replied, "They will respect the Mayor. There is no room for differences."[13] Since Gray had died in the meantime, no one could seek verification from that quarter.

In an interview a few months later, Mayor Noonan recalled that he had thought the trustees should have met at City Hall and recognized the city's overall supervision of Shaw's Garden. The trustees believed, however, that the management of the Garden was not a public matter, but strictly a private affair in which the city should in no way intrude. The mayor thought this "an extraordinary and unreasonable view of the matter" and concluded, "They probably had no cause to regret me, as it was always my object to make the affairs of Shaw's Garden as public as any other matter in which the public is interested."[14]

Shaw had not designated the mayor, or anyone else, as chairman of the board. Since throughout his life he had avoided the political arena, it seems unlikely that he would have let his Garden be under the constant change that City Hall politics brought with it. Further, Shaw usually was specific in giving directions. If in his will he could designate minor items among his vast possessions, such as a watch, a painting, or a bottle of wine, to be left to a particular individual, one might readily presume that if he wanted the mayor to preside, he would have said so. Since he did not do so, one could presume with equal fairness that he wanted to leave the selection of a chairman to the board members.

Early in January 1890, Trelease presented to the trustees an assessment of progress at the Garden that set a pattern for the succeeding years. He described the repairs being done on the stone wall, the

55. The statue of Juno on the right and the first mausoleum on the left flank this sweep of the Garden. Photograph taken in 1907 by C. H. Thompson.

gateways along Tower Grove Avenue, the head gardener's house, and the director's residence. He planned to reroof the plant house, take down a dilapidated ice house east of the Shaw home, and construct a city water line. Because of the needed repairs, he had hired more workers than usual. Their steady toil during the unusually mild fall and winter promised completion by spring.[15]

When he had taken charge of the Shaw School of Botany in 1885, Trelease had pointed to a major difficulty botanists faced at the time in encouraging students to enter their profession: often young men thought of botany as an interest of young ladies—or their mothers.[16] Now he acted immediately on the provision of Shaw's will that called for the training of practical gardeners. Six "garden pupils" would receive free tuition and lodging at the Casino, originally a restaurant but now remodeled into living quarters, and $300 a year scholarships for a six-year course. Candidates had to have a good elementary education, be between fourteen and twenty years of age, be of high moral character, and be courteous. Each student worked five hours a day in manual work, with time for study of horticulture, forestry, botany, bookkeeping, surveying, and other areas that would prepare young men for positions as gardeners at private estates, country clubs, city parks, and college campuses.[17] The directors of Washington University offered free tuition in the School of Botany to the Garden pupils.[18]

Trelease gave this review of activities in the first *Missouri Botanical*

Garden Report, which would become an annual publication. This issue also contained a sixteen-page biography of Henry Shaw by Thomas Dimmock, retired city editor of the *Missouri Republican,* author, and lecturer, who had been an honorary pallbearer at Shaw's funeral. Dimmock wrote a readable, noncontroversial summary of Shaw's life[19] that would remain the accepted account until researchers in the late decades of the twentieth century studied the extensive business papers and other documentation and offered newer interpretations of the merchant-capitalist's career. The trustees approved the purchase of copies of botanical books at a cost of fifteen hundred dollars.[20] This was the first book purchase for the Garden Library since 1858.

Mayor Noonan had called the trustees of the Garden to task the previous fall. Early in 1890, he alarmed the trustees of Tower Grove Park by claiming the park cost too much.[21] A *Republic* editorial agreed with the mayor. Shaw's conditions had stipulated $25,000 a year to maintain Tower Grove Park; the editor believed an outlay of $7,000 enough.[22] A few months later, the *Republic* traced the Tower Grove Park history. In October 1868, Shaw had given the area to St. Louis. The city had issued bonds to the amount of $360,000 to improve the park and had agreed to appropriate $25,000 annually. It carried out this agreement, and Shaw spent the money as he saw fit, improving the property and making it one of the best parks in the country. The surplus over the years allegedly ranged between $75,000 and $80,000. If the city failed to keep its agreement, the park would revert to the Missouri Botanical Garden. City Councilor Leverett Bell urged the city to keep the agreement but to allot money only as needed. If it were not needed, it would revert to the city treasury.[23]

The city government planned a further investigation of Tower Grove Park in May 1890 and set up a joint committee of the Municipal Assembly and the House of Delegates for that purpose. The committee wanted a report on the money the city put into the park fund. Replying for the park board, Charles P. Chouteau pointed out that Shaw had kept a careful account of the money spent. The $47,000 that remained had been invested in city bonds. Whatever remained from the annual city appropriation of $25,000 was invested to build up a fund that would pay interest annually to cover expenses. Ultimately, the park board hoped that it would relieve the city of having to vote money annually. The park commissioners, Chouteau went on, accepted no salaries, the secretary of the board received $400 annually, the superintendent was paid $50 a month, and the laborers took home at most $1.25 a day for ten hours of work.[24] Workers at Forest Park, by contrast, received $1.50 for an eight-hour day.

D. H. MacAdam, secretary of the park commission, recounted the relations of Shaw and the city. When asked if the park could get along with less than the annual appropriation of $25,000, MacAdam asserted that the payroll alone reached $18,000 a year, leaving little for improvements. He reminded the joint committee that the agreement with Shaw called for that amount. Should the city not pay it, St. Louis would lose the park.[25] The joint committee seemed satisfied.

When Shaw had donated his 276 acres for the first large city park in 1868, most of it lay outside the city limits, but the boundaries of St. Louis changed dramatically in the decade immediately following. First the city incorporated its southerly neighbor, Carondelet, in 1870; then in 1876 it extended southwestward to the River des Peres and westward to Skinker Avenue. During that time the expanded city opened three new parks: 1,374-acre Forest Park in the central west end in 1874, and in the following year both 180-acre O'Fallon Park on the north side and 100-acre Carondelet Park in its new area to the south. Prof. M. G. Kern saw these events as related. "This very offer of his [Shaw's] and his influence," he said in a speech in 1890, "paved the way to that system of public parks and prospective boulevards which we have today."[26]

While overseeing tree planting in Tower Grove Park, Shaw had often expressed the conviction that in planting trees and flowers he and James Gurney were doing a more valuable work than many ministers.[27] In his will, however, he expressed more confidence in ministers of the gospel; he called for an annual "Flower Sermon" during the month of May at Christ Church Cathedral on Thirteenth and Locust. The theme was to be "the wisdom and goodness of God, as shown in the growth of flowers, fruits, and other products of the vegetable kingdom."[28] Bishop and Trustee Daniel Tuttle gave the first Flower Sermon, using as his text a passage from the Sermon on the Mount: "Consider the lilies of the field." The eloquent divine pointed to Jesus Christ's concern for things in word and action—the vine and branches, the wheat and tares, the barren fig tree and the mustard seed. "Christ Our Lord," the prelate stated, "institutes the Holy Sacrament for the ever-to-be-continued memorial of His sacrifice on the Cross; He takes from the vegetable kingdom the typical elements: bread and wine."[29] In this talk the bishop set a lofty level for other flower sermonizers, who generally gave excellent messages on the sacredness of things that grew, their sacramentality, beauty, and utility that reflected God's goodness and providence.

On 26 May 1890, the trustees fulfilled an easy task enjoined on them by Shaw's will: they held the first annual banquet. Gov. David R. Francis was there, but not Mayor Noonan, who found the conditions imposed by the trustees insufferable. He could invite six guests, but the trustees would select the six from among twenty names he submitted. He stayed at home. Bishop Tuttle came, as did Rev. Philip P. Brady, vicar general of the Catholic Archdiocese of St. Louis, who represented the octogenarian Archbishop Peter Richard Kenrick. Among editors were Col. George Knapp and Rev. David Phelan. Several university professors came, as well as business and professional men, including Shaw's fellow Englishman Frederick M. Crunden, who was developing the St. Louis Public Library and, like Shaw, leaving the city indebted to him. Many other eminent St. Louisans attended.

In his brief opening remarks, one might have expected the chairman of the program, Maj. Henry Hitchcock, to emphasize the public aspects of the Garden that would be the trustees' chief concern. Instead he insisted that the educational and scientific purposes of Shaw's trust predominate.[30] Perhaps he wanted to reassure Trelease, who obviously had those aspects uppermost in his mind. Director Trelease, scientist and professor of botany, took the approach one might have expected from Hitchcock. "It is impossible to divest the idea of a garden from the idea of a park," he insisted, "a place to which people go for their recreation; a place where the love and the taste for the beautiful may be at once cultivated and gratified."[31] The Garden also had scientific and educational uses, Trelease affirmed. It furnished materials for the study of fruitful and medicinal plants; and to add to the plant materials at the Garden, Trelease recommended that the twenty thousand mounted plants that he had gathered at Washington University be placed at the Garden. The staff would teach botany—"not only how to grow plants, but what those plants are."[32] Henry Shaw had insisted also, Trelease pointed out, on the training of gardeners. The director seconded this concern of Shaw and closed with a strong insistence on the necessity of continued development of herbarium, museum, and library.[33]

In accord with the expressed wishes of Henry Shaw, the trustees held the first banquet for gardeners on 13 October 1890. Sixty men attended this gathering, which was less formal than the trustees' banquet. In his greeting, Trelease recalled that *Hovey's,* "the leading horticultural journal of that time," had, back in 1859, spoken of the Garden as "inspired by Chatsworth."[34] When Henry Shaw enlarged the scope of the Garden with the opening of the museum and library, Trelease pointed out, "the Missouri Garden took . . . a step in advance of its prototype, adopting as its model, the public garden at Kew . . . the leading institution for scientific botany in the world. . . . Mr. Shaw hoped for a somewhat similar career of usefulness for the Garden founded by him."[35]

In a newspaper interview in November 1890, Trelease stated that he was carrying out the program of the trustees based as nearly as possible on the twofold wish of Mr. Shaw: to provide a vision of joy for visitors and a research facility for the professional botanist. Already the Garden staff had mounted one hundred thousand specimens of Dr. Engelmann's and organized the botanical library collections in various languages. They had repaired two miles of fence, rebuilt one of the greenhouses, entirely remodeled several others, placed several miles of gravel walk edged with brick, laid "granitoid" in the main gateway in place of the cobblestones formerly in use, and replaced the coping on the main gate. Introducing city water into the Garden, they had laid pipes to connect with the city water main, and they had also constructed a half-mile of subdrains in the garden and fruticetum to render the soil more congenial to the shrubs and trees.[36]

Trelease called visitors' attention to the fact that Shaw had planned the arboretum as a sylvan wilderness in its original state, unencumbered by gravel walks and "keep off the grass" signs, rather than as a neatly trimmed area reminiscent of the grounds at Chatsworth or the Palace of Versailles. The word *frutus,* further, whence the word *fruticetum,* meant shrub, not fruit tree. Thus Shaw had not intended it to be an orchard as so many visitors presumed. Shaw had followed the English botanist Loudon's threefold division of flowers, trees, and shrubs.[37]

The trustees also in 1890 considered seriously the fitness of Tower Grove House for the needs of its new residents, Director Trelease and his wife and sons. The need for improved plumbing and heating and for enlarged dining facilities at Tower Grove House convinced the trustees to make extensive changes. When they considered the matter carefully, they decided, instead of piecemeal improvements, to enlarge the entire

56. Tower Grove House as it appeared after the rebuilding of 1891.

east side of the residence, the split-level servants quarters, to conform to
the west wing. Contractor Joseph W. Given brought the addition into
reasonable harmony with the older west section, installed modern
plumbing, and painted the entire building red, presumably to unify the
appearance of the two units.[38]

Trelease recommended to the board that the Garden send First
Assistant Albert Spear Hitchcock, a graduate of Iowa State College who
was later to gain a wide reputation as an authority on grasses, as its
representative on a natural history cruise of the Caribbean during
November and succeeding months. The board approved with the condition that all specimens collected must go to the Garden.[39] This was the
first collection undertaken by a member of the Garden staff. Trelease
himself would later undertake expeditions into the field.

When Trelease had accepted the directorship of the Garden in 1889,
he had one assistant at the School of Botany, Louis H. Pammel. The
directors of Washington University would name the assistant an instructor several years later and appoint an additional instructor in cryp-
togamic botany. The school was soon offering fourteen botany courses
in the undergraduate department of the university. Further, Trelease
gave a course of Saturday lectures, and Pammel gave one at the Garden
for children.[40]

In the first available record of special students enrolled in the school, the names of forty individuals appear, including fourteen physicians enrolled in a course in bacteriology. Miss A. Isabel Mulford would receive her doctorate from the Shaw School of Botany in 1895; she would be the first recipient of a doctorate from any branch of Washington University. Eight other doctoral candidates and six master's candidates— four of them women—would receive their degrees in botany before any other section of the university undertook a doctoral program. This record emphasizes another aspect of the great contribution of Henry Shaw in founding a School of Botany in cooperation with the Missouri Botanical Garden: no other division of Washington University had holdings for research adequate to justify a Ph.D. program.[41]

During 1891, in spite of his work in organizing the enterprise and supervising the physical repairs, Trelease still found time to publish a revision of the treatise on willow herbs (*Epilobium*) of North America.[42] It was the first scientific paper that came from the Garden, and a major one that focused attention on Shaw's legacy and its new director. While Engelmann had not made use of the Bernhardi collections for his published papers, Trelease depended on materials in the herbarium for his publications. During that year of his first publication as director, he also presented his private herbarium of eleven thousand specimens of four thousand species and his library of five hundred books and three thousand pamphlets to the Garden.[43] He could exult in directing what a contemporary magazine writer called "the finest institution of its kind in the country,"[44] adjacent to "Tower Grove Park, one of the most beautiful spots on the globe."[45]

Epilogue

❖❖

A number of Americans made huge fortunes in the last half of the nineteenth century. All but two of the richest of these became wealthy by providing supplies for the Union armies during the Civil War. Later in life, at the close of their business careers, some of these men, called both "industrial statesmen" and "robber barons," left to their communities and the nation libraries, schools, and institutes.

Henry Shaw did not increase his already-established fortune in war-related commerce or manufacture. Instead, shortly before the Civil War, he began to devote most of his time, energy, and fortune to the development of the acres he decided to give to the people of the city of St. Louis and the state of Missouri. His gift encompassed more than a mere passing of funds that left him personally untouched; he dedicated his time and involved his mind, hand, and heart in planning and developing a magnificent garden and park.

Sir William Jackson Hooker, director of the world's most famous botanical gardens at Kew near London, saw the unique significance of Shaw's gift. At the very outset of Shaw's effort, Hooker contrasted it with the governmental sponsoring of European botanical gardens. "Yours," he wrote to Shaw in 1859, "is the gift of a public-spirited private gentleman. . . . Such a gift to one's country, anyone may glory in."[1]

Rumors were to spread over the years that the spirit of Henry Shaw watched over the Garden. Perhaps these legends stemmed from the claims of his housekeeper, Rebecca Edom, that the Garden's founder had appeared to her several times shortly after his death. On 14 February 1890, less than six months after Shaw died, the *Post-Dispatch* carried an interview with Mrs. Edom. She alleged that Shaw had visited her three times, once at the Garden and the other times at her home at the northwest corner of Shaw Place. On the first occasion, he asked if she was treated well, and she said she was getting along nicely. During the second apparition, he wondered why she did not go to the Garden more often. She replied that Grand Avenue was torn up and the other road was too muddy. On the third visit, he wondered why David MacAdam had not completed and published his biography. Her answer, if any, was not reported.[2]

When, less than two years later, the trustees began to discuss that part of Shaw's will that required the moving of his city residence to Tower Grove, Mrs. Edom told another newspaper reporter, this one with the *Republic,* that Shaw did not want the town house placed in the Garden, but instead wished it to be moved to the southeast corner of the property, between the Casino and the wall on Tower Grove Avenue. Rebecca insisted that she spoke out so strongly on the matter because Henry had appeared to her in a vision and stated that the plans of the trustees did not meet his wishes.[3]

No doubt the trustees felt that if Shaw had a message for them, he knew where they lived, or he could appear to one of them while they inspected the Garden. Be that as it may, no one could reproach Henry Shaw if he did turn up occasionally in spirit in those early days. One could well picture him, standing on the front steps of Tower Grove House and looking through the opening in the trees to the pagoda, the parterre, and the main conservatory, watching the endless crowds of visitors from St. Louis, from outstate Missouri, from other states, and from many foreign countries.

Henry Shaw might have recalled the first day he looked at the gently sloping, treeless land beyond the Barrière des Noyers seventy years before. Or that other day, thirty years later, when he climbed to the tower of his country residence and took in the sweep of that vast countryside southwest of St. Louis. A smile would have come to his face as he recalled the day two years after that, when he walked along the River Derwent in his native England and saw the lovely gardens of Chatsworth, and had wondered if he could create a similar place of floral beauty on the western frontier of America.

Henry Shaw would have felt elated. The vision that he had first seen at Chatsworth had become a reality. The triumvirate of guiding botanists, Hooker, Gray, and Engelmann, had enriched and deepened his concept of a botanical garden. Gurney and the Bohemian hands had developed flowers and trees. Two teams of interested citizens—trustees for the Garden, and commissioners for Tower Grove Park—gave guidance in their respective spheres. And lastly, the man he had invited to begin the Shaw School of Botany was guiding the Botanical Garden wisely. The land that Henry Shaw had developed would remain forever a "place of floral beauty."

Henry Shaw could well have smiled, for he had succeeded beyond all reasonable expectations.

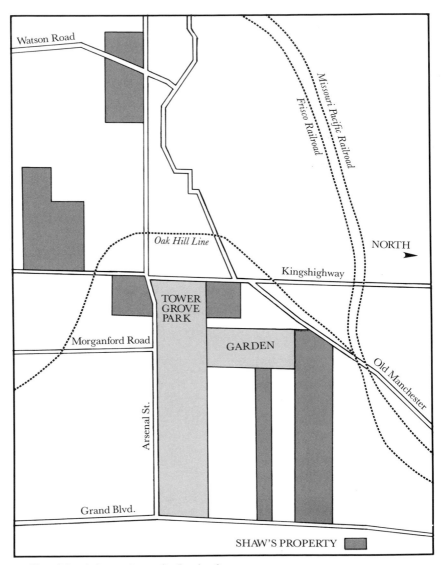

57. Shaw's lands in southwest St. Louis, 1890.

Notes

❖❖

Abbreviations

I. Location of Documents

ARMBG = Archives of the Missouri Botanical Garden
BF = Biographical File, Library of the Missouri Botanical Garden
GD = St. Louis Globe-Democrat
HSAA = Henry Shaw Autograph Album, Library of the Missouri Botanical Garden
HSPAB = Henry Shaw Papers, Account Books, Library of the Missouri Botanical Garden
HSPBP = Henry Shaw Papers, Business Papers, Library of the Missouri Botanical Garden
HSPJD = Henry Shaw Papers, Journals and Diaries, Library of the Missouri Botanical Garden
HSPMC = Henry Shaw Papers, Miscellaneous Correspondence, Library of the Missouri Botanical Garden
HSPPC = Henry Shaw Papers, Personal Correspondence, Library of the Missouri Botanical Garden
MBGB = Missouri Botanical Garden Bulletin
NAL = North American Letters, in the Archives of the Royal Gardens-Kew
PD = St. Louis Post-Dispatch
RHS = "Reminiscences" of Henry Shaw, in the *Missouri Republican,* 4 May 1869
RMBG = Report of the Missouri Botanical Garden
TMBG = Minutes of the Trustees of the Missouri Botanical Garden

II. Persons

AG = Asa Gray
CS = Caroline Shaw
GE = Dr. George Engelmann
HH = Henry Hoole
HS = Henry Shaw
JH = James Hoole

JS = Joseph Shaw
SS = Sarah Shaw

Notes to Introduction

1. Thomas Dimmock, "Henry Shaw, A Biographical Sketch," in *RMBG* 1 (1889): 12. Dimmock was a St. Louis newspaperman who knew Shaw personally. His sixteen-page sketch remained the accepted word on the philanthropist's career until recent times. He told of Shaw's early years, his success in cutlery sales, his opening of the Garden and Tower Grove Park, and his reading interests. He omitted many other facets of Shaw's life. Shortly after the Garden opened in 1859, a correspondent for an eastern journal of horticulture visited and interviewed Shaw, who described his plans for the major greenhouse that would resemble the conservatory at Chatsworth or the Crystal Palace in London. See *The Magazine of Horticulture* (Boston) 25 (1859): 423–25.

Notes to Chapter 1: A Son of Sheffield and Mill Hill

1. David L. Linton, ed., *Sheffield and Its Region—A Scientific and Historical Survey* (Sheffield: Published for the British Association by the Local Executive Committee, 1956), p. 162.
2. William Hulton, "Recollections," manuscript in Sheffield Public Library, p. 787.
3. Linton, *Sheffield,* p. 156.
4. R. E. Leader, *Reminiscences of Old Sheffield* (Sheffield: Leader and Sons, 1876), p. 144.
5. Ibid.
6. Thomas Ramsey, *The Picture of Sheffield* (Sheffield: George Ridge, 1824), p. 154.
7. *Pedigrees of Sheffield.* A copy in the

Sheffield Central Library carries the Hoole genealogy.

8. SS, Pittsford, N.Y., to HS, 9 August 1935, in HSPPC. All Shaw's letters and papers are in ARMBG unless otherwise noted. Shaw's extensive business papers appear to be relatively complete. For a time they were at the Harvard Business School, but they now are back in the Archives in the John S. Lehmann Building at the Garden. His personal letters presumably have not all been preserved; letters to him are more common in the collection.

9. *Trees: The Mill Hill School* (London: The Printing Society, 1957), pp. 1–3.

10. George F. Timpson, "The Boyhood of Henry Shaw," BF. This is a copy of a typed manuscript by a man who attended Mill Hill School early in this century and then took an M.A. at Oxford.

11. Norman G. Brett-James, *The History of Mill Hill School, 1807–1907* (London: Andrew Melrose, 1911), p. 46. In 1866 Rev. Herbert Vaughn, later cardinal archbishop of Westminster, opened a seminary at Mill Hill and began a society of missionaries called the Mill Hill Fathers. This Catholic institution is located in the same general area but had no connection with the older Dissenters' school.

12. Ibid., p. 47.

13. Ibid.

14. Timpson, "The Boyhood of Henry Shaw," page not numbered.

15. Brett-James, *History of Mill Hill School,* p. 49.

16. Ibid., p. 45.

17. *RMBG* 5 (1893): 38.

18. Ernest Hampden-Cook, *The Register of Mill Hill School (1807–1926)* (London: Mill School, 1926), p. 10.

19. JS, Rochester, to HS, 6 September 1840, in HSPPC.

20. Mary Walton, *Sheffield: Its Story and Its Achievements* (Sheffield: Telegraph, 1948), p. 151.

Notes to Chapter 2: Shaw Comes to the States

1. Invoice of Cutlery, Sheffield, July 1818, in HSPBP, Group 2, 1818.

2. HS, New Orleans, to Ben Hart, Esq., 26 February 1819, in HSPBP, Group 2, 1819.

3. RHS.

4. Memoir of James Haley White, typescript, at the Missouri Historical Society.

5. James Essex, "Autobiography" (unpublished), quoted in McCune Gill, *The St. Louis Story* (St. Louis: Historical Record Association, 1952), p. 112.

6. Henry Brackenridge, *Views of Louisiana, together with a Journal of a Voyage up the Missouri River in 1811* (Pittsburgh: Cramer, Spear, and Eichbaum, 1814), p. 120.

7. Selwyn K. Troen and Glen E. Holt, eds., *St. Louis* (New York: New Viewpoints, 1977), p. 27.

8. Brackenridge, *Views of Louisiana,* pp. 123–24.

9. John F. Darby, *Personal Recollections* (St. Louis: G. I. Jones and Co., 1880), p. 14.

10. Richard C. Wade, *The Urban Frontier: Pioneer Life in Early Pittsburgh, Cincinnati, Lexington, Louisville, and St. Louis* (Chicago: University of Chicago Press, 1968), p. 161.

11. Ibid., quoting Thomas Hart Benton to Preston, 14 November 1819, Benton Papers, Missouri Historical Society, St. Louis.

12. John A. Paxton, *The St. Louis Directory and Register* (St. Louis: Printed for the Publisher, 1821; rpt. 1854), p. 263.

Notes to Chapter 3: Budding Businessman

1. HS, St. Louis, to JH, undated, in HSPBP, Group 2, 1819. See also Frederic Billon, *Annals of Saint Louis in Its Territorial Days from 1804 to 1821* (St. Louis: Nixon-Jones Printing Co., 1888), p. 343. The accuracy of Billon's book varies from section to section. Those things he himself could vouch for, such as the location of Shaw's warehouse, coincide with actuality; those he had on hearsay, such as the business of Shaw's father, are inexact.

2. HS, St. Louis, to JS, 27 July 1819, HSPPC.

3. HS, New Orleans, to JH, 10 May 1820, HSPBP, Group 2, 1820.

4. HS, St. Charles, to JS, 4 October 1819, HSPPC.

5. List of Cutlery and Hardware, 25 November 1819, HSPBP, Group 2, 1819.

6. HS, New Orleans, to JS, 17 December 1819, HSPPC.

7. HS, St. Louis, to JS, 16 February 1820, HSPPC.

8. HS, New Orleans, to his mother, 21 May 1820, HSPPC.

9. HS, St. Louis, to JS, 16 February 1820, HSPPC.

10. HS, New Orleans, to his mother, 21 May 1820, HSPPC.

11. Ibid.

12. Ibid.

13. Ibid.

14. HS, St. Louis, to JS, 9 November 1820, HSPPC.

15. HS, St. Louis, to his mother, 11 July 1820, HSPPC.

16. HS, St. Louis, to JS, 20 August 1820, HSPPC.

17. HS, St. Louis, to JS, October 1820, HSPPC.

18. HS, St. Louis, to JS, 16 November 1820, HSPPC.

19. HS, New Orleans, to JS, 7 December 1820, HSPPC.

20. HS, New Orleans, to JH, 12 December 1820, HSPBP, Group 2, 1820.

21. Statement of Goods, 30 April 1821, HSPBP, Group 2, 1821.

22. Paxton, *St. Louis Directory and Register,* p. 270.

23. HS, New Orleans, to his mother, 21 May 1821, HSPPC.

24. HS, St. Louis, to JS, 7 August 1821, HSPPC.

25. HS, New Orleans, to JH, 10 November 1821, HSPBP, Group 2, 1821.

26. HS, St. Louis, to JS, 24 January 1822, HSPPC.

27. SS, Sheffield, to HS, 20 February 1822, HSPPC.

28. JH, London, to Alderson, 25 February 1822, HSPBP, Group 2, 1822.

29. HS, New Orleans, to JH, 3 July 1822, HSPBP, Group 2, 1822.

30. *RMBG,* 1893, p. 39.

31. N. S. B. Gras, "An Early Sedentary Merchant in the Middle West," *Bulletin of the Business Historical Society* 18, 1 (February 1944): 2.

32. Account of Sales of South Alabama Cotton, HSPBP, Group 1, 1822.

33. Tracy and Wahrendorff, St. Louis, to HS, 22 May 1822, HSPBP, Group 2, 1822.

34. Ibid.

35. *Missouri Republican,* 4 September 1822.

36. HS, New Orleans, to his mother, 6 July 1822, HSPPC.

37. Martha Hoole, Sheffield, to HS, 15 November 1822, HSBPC.

38. HS, New Orleans, to JH, 3 July 1822, HSPBP, Group 2, 1822.

39. HS, St. Louis, to JH, 7 December 1822, HSPBP, Group 2, 1822.

40. Wade, *The Urban Frontier,* p. 279.

41. HS, New Orleans, to JH, 12 March 1823, HSPBP, Group 2, 1823.

42. Billon, *Annals of Saint Louis,* p. 343.

43. Ibid.

44. HS, New Orleans, to JH, July 1823, HSPBP, Group 2, 1823.

45. Invoices of Shipments, 16 December 1823, 24 December 1823, HSPBP, Group 2, 1823.

46. Gras, "An Early Sedentary Merchant," p. 2.

47. Ibid.

48. HS, St. Louis, to JH, 18 August 1823, HSPBP, Group 2, 1823.

49. HS, St. Louis, to his mother, 5 September 1823, HSPPC.

Notes to Chapter 4: Sinking Roots in Missouri Soil

1. Tracy and Wahrendorff to HS, 22 May 1822, HSPBP, Group 2, 1822.

2. *St. Louis Enquirer,* 17 November 1823.

3. HS, New Orleans, to JH, 18 December 1823, HSPBP, Group 2, 1823.

4. CS, Pittsford, to HS, 24 January 1824, HSPPC.

5. HS, New Orleans, to JH, 21 March 1824, HSPBP, Group 2, 1824.

6. HS, St. Louis, to JH, 27 July 1824, HSPBP, Group 2, 1824.

7. HS, New Orleans, to JH, 21 March 1824, HSPBP, Group 2, 1824.

8. HS, St. Louis, to JH, 19 May 1824, HSPBP, Group 2, 1824.

9. HS to Alexander Grant, 1 February 1837; HS to Wm. Alderson, passim, in HSPAB, Letter Book, 1828–1840, vol. 34.

10. Accounts, 17 August 1824, in HSPBP, Group 5, 1824.

11. HS, St. Louis, to JH, 19 May 1824, HSPBP, Group 2, 1824.

12. Gras, "An Early Sedentary Merchant," p. 6.

13. HS, St. Louis, to JH, 8 September 1824, in HSPBP, Group 2, 1824.

14. Ibid.

15. HS, St. Louis, to JH, 26 October 1824, HSPBP, Group 2, 1824.

16. RHS; also HSPAB, 3 September 1823, vol. 1; 13 October 1823, vol. 2.

17. Ibid.

18. HS, St. Louis, to JH, 28 December 1824, HSPBP, Group 2, 1824.

19. HS, St. Louis, to JH, 1 December 1824, HSPBP, Group 2, 1824.

20. Ibid.

21. HS, St. Louis, to Turner and Co., 28 December 1824, HSPBP, Group 2, 1824.

22. Ibid.

23. Essex, "Autobiography," p. 113. The *St. Louis Directory, 1826–1840,* locates Shaw's store at 98 North First St.

24. Wade, *The Urban Frontier,* p. 100. When Bishop Louis W. V. Dubourg of the Louisiana Territory asked Bishop Benedict J. Flaget of Bardstown, Kentucky, who had visited Missouri in 1814, whether to locate in St. Louis or Ste. Genevieve as the center of his religious activities, the Kentucky churchman saw advantages in both places. William B. Faherty, S.J., *Dream by the River: Two Centuries of Saint Louis Catholicism* (St. Louis: River City Publishers, 1981), p. 17.

25. Paxton, *St. Louis Directory and Register,* p. 262.

26. Darby, *Personal Recollections,* passim. Frederick E. Voelker pointed out these qualities in the French merchants and mountain men of St. Louis in "The French Mountain Men of the Early Far West," in *The French in the Mississippi Val-* ley, ed. John Francis McDermott (Urbana: University of Illinois Press, 1965), p. 97. In *Introducing America* (London: Methuen, 1963), co-authors Barbara Kreutz and Ellen Fleming saw enduring evidence of the French background in these very qualities.

27. HS, St. Louis, to JH, 23 January-27 June 1826, passim, HSPBP, Group 2, 1826.

28. Ibid.

29. HS, St. Louis, to JH, March (no day given) 1825, HSPBP, Group 2, 1825.

30. Ibid.

31. Ibid.

32. HS, St. Louis, to JH, 12 May 1825, HSPBP, Group 2, 1825.

33. SS, Pittsford, to HS, 21 June 1829, HSPPC.

34. SS, Pittsford, to HS, 3 March 1834, HSPPC.

35. JS, Pittsford, to HS, 12 January 1826, HSPPC.

36. Invoice from James Hoole Correspondence, 6 April 1826, HSPBP, Group 2, 1826.

37. Ibid., 24 August 1826, HSPBP, Group 2, 1826.

38. SS, Pittsford, to HS, 1 February 1826, HSPPC.

39. Ibid.

40. SS, Pittsford, to HS, 8 July 1827, HSPPC.

41. Ibid.

42. CS, Pittsford, to HS, 13 August 1826, HSPPC.

43. SS, Pittsford, to HS, 27 July 1828, HSPPC.

44. SS, Pittsford, to HS, 30 December 1827, HSPPC.

45. SS, Pittsford, to HS, 27 July 1828, HSPPC.

46. SS, Pittsford, to HS, 3 February 1828, HSPPC.

47. CS, Pittsford, to HS, 9 February 1828, HSPPC.

48. CS, Pittsford, to HS, 17 May 1829, HSPPC.

49. Ibid.

50. Bill of Sale, 23 July 1828, HSPBP, Group 3, 1828.

51. Bills of Exchange, 3 January-23 December 1829, HSPBP, Group 5, 1829.

52. Caleb Atwater, *The Writings of Caleb Atwater* (Columbus, Ohio: Published by the author, 1833), p. 212.

53. Ibid.

54. Ibid.

55. Account Books, 1828–1831, passim, HSPBP, 1828–1831.

56. Gras, "An Early Sedentary Merchant," pp. 7–8.

57. Dimmock, "Henry Shaw, A Biographical Sketch," p. 17.

58. SS, Pittsford, to HS, 21 June 1829, HSPPC.

59. Ibid.

60. Billon, *Annals of Saint Louis,* p. 343.

61. Essex, "Autobiography."

62. Darby, *Personal Recollections,* p. 377.

63. William Clark Kennerly, *Persimmon Hill: A Narrative of Old St. Louis and the Far West, as told to Elizabeth Russell* (Norman: University of Oklahoma Press, 1948), pp. 79–80. This book provides a sympathetic view of the outlook of the Southern sympathizers in pre-Civil War St. Louis.

64. Ibid.

65. Elihu H. Shepard, *The Early History of St. Louis and Missouri* (St. Louis: Southwestern Book Publishing Co., 1870), passim. This interesting account by a professor at Saint Louis College covers St. Louis during the first few years Shaw was in the city but never mentions him.

66. Kennerly, *Persimmon Hill,* p. 80.

67. Louis-Hippolyte Gache, S.J., *A Frenchman, A Chaplain, A Rebel,* trans. Cornelius Buckley (Chicago: Loyola University Press, 1981), pp. 144ff.

Notes to Chapter 5: The Thrifty Thirties

1. CS, Pittsford, to HS, 8 August 1830, HSPPC.

2. SS, Rochester, to HS, 5 April 1840, HSPPC.

3. Receipted Bills, 29 February 1844, HSPBP, Group 4, 1844.

4. CS, Pittsford, to HS, 8 August 1830, HSPPC.

5. Ibid.

6. CS, Pittsford, to HS, 28 May 1831, HSPPC.

7. SS, Pittsford, to HS, March 1831, HSPPC.

8. JH, London, to HS, 23 March-10 December 1830, passim, in HSPBP, Group 2, 1830.

9. JH, London, to HS, 18 January-10 December 1831, passim, in HSPBP, Group 2, 1831.

10. JS, Pittsford, to HS, August 1831, HSPPC.

11. SS, Pittsford, to HS, 9 April 1832, HSPPC.

12. Sarah Cornthwaite, Worrall (near Sheffield), to HS, 2 March 1832, HSPPC.

13. CS, Pittsford, to HS, 15 July 1832, HSPPC.

14. SS, Pittsford, to HS, summer 1832, HSPPC.

15. SS, Pittsford, to HS, fall 1832, HSPPC.

16. SS, Pittsford, to HS, 25 December 1833, HSPPC.

17. SS, Pittsford, to HS, 7 January 1834, HSPPC.

18. CS, Pittsford, to HS, 8 July 1834, HSPPC.

19. SS, Pittsford, to HS, 12 May 1834, HSPPC.

20. SS, Pittsford, to HS, 6 October 1834, HSPPC.

21. SS, Pittsford, to HS, 31 August 1834, HSPPC.

22. SS, Pittsford, to HS, 9 November 1834, HSPPC. Following the family custom, when Alathea died, Francis Hoole married a cousin (Hoole Family Tree, Sheffield Public Library).

23. SS, Pittsford, to HS, 9 November 1834, HSPPC.

24. CS, Pittsford, to HS, 8 January 1835, HSPPC.

25. SS, Pittsford, to HS, 8 January 1835, HSPPC.

26. CS, Pittsford, to HS, 3 March 1835, HSPPC.

27. SS, Pittsford, to HS, 12 May 1835, HSPPC.

28. SS, Rochester, to HS, 9 November 1835, HSPPC.

29. Notation, 15 September 1834, HSPBP, Group 2, 1834.

30. Journal 1834–1838, 14 June 1834, HSPAB, vol. 9.

31. J. B. Roy, Black Snake Hills, to HS, 15 September 1834, HSPBP, Group 2, 1834.

32. "Accounts," Ledger, vol. 21 (1835–1838), in HSPAB. See also vol. 34, 16–19 July 1838, HSPAB.

33. Ibid., vol. 21.

34. SS, Rochester, to HS, 8 January 1836; 24 January 1836, HSPPC, 1836.

35. SS, Rochester, to HS, 14 April 1836, HSPPC.

36. SS, Rochester, to HS, 24 January 1836, HSPPC.

37. SS, Rochester, to HS, 8 November 1836, HSPPC.

38. Bill of Sale, 20 May 1836, HSPBP, Group 3, 1836.

39. Bill of Sale, 3 April 1838, HSPBP, Group 3, 1838.

40. U.S. Census, 1850.

41. *French Slave Code, Louisiana.*

42. H. A. Trexler, *Slavery in Missouri, 1804–1865,* vol. 32 of Johns Hopkins University Studies in Historical and Political Science (Baltimore: Johns Hopkins Press, 1914), p. 88n.

43. Will of Henry Shaw, 12 May 1851, in Henry Shaw Inventories, etc., HSPBP, Group 3, 1851.

44. JH, London, to HS, 16 March-3 October 1835, HSPBP, Group 2, 1835.

45. JH, London, to HS, 3 February-22 December, 1836, HSPBP, Group 2, 1836.

46. JH, London, to HS, 25 March-16 October 1837, HSPBP, Group 2, 1837.

47. Property, Rochester, 12 January-17 May 1836, HSPBP, Group 3, 1836.

48. JH, Sheffield, to HS, 25 April 1837, HSPBP, Group 2, 1837.

49. Henry Shaw (a cousin of HS), Sheffield, to JH, 10 October 1837, HSPBP, Group 2, 1837.

50. SS, Pittsford, to HS, 1837, HSPPC.

51. HSPAB, 20 May 1837, Letter Book, vol. 34, 1828–1840.

52. Receipt for Presents, etc., Law

53. JH, London, to HS, February-December 1838, HSPBP, Group 2, 1838, passim.

54. JH, London, to HS, February-December 1839, HSPBP, Group 2, 1839, passim.

55. JS, Rochester, to HS, August 1838, HSPPC.

56. Franco Brichta, Natchitoches, La., to HS, 4 November 1839 and 27 December 1839, in HSPMC.

57. Accounts, 1 January 1839, in HSPAC, Ledger 1839–1846, vol. 15, pp. 2, 4, 8.

58. Manumission, 20 May 1839, HSPBP, 1839.

59. CS, Rochester, to HS, 12 April 1839, HSPPC.

60. SS, Rochester, to HS, 1839, passim, HSPPC.

61. SS, Rochester, to HS, 8 December 1839, HSPPC.

62. SS, Rochester, to HS, 5 April 1840, HSPPC.

63. Ibid.

64. HSPAB, vol. 10, p. 90, 31 December 1839, Journal, 1839-1853.

65. Walton, *Sheffield,* p. 152.

66. James Neal Primm, "Henry Shaw, Merchant-Capitalist," *Gateway Heritage* 5, 1 (Summer 1984): 2–9. In this article, as in his book *Lion of the Valley: St. Louis, Missouri* (Denver: Swallow Press, 1981), Professor Primm showed his expertise in local economic history.

67. Mortgages, HSPAB, 6 July 1840, vol. 10, Journal 1839-1853. J. Thomas Scharf, a contemporary of Peter Lindell and Shaw whose *History of St. Louis City and County,* 2 vols. (Philadelphia: Louis H. Everts and Co., 1883), long remained the standard work on the city, wrote that "the honored Henry Shaw" was one of Lindell's intimate companions (1:568).

68. Bonds and Mortgages, etc., HSPAB, 6 July 1840, 10:155, Journal 1839–1853.

69. Ibid.

70. HSPBP, passim, 1840–1844; mentioned by Primm in "Henry Shaw, Merchant-Capitalist."

Notes to Chapter 6: Years of Travel

1. Henry Shaw's "Journal of a Voyage from Saint Louis . . .," Book 1, 1840, HSPJD.
2. Ibid., 21 July 1840.
3. Ibid.
4. Ibid.
5. Ibid., 29 July 1840.
6. Ibid., 4 August 1840.
7. HSPAB, vol. 60, 1840, p. 39.
8. SS, Rochester, to HS, 10 December 1840, HSPPC.
9. JS, Rochester, to HS, 28 August 1840, HSPPC.
10. JS, Rochester, to HS (then in New York), 6 September 1840, HSPPC.
11. SS, Rochester, to HS, 25 May 1841, HSPPC.
12. "Journal," 18 June 1841.
13. SS, Rochester, to HS, 1841, passim, HSPPC.
14. CS, Rochester, to HS, 9 September 1841, HSPPC.
15. "Journal," Book 3, 9 September 1841.
16. Ibid., passim.
17. Ibid., 4 October 1841.
18. Ibid., 5 October 1841.
19. Ibid., 23 October 1841.
20. Ibid., 25 October 1841.
21. Ibid., 24 October 1841.
22. Ibid., 23 October 1841.
23. Ibid., 2 November 1841.
24. Ibid., 30 October 1841.
25. Ibid., 15 November 1841.
26. Ibid., 7 December 1841.
27. Ibid., 27 December 1841.
28. Ibid., 31 December 1841.
29. Demo Simos, Florence, to HS, 28 December 1841, HSPMC.
30. HH, Sheffield, to HS, 16 March 1842. The marriage of cousins was common in the Hoole family; Betty Gillan of Beaulieu, Warwick, a great-grand-daughter of a cousin of Henry Shaw, attests that two of her great-grand-parents were first cousins. Gillan, Warwick, to Faherty, 21 October 1985, in author's files.
31. HH, Liverpool, to HS, 2 May 1842, HSPPC.

32. SS, Rochester, to HS, Spring 1842, HSPPC.
33. P. Chouteau, Jr., New York, to HS, 4 November 1842, HSPPC.
34. Receipted Bills, Personal, July 1840-September 1842, HSPBP, Group 4, 1842.
35. See above, p. 41.
36. Bankruptcy Petition of J. B. Meachum, 22 June 1842, HSPBP, Group 3, 1842.
37. *MBGB* 31, 7 (September 1942): 138.
38. Undated clipping from the *Missouri Republican,* presumably 25 July 1881, in the Archives of the Missouri Historical Society.
39. Sheriff's Sale, 8 August 1842, HSPBP, Group 3, 1842.
40. Plat Book of property owned by Henry Shaw in the City of St. Louis.
41. Ibid.
42. Indentures, etc., September 1842-December 1843, HSPBP, Group 3, 1842–1843.
43. Ibid., 15 June 1843.
44. SS, Rochester, to HS, 16 October 1842, HSPPC.
45. Receipted Bill, 13 June 1842, HSPBP, Group 4, 1842.
46. SS, Rochester, to HS, 29 January 1843, HSPPC.
47. Ibid.
48. Notebook in Shaw's handwriting in Henry Shaw Papers, Inventories, etc.
49. Agreement between Henry Shaw and Thomas J. Payne, Judge Bryan Mullanphy Arbiter, 28 April 1843, in HSPAB, Account Book, vol. 59, 1840–1849.
50. P. Chouteau, Jr., New York, to HS, 13 April 1843, HSPPC.
51. Charles P. Chouteau, New York, to HS, 18 May 1843, HSPPC.
52. Circuit Court of the City of St. Louis, State of Missouri, 3 July 1843.
53. Court of Common Pleas, Record of, 14 July 1843, HSPBP, Group 3, 1843.
54. Receipted Bills, 31 December 1843, HSPBP, Group 4, 1843.
55. Mary Jones, Prairie des Noyers Fields, to Bernard O'Halloran, 19 July 1843, HSPBP, Group 2, 1843.
56. Ibid.

57. O'Halloran (for HS), Barrière des Noyers Fields, to Mary Jones, 22 July 1843, HSPBP, Group 2, 1843.

Notes to Chapter 7: Caroline Shaw

1. SS, Rochester, to HS, 26 November 1843, HSPPC.
2. Bernard O'Halloran, Barrière des Noyers, St. Louis County, to Henry Shaw (care of James Hoole, London), 19 December 1843, HSPBP, Group 2, 1843.
3. Ibid.
4. Ibid.
5. Ibid.
6. HH, Southampton, to HS, 28 January 1844, HSPPC.
7. HH, Dundee, to HS, 7 April 1844, HSPPC.
8. Ibid.
9. Ibid.
10. HS, "Du Tisne" (unpublished manuscript), ARMBG.
11. SS, Rochester, to HS, 27 April 1844, HSPPC.
12. SS, Rochester, to HS, 10 May 1844, HSPPC.
13. CS, Rochester, to HS, 26 November 1843, HSPPC.
14. Ibid.
15. CS, St. Louis, to HS, 17 July, 16 August 1844, HSPPC.
16. Plat Book of HS Properties.
17. CS, St. Louis, to HS, 13 January 1844, HSPPC.
18. CS, St. Louis, to HS, 16 August 1844, HSPPC. Joseph Robidoux, one of five prominent brothers in the Indian trade, had laid out the city of St. Joseph, Missouri, the previous year.
19. CS, St. Louis, to HS, 12 November 1844, HSPPC. Pierre Chouteau and Col. René Paul, his brother-in-law, were among the most well-known citizens of St. Louis.
20. CS, St. Louis, to HS, 16 September 1844, HSPPC.
21. Mortgages, HSPAB, 6 July 1840, vol. 10, Journal 1839-1853.
22. CS, St. Louis, to HS, 16 May 1844, HSPPC.
23. CS, St. Louis, HS, 13 January 1844, HSPPC.
24. CS, St. Louis, to HS, 15 February 1844, HSPPC. Many other Episcopalians shared Caroline's enthusiasm for the Reverend Cicero. *Green's St. Louis Directory* for 1847 spoke of him as "Rt. Rev. Cicero S. Hawks" (without the e) and referred to him as "Bishop" the following year, 1848.
25. CS, St. Louis, to HS, 17 April 1844, HSPPC. In spite of Caroline's misgivings about the long courtship, Charles P. Chouteau and Julia Ann Gratiot were eventually to marry on 7 November 1845 and rear eight children (Mary B. Cunningham and Jeanne C. Blythe, *The Founding Family of St. Louis* [St. Louis, privately published, 1977], pp. 75-76).
26. CS, St. Louis, to HS, 16 August 1844, in HSPBP, Group 2, 1844.
27. "Agreement for Share-Cropping," 20 October 1845, HSPBP, Group 3, 1845.
28. SS, Rochester, to HS, 25 December 1844, HSPPC.
29. SS, Rochester, to HS, 27 June 1845, HSPPC.
30. CS, St. Louis, to HS, early 1845, HSPPC.
31. B. J. O'Halloran, Barrière des Noyer, to CS, 3 March 1845, HSPBP, Group 2, 1845.
32. CS, St. Louis, to HS, 17 November 1845; 16 December 1845, HSPPC, 1845.
33. CS, St. Louis, to HS, 17 November 1845; 16 December 1845, HSPPC, 1845.
34. CS, St. Louis, to HS, 16 December 1845, HSPPC.
35. HH, London, to HS, 23 June 1845, HSPPC.
36. SS, Rochester, to HS, 26 January 1845, HSPPC.
37. SS, Rochester, to HS, 27 April 1845, HSPPC.
38. SS, Rochester, to HS, 28 May 1845, HSPPC.
39. SS, Rochester, to HS, 27 January 1845, HSPPC.
40. Receipted Bill, 20 January 1845, HSPBP, Group 4, 1845.
41. *Green's St. Louis Directory,* 1845, pp. 123, 127.

42. Aimée Dupont, Paris, to HS, 20 February 1846, HSPPC.

43. Ibid.

44. Francis Grierson, *The Valley of Shadows* (London: Bradbury Agnew and Co. Ltd., 1909), p. 215.

45. Ibid.

46. Ibid.

47. Hotel Receipts, May 1851, HSPBP, Group 4, 1851.

48. CS, Rochester, to HS, 4 August 1846, HSPPC.

Notes to Chapter 8: Loves and Disasters, Houses and Slaves

1. SS, Rochester, to HS, August (no day) 1846, HSPPC.

2. Ibid.

3. SS, Rochester, to HS, 17 September 1846, HSPPC.

4. SS, Rochester, to HS, 5 October 1846, HSPPC.

5. SS, Rochester, to HS, 9 March 1847, HSPPC.

6. Aimée Dupont, Paris, to HS, 25 November 1846, HSPPC.

7. Aimée Dupont, Paris, to HS, 12 January 1847, HSPPC.

8. Aimée Dupont, Paris, to HS, April 1847, HSPPC.

9. Ibid.

10. SS, Rochester, to HS, 15 April 1847, HSPPC.

11. SS, Rochester, to HS, 18 July 1847, HSPPC.

12. SS, Rochester, to HS, 30 April 1848, HSPPC.

13. *St. Louis Directory,* 1848, p. 169. Julius opened a second store just before the Civil War at 285 Broadway. Ibid., 1860.

14. SS, Rochester, to HS, 29 September 1848, HSPPC.

15. SS, Rochester, to HS, 5 April 1849, HSPPC.

16. Scharf, *History of St. Louis City and County,* 2:1143.

17. Jeanne Mino, Rochester Public Library, to Faherty, 10 July 1985, in author's files.

18. *PD,* 21 May 1893.

19. *Republic,* April 1891.

20. SS, Rochester, to HS, 1851 (no month or day), HSPPC.

21. Gerhardt Kramer, "Henry Shaw's Architectural Legacy to the Missouri Botanical Garden," *Gateway Heritage* 5, 1 (Summer 1984): 23.

22. Building Expenses, in HSPBP, Receipted Bills, Group 4, 1852.

23. Ibid., 1849.

24. Bill of Sale, 7 November 1848, HSPBP, Group 3, 1848.

25. Receipted Bills, passim, HSPBP, Group 3, 1850.

26. Bill of Sale, 16 October 1850, HSPBP, Group 3, 1850.

27. Statement of Marshall Brotherton, re: Sale of Jim, 2 January 1851, HSPBP, Group 3, 1851.

28. Thorburn, St. Louis, to HS, 27 October 1849, HSPBP, Group 2, 1849.

29. Receipted Bills, March-November 1850, HSPBP, Group 4, 1850.

30. Receipted Bills, March-November 1851, HSPBP, Group 4, 1851.

31. Ibid.

32. Ibid., 13 March 1851.

33. Legal Document, 19 March 1851, HSPBP, Group 3, 1851.

34. Accounts, 1 July 1846-1 January 1851, HSPBP, Group 5, 1851.

35. Ibid., 2 April 1851.

36. Stocks, etc., 17 June 1851, HSPBP, Group 5, 1851.

37. Receipted Bills, 10 June 1851, HSPBP, Group 4, 1851.

38. Notes, etc., 17 May 1851, HSPBP, Group 5, 1851.

39. Will of Henry Shaw, 12 May 1851, Robert Campbell, Witness. Voided and annulled in the presence of John Shepley, 18 November 1861. Shaw picked up the mortgage on the Shaw home at 17 Atkinson St. in Rochester. Inventories, etc., 7 November 1851, HSPBP, Group 3, 1851.

40. Receipted Bills, Taxes, 3 October 1851, HSPBP, Group 4, 1851.

Notes to Chapter 9: The Challenge of Chatsworth

1. Dimmock, "Henry Shaw, A Biographical Sketch," p. 12. See also footnote 1 of Introduction.

2. Receipted Bills, Hotels, August 1851, HSPBP, Group 4, 1851. J. D. Hooker, *Journey to America, 1877,* unpublished diary in the Archives of the Royal Botanic Gardens, Kew.

3. Receipted Bills, Hotels, 24 September 1851, HSPBP, Group 4, 1851.

4. Ibid., 11 October 1851.

5. Ibid., 12 November 1851.

6. Receipted Bills, Hotels, 17 June 1872, HSPBP, Group 4, 1872.

7. Dimmock, "Henry Shaw, A Biographical Sketch," p. 13.

8. Alphonso Wetmore, *Gazetteer of the State of Missouri* (St. Louis: C. Keemle, 1837), p. 88.

9. *Keemle's Gazetteer of Missouri* (St. Louis: R. A. Keemle, 1874), p. 250.

10. *History of Howard and Cooper County* (St. Louis: National Historical Company, 1883), p. 165.

11. Eric P. Newman, St. Louis, to Author, 3 April 1984, in Author's File.

12. Dimmock, "Henry Shaw, A Biographical Sketch," p. 11.

13. Kennerly, *Persimmon Hill,* pp. 228–29.

14. Ibid., p. 229.

15. Charles Drury, *A Sheaf of Essays by a Sheffield Antiquary* (Sheffield: Northend Ltd., 1929), p. 73.

16. SS, Rochester, to HS, no day given, 1847, HSPPC.

17. Richard Smith Elliott, *Notes Taken in Sixty Years* (St. Louis: R. F. Studley, 1883), p. 279.

18. Ibid.

19. HSPAB, "Notes on Progress of Vegetation, 1853–64," 6 March 1854.

20. HSPJD, Records of Growth, 1853.

21. Tower Grove Workmen's Accounts, 1854–1856, HSPAB, vol. 48.

22. Taxes, City of St. Louis, Downtown Property, HSPBP, Group 4, 1853.

23. HSPBP, Bill of Sale for 16 October 1850. A note scribbled on the back of Brotherton's Bill of Sale—not in Brotherton's handwriting—stated: "Child a fugitive in Chicago with the mother, 1854."

24. The *St. Louis Directory* for 1849 listed two slave dealers in St. Louis, Bernard Lynch and Corbin Thompson. While slave dealers were generally considered obnoxious to all citizens, H. A. Traxler, an authority on slavery in Missouri, wrote in 1914: "Lynch could not have been the terror-inspiring ogre that the slave-dealer is pictured to be" (*Slavery in Missouri, 1804–1865,* vol. 32 of Johns Hopkins University Studies in Historical and Political Science [Baltimore: Johns Hopkins Press, 1914], p. 49).

25. Slave Trade, 17 June 1854, HSPBP, Group 4, 1854.

26. Taxes, City of St. Louis, 30 September 1854, HSPBP, Group 4, 1854.

27. *Missouri Republican,* 22 May 1855; *Saint Louis Pilot,* 26 May 1855.

28. See above, Chapter 7, note 22. Also CS, St. Louis, to HS, 16 May 1844, in HSPPC.

29. *Missouri Republican,* 22 May 1855.

30. Slave Trade, May-July 1855, HSPBP, Group 4, 1855. Rev. Lloyd A. Hunter, in "Slavery in St. Louis, 1804–1860," *Bulletin of the Missouri Historical Society,* July 1974, pp. 258–59, describes the practices of B. M. Lynch and other slave dealers in St. Louis during the 1850s.

31. Slave Trade, 29 July 1855, HSPBP, Group 4, 1855.

32. Slave Trade, Itemized Expenses, 29 July 1855, HSPBP, Group 4, 1855. The last name of the purchaser is difficult to make out but appears to be *Fondren.*

33. Taxes, City of St. Louis, 29 October 1856, HSPBP, Group 4, 1856.

34. Interview with Louis Kittlaus, Director of Physical Education, St. Louis Public Schools, gymnast, descendant of members of early Turner societies, June 1982.

Notes to Chapter 10: Shaw's Mentors

1. HS, St. Louis, to Sir William Jackson Hooker, 11 February 1856, in NAL, 1851–1858, LXIV.

2. Ibid.

3. Ibid.

4. HS, St. Louis, to William Hooker, 10 August 1856, NAL 1851–58, LXIV, 360.

5. Ibid.

6. Henry Shaw's Lands and Mansions at the Prairie des Noyers . . . etc., ibid., LXIV, 443. Indexed at 377.

7. GE, St. Louis, to AG, 9 April 1856, quoted in *MBGB* 30, 5 (May 1942): 101.

8. Ibid.

9. AG, Cambridge, to GE, 15 April 1856, ibid.

10. GE, St. Louis, to AG, 13 May 1856, ibid.

11. "Henry Shaw's Idea of a Botanical Garden," *Washington University Magazine,* Spring 1969, p. 39.

12. In an address to science and mathematics teachers in February 1908, William Trelease, director of the Garden after the death of Henry Shaw, pointed out that Shaw "put into shape a beautiful flower garden " At the advice of Dr Engelmann, Sir William Hooker, and Dr. Asa Gray, he broadened his plans to include the training of botanists and gardeners and scientific investigations into plant life. "Research received a small but continuous part of the time and effort of capable employees" ("The Missouri Botanical Garden," *School Science and Mathematics,* February 1908, p. 1).

13. Elizabeth Shaw, "George Engelmann: Frontiersman," a speech given at the 27th Annual Systematics Symposium, Missouri Botanical Garden, 20 October 1984; copy in ARMBG

14. A. Hunter Dupree, *Asa Gray, 1810–1888* (Cambridge: Harvard University Press, 1959), p. 97. A definitive biography.

15. Ibid., p. 158.

16. "Inaugural Exercises, School of Botany, Reminiscences of William G. Eliot," 6 November 1885, in *RMBG,* 1890, p. 56.

17. *Proceedings of the American Academy of Arts and Sciences,* 19:520, 522.

18. Ibid., 521.

19. AG, "Engelmann," in *Proceedings of the American Academy of Arts and Sciences,* 19:516.

20. Ibid., 522.

21. GE, St. Louis, to C. C. Parry, 7 December 1873, quoted in Andrew Denny Rodgers, *American Botany,*

1873–1892: Decades of Transition (Princeton: Princeton University Press, 1944), p. 57.

22. Dupree, *Asa Gray,* p. 67.

23. Howard A. Kelly, M.D., *Some American Medical Botanists* (Troy, N.Y.: The Southward Company, 1914), pp. 165ff.

24. Quoted in ibid., p. 173.

25. Ibid., passim.

26. AG, Correspondence, Archives of the Royal Botanic Gardens, Kew.

27. Dupree, *Asa Gray,* p. 406.

Notes to Chapter 11: Guidance by Correspondence

1. HS, St. Louis, to William Hooker, 10 August 1856, in NAL, XLIV, 360.

2. Ibid.

3. HS, St. Louis, to GE, 18 October 1856, HSPPC.

4. Ibid.

5. HS, St. Louis, to Hooker, 28 April 1857, in NAL, XLIV, 361.

6. Ibid.

7. HS's Diary, 1857, HSPJD, 1857.

8. Ibid.

9. *St. Louis County Deed Book,* 192, p. 205.

10. W. J. Hooker, Kew, to HS, 10 August 1857, in Scrapbook I to 1890.

11. Ibid.

12. Ibid.

13. GE, Kew, to HS, 11 August 1857, MBG Scrapbook I, to 1890.

14. HS, St. Louis, to Engelmann, 15 September 1857, HSPPC.

15. Ibid.

16. HS, St. Louis, to Hooker, 18 December 1857, in NAL, XLIV, 362.

17. HS's Diary, 1857–1858, HSPJD, 1857–1858.

18. HS, St. Louis, to Hooker, 18 December 1857, in the Archives of Kew, NAL, XLIV, 362.

19. William G. D'Arcy, "Mysteries and Treasures in Bernhardi's Herbarium," *MBGB* 69, 1 (1971): 20–25.

20. Ibid.

21. Edgar Anderson, "Personal Reflections," p. 42, in ARMBG.

22. Ibid.

23. Hooker, Kew, to HS, 17 January 1858, MBG Scrapbook I, to 1890.

24. HS, St. Louis, to GE, 13 January 1858, HSPPC. Henry S. Clarke and Co. had begun the fencing in 1856, and Charles Boswell worked in 1857. In that same year Shaw commissioned the O'Fallon Stone Co. to do the stone work. Receipted Bills, 1856, 1857, HSPBP, Group 4, 1856, 1857.

25. GE, Florence, to AG, 2 May 1858, *MBGB* 30, 5 (May 1942): 101.

26. HS, St. Louis, to AG, 28 September 1858, ibid., p. 102.

27. Ibid.

28. Ibid.

29. "Building Plans," made available by Assistant Librarian Leonore Thompson, Archives, Royal Botanic Gardens, Kew.

30. Anderson, "Personal Reflections," p. 42.

31. AG, Cambridge, to GE, 14 October 1858, *MBGB* 30, 5 (May 1942): 103.

32. GE, St. Louis, to AG, 30 October 1858, ibid.

33. AG, Cambridge, to GE, 8 November 1858, ibid.

34. Perley Spaulding, "A Biographical History of Botany at St. Louis, Missouri," *Popular Science Monthly* 4, 2 (March 1909): 240–41. See also "Letters from Augustus Fendler, Plant Collector, to Dr. George Engelmann, Physician and Botanist," translated and compiled by Carla Lange, manuscript copy in ARMBG, p. 38.

35. AG, *American Journal of the Sciences and Arts,* 34th series.

36. Dupree, *Asa Gray,* p. 336. Rodgers, in *American Botany, 1873–1892,* called Fendler "an able, notable and worthy collector" (p. 118).

37. Inventory of Henry Shaw's Personal Library.

38. GE, St. Louis, to AG, 25 February 1859, *MBGB* 30, 5 (May 1942): 103.

39. GE, St. Louis, to AG, 15 April 1859, ibid.

40. Ibid.

Notes to Chapter 12: Female Friends and Would-Be Wife

1. Thomas Dimmock, *Henry Shaw,* pp. 9–10.

2. See above, p. 32, and Chapter 5, note 6.

3. "Journal," Book 3, passim.

4. Ibid., 30 October 1841.

5. Aimée Dupont, Paris, to HS, 12 January 1847, HSPPC.

6. Honorine Douard, St. Louis, to HS, 5 March 1849, HSPPC.

7. Honorine Beranger, St. Louis, to HS, 1849, HSPPC.

8. Recollections of Rebecca Edom, *GD,* 30 August 1889.

9. Ibid.

10. Agreement, 28 February 1856, HSPBP, referred to in *Missouri Democrat,* 16 October 1858.

11. Agreement, 19 May 1857, HSPBP, referred to in *Missouri Democrat,* 16 October 1858.

12. Agreement, 6 August 1857, HSPBP, Group 3, 1857.

13. Records of the Court of Common Pleas, St. Louis, 19 July 1858, Civil Courts Building, St. Louis, Mo.

14. Shaw's Testimony, quoted in *Missouri Democrat,* 16 October 1858.

15. Ibid.

16. Ibid.

17. *Missouri Democrat,* 27 May 1859.

18. Ibid.

19. Ibid.

20. Tomique, "Back Talk," in *Reedy's Mirror* 16, 12 (17 May 1906), pp. 14–15. Copy in Shaw's Miscellaneous Files.

21. *Missouri Republican,* 30 May 1859.

22. *Missouri Democrat,* 1 June 1859.

23. Ibid., 2 June 1859.

24. Ibid.

25. *Missouri Republican,* 25 June 1859.

26. Effie Carstang, St. Louis, undated, to HS, quoted in *Missouri Democrat,* 3 April 1860; copy in ARMBG Library.

27. *Daily Missouri Democrat,* 3 June 1859.

28. Ibid.

29. Ibid.

30. *Missouri Republican,* 3 June 1859.

31. *Missouri Republican,* 21 January 1860.

32. Records of the Court of Common Pleas, p. 462, 2 June 1859.

33. *The Diary of Edward Bates, 1859–1886,* ed. Howard K. Beale (Washington: U.S. Government Printing Office, 1933), p. 20.

34. Ibid.

35. Ibid.

36. *Missouri Democrat,* 1859 passim.

37. Records of the Court of Common Pleas, 4 June 1859.

38. *Missouri Democrat,* 8 June 1859.

39. Ibid., 14 June 1859.

40. No recent account of Shaw's career elaborated on the trial until Jack Maier, special correspondent for the *Southside Journal* of St. Louis, entitled an article "Henry Shaw's Piano Spelled Matrimony to Effie Carstang," in the 3 April 1985 edition, p. 2H.

41. List of letters received by Shaw, June 1859, in Shaw Account Book, 1859.

42. Ibid.

43. *New York Illustrated News,* 14 April 1860.

44. *Harper's Weekly,* 31 March 1860, p. 201.

45. Ibid.

46. Records of the Court, 10 April 1860.

47. *New York Illustrated News,* 14 April 1860, p. 348.

48. *Missouri Democrat,* 3 April 1860.

49. Ibid.

50. Ibid.

51. *Missouri Republican,* 2 April 1860.

52. Ibid.

53. *Missouri Democrat,* 19 April 1860.

54. *New York Illustrated News,* 4 April 1860, p. 338.

55. Ibid.

56. Ibid.

57. Ibid.

58. *St. Louis Times,* 2 April 1860.

59. Ibid.

60. *The Diary of Edward Bates,* pp. 114ff.

61. Ledger, HSPAB, vol. 62 (1856–1866), p. 41; 25 October 1859, p. 46; 6 July 1860.

62. *Reedy's Mirror,* undated clipping, pp. 14–15. Copy in Shaw's Miscellaneous Files.

63. *Ledger,* HSPAB, vol. 62 (1856–1866).

64. SBP, passim, HSPBP, Group 4, 1870–1888.

65. *St. Louis Directory,* 1857–1859.

66. Ibid., 1860.

67. *Republic,* 27 August 1911.

Notes to Chapter 13: The Garden Opens

1. Enabling Act, Missouri Legislature, 14 March 1859 (Missouri Session Acts of 1859, p. 434).

2. HSAA.

3. Ibid., 15 July 1859.

4. Ibid., 3 June 1860.

5. GE, St. Louis, to AG, 13 May 1859, *MBGB* 30, 5 (May 1912): 104.

6. AG, Cambridge, to GE, 18 May 1859, ibid.

7. GE, St. Louis, to AG, 2 June 1859, ibid.

8. Ibid.

9. AG, Cambridge, to GE, 6 June 1859, ibid., p. 105.

10. GE, St. Louis, to AG, 15 June 1859, ibid.

11. GE, St. Louis, to AG, 3 August 1859, ibid.

12. Ibid.

13. AG, Cambridge, to GE, 8 August 1859, ibid., p. 106.

14. *The Magazine of Horticulture* (Boston) 25 (1859): 425.

15. Ibid.

16. Ibid.

17. Ibid., p. 424.

18. Ibid.

19. Ibid., p. 425.

20. Ibid.

21. GE, St. Louis, to AG, 17 October 1859, *MBGB* 30, 5 (May 1942): 106.

22. GE, St. Louis, to AG, undated, presumably November 1859, ibid.

23. GE, St. Louis, to AG, 30 December 1859, ibid.

24. W. B. Baker, *Fourth Annual Report of the St. Louis Chamber of Commerce for 1859* (St. Louis: Baker and Hammond, 1860), pp. 6–7.

25. *The Magazine of Horticulture* 25 (1859): 423–24.

26. Receipted Bills, January-December 1860, HSPBP, Group 4, 1860.

27. AG, Cambridge, to GE, 20 March 1860, *MBGB* 30, 5 (May 1942): 106.

28. GE, St. Louis, to AG, 10 April 1860, ibid.

29. Ibid.

30. GE, St. Louis, to AG, 12 June 1860, ibid., p. 107.

31. GE, St. Louis, to AG, 4 October 1860, ibid.

32. GE, St. Louis, to HS, 1 November 1860, ibid.

33. Ibid.

34. AG, Cambridge, to GE, 6 August 1860, ibid.

35. GE, St. Louis, to C. C. Parry, 24 January 1861.

36. Ledger (1859–1861), HSPAB, vol. 22, p. 80.

37. Spaulding, "A Biographical History of Botany at St. Louis, Missouri," *Popular Science Monthly* 4 (1909): 240. Also William Trelease, "The Missouri Botanical Garden," in *Popular Science Monthly* 62, 13 (January 1903): 195.

38. Spaulding, "Biographical History," *Popular Science Monthly* 3 (1908): 130; Trelease, "Missouri Botanical Garden."

39. "Notes on Progress of Vegetation," 1861–1864, HSPBP, Group 4, 1861–1864.

40. Will of 12 May 1851, annulled 18 November 1861, in Shaw Papers.

41. Jeanne Mino, Rochester Public Library, to Faherty, 8 May 1985, in author's files.

Notes to Chapter 14: Civil War Comes to Missouri

1. Grierson, *The Valley of Shadows,* p. 203.

2. GE, St. Louis, to AG, 17 August 1861, *MBGB* 30, 5 (May 1942): 107.

3. Ibid.

4. AG, Cambridge, to GE, 9 June 1862, typed copy in Library, Gray Herbarium, Harvard University, Cambridge, Mass.

5. GE, St. Louis, to AG, 9 December 1861, in Library, Gray Herbarium, quoted in Dupree, *Asa Gray,* p. 310.

6. HSAA.

7. Recollections of Rebecca Edom, in *GD,* 30 August 1889.

8. Ibid.

9. Receipted Bills, 14 March 1878, HSPBP, Group 4, 1878.

10. Accounts Receivable 1862–1889, passim, HSPBP, Group 1, 1860–1889. As late as 1887 these rented properties would bring in an average of $7,000 a month. Report of J. E. Kaime, in MBG Scrapbook, 1879–1890.

11. "Sketches of the Garden Area," in Shaw Papers.

12. Julius Hutawa, *Atlas of St. Louis County,* 1862.

13. J. H. Fisher, *Map of the City of St. Louis,* undated, presumably in the 1860s.

14. Ibid.

15. Scharf, *History of St. Louis City and County,* p. 353.

16. William E. Parrish, *Missouri Under Radical Rule, 1865-1870* (Columbia: University of Missouri Press, 1965), p. 83.

17. HSAA.

18. Ibid.

19. Scharf, *History of St. Louis City and County,* pp. 896-97.

20. Missouri Historical Society, *Collections* 1, 11 (1880): 13–14.

21. Quoted by Rev. Montgomery Schuyler, in the Second Annual Flower Sermon, in *RMBG,* 1892, p. 24.

22. Time Book, January 1867–1871, vol. 49, HSPAB. A grand-daughter of James Gurney, Clara Compton of Nixa, Missouri, recounted (on 26 April 1987) a family tradition that Shaw met Gurney during Shaw's visit to England in 1851. In a newspaper interview, however, Gurney stated that he had not known Shaw before coming to St. Louis, but asserted that Shaw had heard of his work at the Kew Gardens (*Republic,* 27 August 1911).

23. Elizabeth Bacon Custer, Fort Riley, Kansas, to Rebecca Richmond, 6 December 1866, quoted in *Kansas Historical Quarterly* 40, 1 (Spring 1974): 65.

24. Ibid.

25. *Stranger's Guide to St. Louis* (St. Louis: G. B. Wintle, 1867), p. 22.

26. Thomas Meehan, ed., *The Gar-*

dener's Monthly . . ., 10, 8 (August 1868): 244–45.

27. Account Books, Ledger, 1859–1861, HSPAB, vol. 22, p. 80.

28. HS, Plat Books, p. 99.

29. Record of Deeds, Julius Conrad, Recorder, 5 March 1867. Also, *GD,* 11 December 1949.

30. Receipted Bills, 1 October 1869, HSPBP, Group 4.

31. "Joseph Tarrigan Monell," in *Entomological News* 26 (October 1915): 380–83.

32. *The Gardener's Monthly* 10, 8 (August 1868): 244.

Notes to Chapter 15: Tower Grove Park Through Two Decades

1. David MacAdam, *Tower Grove Park* (St. Louis: R. P. Studley and Co., 1883), p. 7.

2. Scharf, *History of St. Louis City and County,* p. 697.

3. MacAdam, *Tower Grove Park,* p. 10.

4. Ibid., p. 20.

5. Ibid., p. 67.

6. Ibid., p. 67.

7. *Tower Grove Park Second Annual Report,* 1871.

8. Ibid.

9. Gerhardt Kramer, "Shaw's Architectural Legacy," pp. 21–22.

10. W. A. Kelsoe, *St. Louis Reference Record* (St. Louis: Von Hoffman Press, undated), p. 93.

11. MacAdam, *Tower Grove Park,* p. 80.

12. Ibid. p. 36.

13. Ibid., pp. 77–79.

14. W. T. Harris, "Humboldt," quoted in MacAdam, *Tower Grove Park.*

15. Mathilde von Humboldt, Ott. Machan, Germany, to HS, 18 January 1879, quoted in *The Exporter and Importer,* June 1879, p. 6.

16. MacAdam, *Tower Grove Park,* p. 66.

17. Ibid., p. 60.

18. Quoted in ibid., p. 65.

19. Ibid.

20. George McCue, "Old Patron, etc.," in *PD,* 27 October 1974, 5B.

21. HS, St. Louis, to James O. Broadhead, 17 March 1884, in Broadhead

Collection at Missouri Historical Society.

22. Receipted Bills, HSPBP, Group 4, 1860. The following statement appears: "Thomas O'Reilly, M.D., Attendance on Mary Ann; obstetrical attendance on Maria; attendance on children; on Bridget's children; on *self*; on Cass."

23. *Republic,* 25 August 1889.

24. Ibid.

25. William Hyde and Howard L. Conard, *Encyclopedia of the History of St. Louis,* 2:1675.

Notes to Chapter 16: Progress at the Garden

1. HSAA, 1867, passim.

2. *Missouri Republican,* 5 May 1869.

3. Ibid.

4. HSAA, 1867, 4 May 1869.

5. *Missouri Republican,* 5 May 1869.

6. Ibid.

7. Ibid.

8. Scharf, *History of St. Louis City and County,* p. 890.

9. Receipted Bill, 17 June 1872, HSPBP, Group 4, 1872.

10. Waterhouse to HS, 22 April 1879, in HS's Scrapbook, 1879–1890.

11. HSAA, 20 July 1874.

12. Quoted by the Rev. Montgomery Schuyler, in the Second Annual Flower Sermon, in the *RMBG,* 1892, p. 23.

13. W. H. Ragan, "Ramblings of a Hoosier," in *Transactions of the Indiana Horticultural Society,* 1874, p. 29.

14. *Compton's Pictorial St. Louis* (St. Louis: Compton, 1875), p. 110.

15. Ibid.

16. Kelsoe, p. 133.

17. GE, St. Louis, to Joseph Hooker, 16 March 1866; in Kew, U.S. Letters, South and West, 1865–1900, vol. 199, no. 128.

18. GE, St. Louis, to Hooker, 14 February 1873, ibid.

19. J. D. Hooker, "Journey to America, 1877," an unpublished diary in the Archives of the Kew Gardens.

20. Ibid.

21. Quoted in Henry Shaw, "Sir

Joseph Hooker," an unpublished manuscript in the ARMBG.

22. Ibid.

23. *The Exporter and Importer,* June 1879,
p. 6. Since few blacks visited the Garden
or recreated in Tower Grove Park, a
rumor grew over the years that they were
excluded from the Shaw properties.
Careful investigation has uncovered no
rule of exclusion. The present author
asked two prominent black historians of
the area if blacks felt they were excluded
from the Garden and Park. They knew
of no such attitude or understanding in
the black community.

24. HS, quoted in ibid. Presumably
Shaw was referring to Joseph Tibeau, a
neighbor during his early days in St.
Louis.

25. J. A. Dacus and James W. Buel,
Tour of St. Louis (St. Louis: Western Publishing Co., 1878), p. 50.

26. Ibid., pp. 51–52.

27. Eliot, p. 280.

28. HSAA, 1879.

29. HS's Scrapbook.

30. Walter J. Monaghan, "John Feugh
Was the Personal Servant of Henry
Shaw," *GD Sunday Magazine,* 9 October
1932, p. 15.

31. "Reminiscence" of Marguerite
Irish Norville, daughter of Superinten-
dent H. C. Irish, who lived at the
Garden in the early years of the century.
Written in 1980, ARMBG.

32. Monaghan, "John Feugh," p. 15.

33. Ibid.

34. *Missouri Republican,* undated, on
occasion of Shaw's eighty-first birthday.

35. Ibid.

36. Mark Twain, *Life on the Mississippi*
(New York: Harper and Brothers, Publishers, 1883), p. 192.

37. Ibid.

38. Receipted Bills, 5 February 1884,
HSPBP, Group 4, 1884.

39. *Missouri Republican,* 5 May 1869.

40. *Biographical Directory of the American
Congress,* 1774-1961 (Washington: U.S.
Government Printing Office, 1961),
p. 606.

41. Privileged sources.

42. Ibid.

43. Unidentified newspaper clipping,
27 August 1889.

Notes to Chapter 17: Prolific Writer and School Founder

1. Henry Shaw, *The Rose* (St. Louis:
R. P. Studley and Co., 1879).

2. Henry Shaw, *The Vine and Civilization*
(St. Louis: Tower Grove, 1884), pp.
17–18.

3. Ibid., p. 27.

4. Ibid., p. 29.

5. Ibid., p. 30.

6. Ibid., p. 27.

7. Ibid., p. 33.

8. Ibid., p. 32.

9. Ibid., pp. 62–64.

10. Ibid., p. 64.

11. MacAdam, *Tower Grove Park,* p. 66.

12. HS, "Guide to the Trees and
Shrubs in the Arboretum of the Mis-
souri Botanical Garden." Manuscript
Copy, 1880, in ARMBG.

13. Ibid.

14. Ibid.

15. Ibid., p. 2.

16. HS, "Gardens and Botanic Gardens," in *MBGB* 31, 7 (September 1943):
140ff.

17. Ibid., p. 143.

18. Ibid., p. 145.

19. Quoted in *MBGB* 72, 2 (April
1984).

20. "Treatise on Birds," in Shaw
Papers, quoted extensively in *MBGB* 36,
4 (April 1948): 67–72.

21. Ibid., p. 68.

22. Ibid.

23. Ibid.

24. Ibid., pp. 68–69.

25. HS, "A Brief History,"
unpublished, in ARMBG.

26. Ibid.

27. Benjamin Franklin French pub-
lished *Historical Collections of Louisiana.*
His life story appears in Appleton's
Encyclopedia of American Biography (New
York: D. Appleton, 1887), 2:510.

28. Francis Xavier Martin, chief justice of the Supreme Court of Louisiana,
published thirty-four volumes, many of
them dealing with the history of colonial

Louisiana. See the *Dictionary of American Biography,* 12:335–37.

29. HS, "A Brief History."

30. Ibid.

31. HS, "Du Tisne," unpublished.

32. Ibid.

33. Ibid.

34. HS, "Jesuits," in "A Brief History."

35. "DeSoto," ibid.

36. "La Salle," ibid.

37. Unidentified newspaper clipping, 27 August 1889. Xerox copy in files of author.

38. James Reed, "Notes," presented to the Trustees, November 1979.

39. Sylvester Waterhouse, St. Louis, to HS, 22 April 1879, in HS's Scrapbook, 1879–1890.

40. HS, St. Louis, to Waterhouse, 14 April 1879, in HS's Scrapbook, 1879–1890.

41. Ibid.

42. Waterhouse, St. Louis, to HS, 20 April 1879.

43. HS, St. Louis, to Eliot, 16 January 1884.

44. HS, St. Louis, to James O. Broadhead, 17 March 1884, in Archives, Missouri Historical Society.

45. C. C. Parry, Davenport, to HS, 7 April 1884, in HS's Scrapbook, 1879–1890.

46. Memorandum of GE, originally written in 1879 and copied on 5 December 1885, in HS's Scrapbooks.

47. Spaulding, "A Biographical History of Botany at St. Louis, Missouri," *Popular Science Monthly* 4 (1909): 253–56.

48. C. C. Parry, Davenport (?), to AG, 2 April 1884, quoted in Rodgers, *American Botany, 1873–1892,* p. 222.

49. Ibid.

50. GE, St. Louis, to C. C. Parry, 13 February 1885.

51. HS, St. Louis, to AG, 16 June 1884.

52. Ibid.

53. Rodgers, *American Botany, 1873–1892,* p. 224.

54. Yeatman, St. Louis, to HS, 12 April 1884.

55. AG, Cambridge, to HS, 29 May 1884.

56. HS, St. Louis, to Sir Joseph Hooker, 19 December 1884, NAL, 1065, Archives at Kew.

57. Hooker, Kew, to HS, 7 January 1885, quoted in *MBGB* 20, 103 (1932).

58. HS, St. Louis, to Sir Joseph Hooker, 24 February 1885, NAL, 1070, Archives at Kew.

59. James Butler, Madison, to HS, 26 February 1885, in HS's Scrapbook, p. 131.

60. Edward S. Holden, Madison, to W. G. Eliot, 18 February 1885, ibid., p. 30.

61. AG, St. Louis, to Trelease, 11 May 1885, ibid., p. 33.

62. HS, St. Louis, to Trelease, 16 May 1885, ibid., p. 35.

63. Eliot, St. Louis, to HS, 1 June 1885, ibid., p. 37.

64. Eliot, St. Louis, to Trelease, 9 June 1885, ibid., p. 41.

65. *MBGB* 39 (November 1951): 181.

66. For more on Dr. George Julius Engelmann, see *Dictionary of American Biography,* 6:160.

67. Eliot, St. Louis, to Trelease, 19 June 1885, in HS's Scrapbook, p. 45.

68. Eliot, St. Louis, to Trelease, 4 July 1885, ibid., p. 1880.

69. Edgar Anderson, "Personal Reflections," in ARMBG.

70. Shaw's Will.

71. J. D. Butler, postcard in HS's Scrapbook, postmarked Madison, 19 August 1885.

72. William Trelease, Jr., Pacific Grove, Calif., to Faherty, 7 October 1984.

73. William Trelease, Jr., Pacific Grove, Calif., to Faherty, 16 October 1984.

74. William Trelease, "Inaugural Address," in *RMBG,* 1890, pp. 63–83.

75. Ibid.

76. "Washington University, 1887–1888" (Washington University catalogues are in the Olin Library, Washington University).

Notes to Chapter 18: Sunset at Tower Grove House

1. Inventory of Books, HSPBP, 1889.

2. *The Church News,* St. Louis, April 1979, pp. 32–33. Also *SBP,* 27 August 1881; 9 October 1882; and 1884, 1885, 1887, passim. *First Annual Report of the Board of Directors of St. Luke's Hospital,* 1880, reprinted in 1981; *Annual Journal,* Diocese of Missouri, pp. 102–4.

3. *Annual Journal,* Diocese of Missouri, pp. 102–4.

4. F. M. Cockrell, Washington, to HS, 11 January 1887, HSPBP, Group 2, 1887.

5. John Gilmary Shea, Elizabeth, N.J., to HS, 4 January 1887, ibid.

6. Francis Parkman, Boston, to HS, 13 January 1887, ibid.

7. Dimmock, p. 19.

8. Ibid.

9. *Entomological News* 26 (October 1915): 380.

10. Joseph Monell, Cooney, N.M., to HS, 6 February 1887, HSPPC, Box 6. Monell kept scientific scrapbooks at various times, pasting articles of scientific interest in an old magazine or abandoned book. One of these contains these words, possibly in Shaw's handwriting: *"Ex libris Josephi Monell Shaw."* Joseph Monell, Scrapbooks, I.

11. Monell, Mine La Motte, Mo., to HS, 18 May 1887, HSPPC, Box 6.

12. HS, St. Louis, to Trelease, 24 November 1887, in HS's Scrapbooks.

13. Rodgers, *American Botany, 1873–1892,* p. 224.

14. HS, St. Louis, to AG, 19 March 1887.

15. *Botanical Works of George Engelmann* (1887), title page.

16. HS, St. Louis, to AG, 9 March 1887.

17. HS, St. Louis, to AG, 26 October 1887.

18. *Botanical Works of George Engelmann* (1887), copies inscribed in Shaw's own handwriting to various botanists and botanical centers.

19. HS, St. Louis, to AG, 26 October 1887.

20. Monell, Mine La Motte, Mo., to HS, 15 March 1888, HSPPC, Box 6.

21. HSAA, 4 May 1888.

22. Ibid., 28 May 1888.

23. Ibid., 4 June 1888.

24. *PD,* 25 September 1892.

25. Ibid., 2 October 1888.

26. MacAdam, p. 10.

27. *Record* of TMBG, 12 November 1889.

28. *Republic,* 26 August 1889.

29. D. Gould, *Official Map of the City of St. Louis,* 1901.

30. HSAA, 1 January 1889.

31. M. M. Yeakle, *The City of St. Louis of Today* (St. Louis: J. Osmund Yeakle and Co., 1889), p. 124.

32. Ibid.

33. Ibid., p. 126.

34. Ibid., p. 126.

35. *Republic,* 26 August 1889.

36. *PD,* clipping for 27 August 1889, in HS's Scrapbook, p. 78.

37. *PD,* 4 September 1889.

38. "Inventory of Shaw's Estate," 2 September 1889, HSPBP, Inventories.

39. *Mirror, loc. cit.*

40. George T. Moore, "Henry Shaw," in *The Dictionary of American Biography,* 17:39.

41. HS's Will, in *RMBG* (1890), pp. 29–55.

42. Rochester *Union and Advertiser,* 9 September 1891.

43. Bonds and Mortgages, 1 April 1884, HSPBP, Group 3, 1884.

44. *PD,* 4 September 1889.

45. *Chicago Tribune,* 26 August 1889.

46. *Republic,* 8 September 1889.

47. Ibid.

Notes to Chapter 19: The Three Legacies of Henry Shaw

1. HS's Will, establishing the Missouri Botanical Garden, admitted to Probate at St. Louis, Mo., 2 September 1889, p. 3.

2. Noonan, St. Louis, to Kaime et al., 6 September 1889, TMBG.

3. Hitchcock, St. Louis, to Noonan, 7 September 1889, TMBG.

4. *The Mirror* 4, 13 (20 May 1894): 8.

5. Ibid.

6. *PD,* 9 September 1889.

7. Yeatman, Philadelphia, to Kaime, 9 September 1889, TMBG.

8. Noonan, St. Louis, to Board, 9 September 1889, TMBG.

9. Ibid., 10 September 1889.

10. Ibid.

11. Ibid., 30 September 1889.

12. Ibid., October 1889.

13. *PD*, 18 December 1889.

14. *Republic*, 27 May 1890.

15. *RMBG*, 1890, pp. 91–102.

16. Ibid., p. 64.

17. Ibid., pp. 94–98.

18. Ibid., p. 98.

19. *RMBG*, 1890, pp. 7–25.

20. TMBG, 22 January 1890.

21. *PD*, 17 February 1890.

22. *Republic*, 18 February 1890.

23. Ibid., 10 May 1890.

24. Ibid., 29 January 1891.

25. *GD*, 29 January 1891.

26. *RMBG*, 1891, p. 62.

27. Privileged sources.

28. HS's Will.

29. *RMBG*, 1890.

30. Ibid.

31. Ibid.

32. Ibid., pp. 89–90.

33. Ibid.

34. Ibid., 1891, p. 38.

35. Ibid.

36. *Republic*, 24 November 1890.

37. Ibid.

38. Kramer, "Shaw's Architectural Legacy," p. 29.

39. TMBG, 8 October 1890. Albert Spear Hitchcock, a native of Michigan, came to the Garden from Iowa State College, where he was to earn his Doctor of Science degree many years later (1920). After two years at the Garden (1889–1891), he was to teach at Kansas College, Manhattan, Kansas, for nine years. In 1901 he became an agrologist and later principal botanist with the U.S. Department of Agriculture. He won a wide reputation as an authority on grasses. BF.

40. Ibid.

41. Interview with Beryll Manne, archivist, Washington University, 29 August 1985. "Until the year 1911, the degrees were limited chiefly to the master's degree with an occasional degree of Doctor of Philosophy in the Shaw School of Botany." "Historical Statement" on the Washington University Graduate School of Arts and Letters, in Ninety-eighth Annual Catalogue (1954-1955), p. 5.

42. *RMBG*, 1891.

43. TMBG, 10 December 1891.

44. Anna Hinrichs, "The Missouri Botanical Garden and the Henry Shaw School of Botany," in *Chaperone Magazine*, 1892, p. 105.

45. Ibid., p. 112.

Notes to Epilogue

1. J. W. Hooker, Kew, to HS, 10 August 1857, in Scrapbook I, to 1890.

2. *PD*, 14 February 1890.

3. *Republic*, 13 April 1891.

Bibliographical Essay

◆◆◆

In view of the wide acclaim given to Henry Shaw as a public benefactor and the international reputation of the Garden he founded, one is rightly surprised at the relatively meager amount of researched writing that has been done on the man and his Garden. Neither a full-length biography of Shaw nor an objective study of the Garden has yet appeared.

Research materials are plentiful. Shaw the businessman carefully kept all his accounts—even hotel bills from his travels. He listed the goods he ordered from England to be sold on the Missouri frontier and the boats that brought them over. Letters from his family are extant for his first thirty years in America. While some letters seem to be missing, many remain, some on personal matters. He liked to write colonial history of the Mississippi Valley, presumably intending to publish the material later. He kept a diary on some of his journeys. All these materials are available at the Library of the Missouri Botanical Garden in the John S. Lehmann Building.

The *Report of the Missouri Botanical Garden* (published annually from 1889–1912) and the *Missouri Botanical Garden Bulletin* (1913–) regularly carried articles on the history of the Garden and the story of its founder, and of staff members over the years. None of these broke new ground.

Thomas Dimmock, a Saint Louis newspaperman who knew Shaw personally, wrote a short biography of the founder of the Missouri Botanical Garden that remained the basis of almost everything written about Henry Shaw until recent years. This sixteen-page account, "Henry Shaw, a Biographical Sketch," which appeared in *Report of the Missouri Botanical Garden* 1 (1889): 7–25, told of Shaw's early years, his coming to Saint Louis, his success in cutlery sales, his opening of the Garden and Tower Grove Park, and his reading interests. It said little of his slaveholding, his money-lending, his amassing of rental properties, and his court cases.

In a personal reminiscence published in the *Report of the Missouri Botanical Garden* 4 (1893): 37–43, J. D. Butler recalled the octogenarian Shaw's statement of a youthful interest in botany. Dr. William Trelease, head of the Henry Shaw School of Botany, who also knew Shaw personally, added a few reminiscences not discussed by Dimmock or Butler in "The Missouri Botanical Garden," *Popular Science Monthly* 62 (January 1903): 193–221.

For many years, Dimmock's picture set the pattern for articles that touched on Shaw's career, such as H. V. Blaise's "Mister Shaw's Garden," *Saturday Evening Post* 175 (January 1903): 16, 52, and Dana C. Jensen's "The Enigma of Mr. Shaw," *Bulletin of the Missouri Historical Society* 15 (July 1959): 311–18.

Many short accounts of Shaw, the Garden, and Tower Grove Park appeared in a succession of guidebooks about St. Louis over the years, such as *Stranger's Guide to St. Louis* (St. Louis: G. B. Wintle, 1867), pp. 22ff.; Thomas Meehan's *The Gardener's Monthly* 10, 8 (August 1868): 244–45; and *Compton's Pictorial St. Louis* (St. Louis: Compton & Co., 1875), p. 110. These were factual rather than analytic.

In *A Sheaf of Essays by a Sheffield Antiquary* (Sheffield: North End Ltd., 1929), pp. 73ff., author Charles Drury included a short biography of Shaw that followed the Dimmock pattern, except in asserting that Shaw was a nature lover from youth. He based the assertion that Shaw planted anemones and buttercups while a boy in England on reminiscences of Shaw as a man of eighty—perhaps relying on the statement of J. D. Butler. George F. Timpson, like Shaw an alumnus of Mill Hill School near London, wrote "The Boyhood of Henry Shaw." This unpublished manuscript moves on the presumption that since Shaw was interested in flowers in later life, he must have developed that bent at the Mill Hill, a school that had a history of associations with botanists. A copy of this manuscript is in the Garden Library. Even Garden director George Moore's sketch of Henry Shaw in *Dictionary of American Biography*, 17:39, hews closely to the Dimmock pattern. Moore does have a richer account of Shaw's legacy, the Garden.

The first director of public relations for the Garden and Tower Grove Park, David MacAdam, wrote a seventy-page book, *Tower Grove Park* (St. Louis: R. P. Studley and Co.), in 1883. Robert Knittel wrote *Walking in Tower Grove Park* (St. Louis: Grasshopper Press, 1978). NiNi Harris described Tower Grove Park, the Garden, and the neighborhood in a ninety-four-page book, *Grand Heritage* (St. Louis: De Sales Community Corporation, 1984). She also described the park historically in *Henry Shaw's Living Legacy* (St. Louis: Tower Grove Park, 1986).

The catalogs of Washington University regularly contained information on the Shaw School of Botany, especially those for 1887–1888 and 1954–1955. Anna Hinrichs included an account of the school in "The Missouri Botanical Garden and the Shaw School of Botany," *Chaperone Magazine* (1892): 104–20. Director George Moore gave an overview of the school's history in "The Henry Shaw School of Botany," *Missouri Botanical Garden Bulletin* 39, 9 (November 1951): 181–87. This last article typified the many articles appearing in the *Bulletin* over the years that throw light on Shaw's life and legacies.

Gerald Brown's M.A. thesis at St. Louis University in 1967, "The Missouri Botanical Garden," gave little new on Shaw's life but gave a good view of the history of the Garden.

In "The Vision of Henry Shaw," *Missouri Botanical Garden Bulletin* 72, 1 (February 1984): 3–7, the present writer put into historical focus the achievements of the Garden's founder. NiNi Harris described Shaw and architect George I. Barnett in "The English Arrive," *The Market Place—A Forum* 1, 2 (Fall-Winter 1983): 36–37. The present writer told of two Garden staffers, George Pring and James Gurney, in "More St. Louisans Who Were British-born," *The Market Place—A Forum* 3, 4 (Winter 1985–1986): 5–10.

The first scholarly rebuttal of the Dimmock allegation that Shaw quit business in 1840 came from James Neal Primm, "Henry Shaw: Merchant Capitalist," *Gateway Heritage,* 5, 1 (Summer 1984): 2–9. Primm explored in detail Shaw's business ventures and his sorties into the Indian trade and showed that Shaw did not retire from business, but simply moved from selling cutlery to lending money and leasing properties.

The editors of the *Gateway Heritage* devoted the entire Summer 1984 issue to the 125th anniversary of the Garden. Architect Gerhardt Kramer wrote on "Henry Shaw's Architectural Legacy to the Missouri Botanical Garden" (pp. 20–29), Barbara Lawton on "The Gardens of the Missouri Botanical Garden" (pp. 30–39), Dr. Peter H. Raven on "The Missouri Botanical Garden in the World's Service" (pp. 40–48), and the present writer on "The Missouri Botanical Garden through 125 years" (pp. 10–19).

Index

Credits for Illustrations

Author's collection, 6, 7, 9

Lisa DeLorenzo, 4

Harvard University Herbaria, 40

Historic American Buildings Survey, Library of Congress, 39

Jesuit Missouri Province Archives, 19 (reproduced by Tom Dewey from a glass-lantern slide)

Missouri Botanical Garden Archives, frontispiece, vi, 11, 14, 17, 18, 22, 23, 24, 25, 26, 29, 30, 31, 32, 33, 36, 37, 38, 41, 42, 43, 44, 45, 46, 47, 49, 50, 51, 52, 54, 55, 56

Montana State Historical Society, 8

Sheffield Central Library, 27

Sheffield Newspapers Ltd., 1

State Historical Society of Missouri, 3, 12, 16

Swekosky Photo Collection, School Sisters of Notre Dame, 15, 20, 21, 28, 34, 35, 48

Norbury Wayman, 2, 10, 13

Gottemann, Rosemary Thomas